THE SLASHER KILLINGS

D1500704

Windsor riverfront as viewed from Detroit, 1945. Courtesy Sharon Masse.

THE SLASHER
KILLINGS

A CANADIAN
SEX-CRIME PANIC,
1945–1946

**PATRICK
BRODE**

A PAINTED TURTLE BOOK

Detroit, Michigan

13 12 11 10 09   5 4 3 2 1

Library of Congress Cataloging-in-Publication Data

Brode, Patrick, 1950–
The Slasher killings : a Canadian sex-crime panic, 1945–1946 / Patrick Brode.
p. cm.
"A Painted Turtle book."
Includes bibliographical references and index.
ISBN 978-0-8143-3448-5 (pbk. : alk. paper)
1. Sears, Ronald, d. 1956. 2. Serial murderers—Ontario—Windsor. 3. Gays—Crimes against—Ontario—Windsor. 4. Gays—Social conditions—Ontario—Windsor. 5. Windsor (Ont.)—History—20th century. I. Title.
HV6535.C33W565 2009
364.152′32092—dc22
2009008322

Designed by Isaac Tobin
Typeset by Maya Rhodes
Composed in Gotham and Adobe Caslon Pro

CONTENTS

Introduction · 1

INTRODUCTION

During the final days of World War II, one individual in Windsor, Ontario, defied accepted codes of conduct and began to enforce his own kind of justice. Dubbed "the Slasher" because he attacked and killed with a knife, this individual carried out a series of assaults and murders that created a moral panic, a hysteria that swept the city and called into question the ability of modern authorities to maintain law and order.

The panic that resulted from the Slasher attacks gripped a community not typical of Canada for the period. For decades, Windsor had been an industrial city focused on automotive production. During Prohibition, it had developed a reputation as an open city, where first liquor and then other vices, including prostitution and gambling, were readily available. As a result, criminal laws were neither widely observed nor strictly enforced in Windsor. The dislocation caused by the war only accentuated this lack of control. Society had been turned upside down. Women were leaving their homes to work in the factories, and in the factories themselves, there were the beginnings of labor unrest. These changes met with resistance from many of Windsor's leaders, who seemed eager to retreat to prewar conventions.

The sudden spate of knifings and murders in July and August 1945 brought several uncomfortable realities to the surface of this evolving community. The most obvious fact was that there was a killer in their midst, one who killed brutally and seemingly at random. The hidden presence of such a monster, combined with the turbulence of the times and the inability of the police to catch the killer, plunged the city into a panic. The panic, in turn, justified a ruthless police reaction out of proportion to the threat. But above all, the panic generated a vicious press campaign that vilified all those who did not belong: drifters, the unemployed, racial minorities, and, ultimately, sexual outsiders. It led to a crackdown on suggestive literature and to the heightened surveillance of young people. The media reaction to the hysteria validated the public's disgust with those who did not conform to the norms of mainstream society—especially those with "deviant" sexualities—and justified driving them underground. However, none of this paranoia led to a resolution, and for a year, Windsor lived under a cloud of fear, not knowing what had triggered the killings, who was behind them, or how the killer selected his victims.

The subsequent panic of 1946 occurred during a period of growing insecurity. Instead of basking in their victory over the fascist powers, North Americans were wary of Soviet intentions and concerned about the possibility of another war—this time featuring the use of atomic weapons. The mood prevailed that society was at risk of attack by enemies both abroad and at home. One aspect of this subtle but pervasive fear was a belief that "perverts," or sexual misfits, would, if allowed, take over public spaces so they could assault and infect children. In the postwar era, those who were seen as deviating from the norm were not only characterized as immoral but also as an active threat to the innocent. While the panic was particularly acute in Windsor, it flared up in other places as well: Slasher sightings occurred in Detroit; and in Chicago, a similar trauma resulted in a mass roundup of gay men by police.

Only a few decades before the Slasher murders, outraged citizens would have demanded that the perpetrator be apprehended and executed. Death was believed to be the only appropriate retribution for such crimes. But the Slasher case was significant in demonstrating the shift in public sympathies toward deviant criminals. While Windsorites were afraid and wanted the killer caught, they recognized almost from the beginning that any person who had committed such depraved acts was mentally ill and not necessarily wholly responsible for his actions. It was just as much a health issue as a criminal one, for the murderer obviously had a defective personality. In the modern age, when humanity had harnessed the power of the atom, corrective treatment rather than brute punishment seemed the appropriate response. But psychiatric therapy could not help an individual who, despite taunting the police about his intentions, remained maddeningly at large, relishing his public notoriety.

Ultimately, the hysteria in Windsor was followed by due process as the duly appointed authorities sought to regain control. Their handling of the case was, however, far from clean, dispassionate, or factual. The lawyers, trial judges, juries, and appeal judges involved in the case seemed to steer away from the historical reality of what had occurred, making findings that were unsupported by the facts before them. They ignored clear, persuasive evidence while giving weight to appearances and suggestions. While there is always an element of theater in the law, the illogical and melodramatic conduct of those involved in the Slasher trials indicated that the process could all too easily veer from a search for justice to a public condemnation of the unconventional.

Finally, rather than shocking the community into questioning the status quo, the Slasher case was so disturbing that it was quietly forgotten, as though to pretend it had never happened. It had become apparent that the attacks were an isolated outbreak and that there no longer existed any imminent threat. However, seen within its context, the Windsor Slasher case was one of several similar, highly publicized events that occurred across North America and added to the insecurity of the postwar climate. As a result of these events, the pressure to conform became more intense than ever, and for the first time, a type of psychopathic criminal personality was defined. The Slasher case would be raised in the Canadian Parliament and openly discussed as one of the reasons society needed protection from psychopaths. The case's only reverberation was its contribution to the list of criminal sanctions against those who were sexual "deviates." In a postwar world in which mainstream society demanded protection from undefined evils, that seemed a satisfactory result.

1

VICTORY

By rights, it should have been the best of times.

Shortly after 11 a.m. on Monday, May 7, 1945, residents of Windsor, Ontario, received news that the war in Europe was over. Gigantic headlines in the *Windsor Daily Star* proclaimed "Germany Quits." That afternoon, as excited citizens began to gather downtown, a roaring RAF Mosquito "F for Freddy" swooped low over the streets to join in the jubilation. By Tuesday night, a huge spontaneous celebration had broken out, and, as one journalist described it, "Happy milling thousands marched up and down sidewalks, waving flags, blowing horns, throwing confetti and imbibing in the holiday spirit."[1] Yet, even as the snake-dancing lines of teenagers careened through traffic, casualty lists were still coming back from Europe. While no one knew the final reckoning, at least the war was over, and those who had survived would soon be coming home.

Among these men and women would be hundreds of soldiers believed lost during an ill-fated raid on Dieppe, France, on August 19, 1942. During the raid, almost all of the more than five hundred men of the local regiment, the Essex Scottish, were captured and presumed dead, giving the name Dieppe a special significance in Windsor's collective memory.

Within weeks after the raid, however, word came from Europe that most of the men at Dieppe had not been killed but rather were being held as prisoners of war. Two months after the war's end, on July 12, 1945, a contingent of Dieppe prisoners and other repatriated soldiers was scheduled to arrive at the Canadian National Station in Windsor. The celebration of their arrival eclipsed the earlier V-E celebration, for many of these men had been overseas since 1939 and held in prison for two and a half years. The train arrived just before midnight, and according to local news accounts, "By the time the train pulled cautiously into the station there wasn't an inch of standing room available within two blocks of the depot."[2] Ironically, some of the men were waving captured Nazi flags as the train ground to a halt. There followed delirious reunion scenes as entire families piled on sons and fathers. Led by the Essex Scots piper Jock Copland, a spontaneous parade of returned men and their families marched up Ouellette Avenue.

———————————

Ten days after this wild reception, on July 24, 1945, a stabbing occurred on Windsor's waterfront. The attending constables, Ted LePage and Bob Anderson, received the call at 1:30 a.m. and arrived on Sandwich street to find that George Mannie, a middle-aged man from the west side of the city, had been stabbed twice in the back. Nearly dead, his shirt soaked with blood, Mannie had been found by a military provost officer. Mannie was rushed to Grace Hospital, where doctors discovered that one of the deep stab wounds had penetrated his lung.

Once Mannie's condition was stable, LePage and Anderson took his statement. He told them that two men in brown suits—"they looked like zoot suits"—had stabbed him at the foot of California Street and pushed him down the embankment toward the Detroit River. He had managed to crawl back up the embankment to Sandwich Street. At first light, LePage and Anderson returned to the riverfront to see what evidence they could find. What they discovered indicated that there was little or no truth to Mannie's story. First, there was a row of bushes between the street and the river embankment, which would have prevented Mannie from falling down the hill, even if he had been pushed. Additionally, near the edge of the riverbank, LePage and Anderson discovered a "sort of a nest or space amongst the grass and bushes," containing a flattened straw hat and several discarded bottles of rubbing alcohol. There appeared to have been a struggle in the vicinity. The officers found blood on the grass and a trail of blood up the hill toward the street. Even this cursory examination suggested that Mannie's story was fictitious. "It appeared to us," the officers wrote in their report, "that the stabbing took place at the bottom of the river bank."[3]

The two detectives assigned to the case, Sam Royan and Jim Hall, followed up and took some photographs of the "nest." They agreed that Mannie had crawled up the embankment rather than having been thrown down it. When they visited Mannie in the hospital, he was awake and reading a newspaper. By that time, the police knew more about George Mannie. He was an occasional dock laborer who, despite the wartime press for workers, had successfully avoided permanent employment. Confronted with Royan and Hall's partial reconstruction of the events of July 24, Mannie admitted that he had been stabbed down by the river rather than near the street. Mannie also revealed that he led a less than edifying social life. The truth was, he claimed, on the night of the stabbing, he had been drinking rubbing alcohol with two acquaintances of no fixed abode and one "Pete the Swede." When the others left, Mannie decided to sleep it off. He awoke to find a "light-coloured negro" or a well-tanned white man of about twenty-five standing over him. "Are you all alone, pal?" the man said. Mannie, groggy and suspicious, began to walk up the hill to escape the man when, without warning, he was stabbed in the back.

Skeptical, the detectives reported that Mannie "may not tell the true Story even if he does remember it."[4] With no motive or reliable description of the attacker, and a victim who appeared to be far from trustworthy, the police had very little to work with. They decided that alcohol "in a questionable mixture" had probably played a key role in the incident and resigned themselves to never solving the case.

The *Windsor Daily Star*'s account of the stabbing was confined to a remote corner of the newspaper, most likely because Mannie's attack coincided with the public reception for Windsor's only recipient of the Victoria Cross for valor. Major Frederick Tilston, "the Hochwald Hero" received a tumultuous civic reception at Jackson Park on the same night that Mannie's nearly lifeless body was discovered on Sandwich Street. With banks of wounded comrades looking on, Tilston modestly accepted the crowd's adulation, and a crew from the National Film Board recorded the event for the newsreels. Following the reception for Major Tilston, one of the area's most vibrant annual celebrations, Emancipation Day, was held at Jackson Park. The festival, which celebrated British Empire emancipation, drew large crowds of African American revelers from Michigan and Ohio. Bands and dancers paraded up Ouellette Avenue and gathered in the park for jitterbug contests, a massive barbecue, and the crowning of the beauty queen "Miss Sepia." Amid all the excitement, the "Mysterious Stabbing," as the *Star* called it, was all but forgotten.

By 1945, Windsor had become one of Canada's principal manufacturers of war machinery, although the city's early history seemed to belie this destiny. At the turn of the century, the Canadian side of the Detroit River was composed of a number of sleepy Victorian towns called the "border cities." From west to east, Sandwich, Windsor, and Walkerville were a string of small municipalities dwarfed by the emerging industrial metropolis of Detroit. The border cities' only distinguishing features were the railways that passed through and placed the towns on the New York–Chicago line.[5] While they supported a few large concerns, such as the Hiram Walker Distillery, for the most part, the border cities served as sites for small, transitory manufacturers. Then Henry Ford happened.

In 1904, an ambitious wagonmaker, Gordon McGregor, contacted the Detroit automaker and suggested that Ford assemble cars on the Canadian side of the river. As a result of McGregor's initiative, by the 1920s, Ford of Canada was the largest automaker in the British Empire and the dynamo of the border cities. In 1922, Ford of Canada produced almost 80,000 cars and, with the help of an aggressive marketing program, exported them around the world.[6] However, during the Great Depression of the 1930s, car production fell drastically, and there were massive layoffs at Ford of Canada plants. In 1935, economic conditions compelled the border cities to amalgamate; together they became the City of Windsor.

The Second World War revitalized industrial production in Windsor, and the Ford plant was called upon to produce the trucks and universal carriers used to transport Allied armies across North Africa, Italy, and France. Almost half of all the military vehicles produced in Canada during the war were made in Windsor. Workers, many of them immigrants from Eastern Europe, flooded into the city to work on the assembly lines, and for the first time, many women were employed in the factories.

In spite of the reinvigorated economy, the war years were filled with hardship and uncertainty. Meat and butter were rationed, and those families without enough coupons had to do without. Prominent Windsor lawyer Leon Paroian recalled growing up near Parent Avenue: "Nothing got thrown out . . . the whole philosophy of the community was 'waste nothing.'" Newspapers were either bundled up for recycling or burned to ash to be sprinkled on the sidewalks. If a family lost a son overseas, "We young kids were warned on pain of physical harm to recognize the grief these people were in and to make sure we didn't play kick the can near their house." In the schools, the children were drilled in patriotic tunes such as "There'll Always Be an England" or "Coming in on a Wing and a Prayer," and when not in school, they were organizing paper or scrap-metal drives. Neighborhoods in Windsor were intensely proud of their sons' accomplishments on the battlefield, but by May of 1945, everyone was profoundly relieved that the dreary reality of the war in Europe was finally over and that the survivors were on their way home.[7]

In Windsor, the growth of major war industries had resulted in a grimly utilitarian landscape. The enormous Ford complex spanned 245 acres along the Detroit River, extending to the east of Drouillard Road and over a mile to the south. Since the completion of the Ambassador Bridge in 1929 and the Detroit-Windsor Tunnel in 1930, motorists could simply drive between the two countries, and the riverfront was no longer needed as a ferry crossing. While the railways still maintained two cross-border freight-ferry services, the riverfront was becoming increasingly run down, and it was blighted with a number of hotels of dubious reputation.

Downtown Windsor was an active commercial area that supported several department stores and major hotels. Just to the west of the downtown, however, was Government Park, a largely neglected patch of open land next to the government wharf and one of the few public areas near the river. Overlooking the park were the silos of the Canada Cement Company and the huge piles of sand used to make the cement. Oblivious to the churning propellers of docking freighters, neighborhood boys would mount the sand piles and dive into the river. Just to the west of the park, on the other side of Sandwich Street, was a large plot of vacant land that had been the site of the Canada Salt Company mine. Since 1920, it had lain vacant and become wild and overgrown. These vacant spaces were an eyesore, a no-man's-land that separated the downtown from the more presentable residential areas of west Windsor.

––––––––––

Earl McMaster, a Canadian Pacific Railway employee, usually had no cause to leave the rail-yard cutting that lay several feet below ground level. But around noon on August 7, 1945, McMaster was climbing up the embankment from the trench where the tracks lay, when he spotted something unusual: there was a body in the weeds, lying about a hundred feet south of Sandwich Street and a hundred feet in from Caron Avenue, near the old salt mine, but on railway land. The vacant lot was so overgrown with tall weeds that it took the full light of day to make the body visible to a passerby.

Detectives John Mahoney and Alfred Carter arrived at the scene to find the lifeless body of a man of forty to forty-five years old. Even for detectives with little experience with homicide, it was a most peculiar murder scene. The grass near the body had not been trampled down, and there appeared to be no signs of a struggle. In fact, the victim was still wearing his eyeglasses and straw hat. And yet the attack had been so furious that in addition to receiving several stab wounds in the back, the victim had been slashed repeatedly in the buttocks until "his trousers [were] almost cut from the body."[8]

The following day, the detectives learned that the dead man was Frank Sciegliski, a fifty-six-year-old man who had worked for the Windsor Bedding Company. He was rumored to have had a wife in Europe whom he had left behind, and by all accounts, he had mainly kept to himself. His landlady recalled that he had come home from work the night of August 6, changed his clothes, shaved, and left. His car was found a block away from the murder scene. There was nothing unusual about the car, and it appeared that he had simply parked it and ventured into the weeds. The coroner reported that there were a total of six stab wounds in the victim's back and that they had been inflicted, roughly, in the shape of a cross. Any one of the wounds would have been enough to cause death.

At that time, there existed an easy, if inappropriate, rapport between the police investigators and the reporters for the *Windsor Daily Star,* which led to the detectives' musings about the murder ending up on the local news page: two days after the killing, the newspaper published the detectives' speculation that although the victim's wallet was missing, Sciegliski's death was a "grudge killing." By the end of the week, the Inspector of Detectives, Duncan MacNab, was assuring reporters that they had several leads and that he expected "an early arrest in the case."[9]

In reality, such assurances were baseless, since the police had no leads. Additionally, the comforting but false reports most likely contributed to the later collapse of public confidence when it became apparent that the police were at a complete loss as to the killer's identity. Stunningly, in spite of the similarities, no one at the police department connected Sciegliski's murder to the attack on George Mannie.

The body in the weeds was an ominous sign, for in the previous year, Windsor, a city with a population of over 100,000, had experienced no murders. The police had no homicide squad, since there had appeared to be no need for one. Violent attacks, such as murder and rape, were rare occurrences in Windsor, and consequently, the police had little experience in such investigations.[10]

Although serious crime was rare, common assaults and offenses against public decency were commonplace. In 1944, there were twenty-seven charges against bawdy houses and thirteen against illegal betting establishments. In 1945, the number of bawdy-house charges rose to thirty-six. A veteran police officer recalled that "it was just wild" downtown and that on weekends, officers walked their beats in pairs for their own safety. The hotels on the waterfront, such as the British American and the Ambassador, provided rooms for prostitutes, while those a block or so from the river, such as the Munro, were the sites of constant brawls. "Pitt Street was wall-to-wall whores . . . the downtown hotels on Pitt Street were all hooker hangouts," another officer recalled. One of the most infamous houses was located at 359 Brant Street, just behind the Windsor Arena. There, a Quebec Madame, Cecile Lamontagne, ran one of the largest and most profitable brothels in the city. It was so popular "that the old gal had business cards printed up with maps and everything. I can remember such a lineup there on weekends. [The customers] would go in and pay their money, and they would have to wait out on the street with their chit, and then they would be called in."[11]

Gambling was also widespread in many areas. A *Star* reporter visited a pool hall on Ouellette Avenue, noting that "after 1:30 p.m. it is becoming difficult to make the eight ball without a blast reaching your ear to the effect that 'Chicago track, Ocean Cup Cake scratched in the first.'" While "sharpies" made their wagers, an imposing man guarded the front door to sound a warning if any authorities should appear.[12] On Drouillard Road in the east end, illegal gambling spots were common. While other suburbs, notably Walkerville, could be primly respectable, it seemed as if parts of Windsor were open to any activity that catered to vice.

Gerald Hallowell, in his study of Prohibition in Ontario, has suggested, "Although there was trouble all along the international boundary, the heart of the problem centred around the City of Windsor." Windsor's "reputation for lawlessness and insobriety" seems well deserved.[13] Organized crime in Detroit, namely the Purple Gang, dominated the liquor trade and used Windsor as a funnel for supplies that entered the American Midwest and found their way to the Capone syndicate in Chicago. A 1927 inquiry into police corruption proclaimed that Windsor was the "Monte Carlo of the North American Continent" and that the Chief Constable, David Thompson, tolerated gambling and prostitution. One witness described Stephen's Inn on Sandwich Street this way: "I've been on the Barbary Coast, but there's not a place to compare to Stephen's Inn. It's a tough joint." There he saw "beer and painted women who flitted from table to table like vultures."[14] Even after the repeal of Prohibition, these free wheeling ways continued and seemed to be augmented by the dislocation caused by the war years. For many of the returning soldiers, gambling had become a part of life. But while sections of the city seemed lawless, the murder of a man in a public place should have been seen as a serious threat to Windsor's law-abiding citizens.

Greater events conspired to ensure that the mysterious death of one loner remained buried in obscurity. Two days after Frank Sciegliski's body was found in the high weeds, the *Star* announced, "Japan Offers Peace." Even if the war in the Pacific was not officially over, it was clear that the fighting would soon end there as well. Many men had returned from Europe with the understanding that they would be deployed against Japan. Now they were instead on the verge of being demobilized and returned to civilian life. That Saturday, August 12, massed bands in Jackson Park celebrated the Japanese surrender. On "Victory in Japan" day, Tuesday, August

14, there was yet another impromptu celebration in what had become a summer of celebrations. Neighbors held block parties, and as the parties became wilder, entire blocks of people marched (beer bottles in hand) to the central festivities downtown, where "insanely-happy paraders took over the street" and "as late as 4 o'clock this morning downtown Windsor continued to echo with the sound of car horns and the high crescendo of human voices."[15] Bonfires were set all over the city, usually with effigies of Hideki Tojo suspended over them. Homemade paper confetti was hurled from the high windows of office buildings and hotels, and when celebrants ran out of paper, they shredded pillowcases and sent them billowing downward.

The revelry continued into Wednesday morning, even as public works crews tried to clear the streets and sweep up the confetti. That evening, as the victory celebrations finally wound down, another man was murdered in downtown Windsor.

2

PANIC

Now that the war was coming to an end, the G. Tate Easton garage on Goyeau Street was doing a respectable business. People could afford to have repairs done on their cars, and there were hopes that civilian production at Ford would start up again soon. When Ted Tellier and Leandore Godin reported for work at 7 a.m. on Thursday morning, August 16, 1945, they found the garage strangely silent. The Canadian National express truck, which the night watchman was supposed to drive inside the garage, was still parked outside. On further inspection, Tellier and Godin found the body of the watchman, sixty-seven-year-old William Davies, on the second floor of the garage. It was a sight neither of them would ever forget. Davies's head had literally been beaten to pieces. His face was largely unrecognizable, and there were bits of skull and flesh scattered about the garage floor. The killer had apparently opened a window on the ground floor, climbed over a radiator and surprised Davies at his desk. Then the killer had dragged him up to the second floor and finished him off with a machinist's hammer.

The sheer violence of the attack on the hapless watchman shocked even the investigators, who "said it was one of the most brutal murders in Windsor's history." The *Star* spared no sensational detail, speculating that "The murderer must have been out of his mind, hammering away at Davies long after he was dead," and that "In addition to the blows which shattered Davies' skull, several blows were aimed directly at his face." The newspaper even conjectured on the victim's final moments: "that the man held his hands over his head in a vain effort to protect his skull from the crushing impact of the hammer blows."[1] A photograph on the third page of the *Star* showed Davies's lifeless body partially covered with a tarp, giving readers a glimpse of the horrors the detectives found in the garage that morning.

As a disseminator of news (and often of raw emotions), the *Star* played a crucial role in the community. The newspaper's paid circulation was 61,630, and 38,938 of these subscribers lived in the greater Windsor area. In the absence of television and with limited local radio broadcasting (the area's only station was CKOK) the *Star* was a pervasive influence in shaping public views. The newspaper's president, Hugh Graybiel, was a solid conservative whose anti-union leanings would become apparent during the labor unrest of the late 1940s. The columnists, W. L. Clark writing the "As We See It" column and R. M. Harrison writing the "Now" column, carefully hewed to Graybiel's line. At one point, Harrison went so far as to link the Canadian Labour Congress and the democratic socialists in the Canadian Commonwealth Federation as similarly dedicated to creating a new order based on "the Communist policy of chaos and collapse."[2] With regard to the recent murders, the newspaper stressed the savagery of the killings and the need to hunt down any person or group who might be responsible.

The public perception of the garage killing was vastly different from that of the murder near the abandoned salt mines. First, William Davies was not a peculiar loner like Frank Sciegliski. A veteran of the First World War, Davies had served almost four years overseas and had been wounded twice. He had been living quietly in Windsor for twenty-six years, when he was viciously attacked as the rest of the city was preoccupied by the V-J celebrations. Early in the Davies investigation, police ruled out any connection between the Davies and Sciegliski murders. The "fiendish hammer murder," they reasoned, was a botched robbery unrelated to the Sciegliski killing, which Inspector MacNab insisted—even though Sciegliski's wallet had been taken—was an act of vengeance. The

Star, however, disagreed. "The two crimes have something in common," a reporter concluded, "in that each of them appears to have been committed by a murderer possessed by an unusual desire to kill."[3] In both cases, the attacks had been prolonged and had continued postmortem.

For better or worse, in the space of a week, the double slaying had focused the public's attention on the Windsor Police Department. Even without multiple homicides, it was a tall order for the force of 107 officers to police an often raucous community of over 100,000. Chief Constable Claude Renaud had repeatedly requested (and been denied) more officers. Despite the increase in population and sprawl that had resulted from the border-city amalgamation of 1935, the existing police force had even shrunk as a result of layoffs due to the Great Depression. By 1936, city funding was so low that the Windsor police could not afford ammunition for target practice. When the war began, the size of the force was effectively frozen, even as several officers volunteered for military service and one of them, Constable A.K. Green, was killed flying with the RCAF. The war had made novel demands on the Windsor force. A "Special Division" was formed to investigate subversive activities, and by 1944, this division had files on 635 Germans, 810 Italians and 108 Jehovah's Witnesses.[4] Nevertheless, most of the Special Division's work involved native Canadians trying to avoid military service.

In many instances, Canadian police were viewed as a heavy-handed force exerting urban discipline over the working poor. Additionally, they were often considered a foreign force, physically and ethnically removed from those they policed. In Toronto, for example, in the late nineteenth century, the police force consisted for the most part of Irish Protestants who lived in the wealthier parts of the city.[5] In Windsor as well, the police nominal roll was almost completely Anglo-Saxon or Celtic in a community with a substantial French-Canadian presence, as well as many recent Italian and Eastern-European immigrants. Few representatives of these populations (Chief Claude Renaud being a conspicuous exception) appeared on the police roster. In fact, it had taken considerable pressure from black community leaders for the Windsor force to accept its first black constable, Alton Parker, in 1942. Its only Italian constable had been dismissed when Italy had declared war on the Allies. Yet, despite its ethnic remove, the Windsor force was well known for casting a blind eye on gambling and prostitution in various parts of the city. Unlike other forces, whose members often considered themselves "domestic mission-aries" with the goal of coercing the working class toward a more elevated morality, Windsor police seemed quite willing, within reason, to let the citizens enjoy their carnal pleasures.

Of course, the police worked to control vice to a certain extent. The press regularly reported raids on bordellos and illegal betting shops. Typi-cal headlines in July 1945 announced "15 Caught in Police Raid" and that an Ottawa Street bookie had been shut down. Yet, considering the extent of the local prostitution trade, there were statistically very few arrests for persons found in bawdy houses. In the early war years, there were ten or fewer arrests per year. The figure spiked to twenty-seven in 1944, when the military insisted on more policing due to the threat of venereal disease.

As the numbers indicate, there was little enthusiasm for shutting down prostitution or gambling. As Bruce Macdonald, a lawyer who later be-came a reform-minded Crown Attorney in 1950 remarked, "It was just general laxity. . . . Cases were not being vigorously prosecuted. The police were not doing good work and aggressively pursuing their cases."[6] Many officers felt that something far more serious than laxity was to blame for the state of vice in Windsor. Senior officers, it seemed, were more than willing to shelter favored gambling and prostitution operations. One officer remembered, "There were deals made."[7] Another former officer recalled how reports on suspected bawdy houses were submitted to the morality squad, only to be thrown away and the officer told in no un-certain terms, "You dust them fucken doorknobs—we'll take care of the whores."[8] Officers brought onto the morality squad were instructed which side of the city to lay off. Any eager type who "went out and did something where you shouldn't have been, you weren't on [the morality squad] next week."[9] The bordellos on Pitt Street operated with the full knowledge and tacit approval of the police. The gambling houses on Ouellette Avenue broadcast the Chicago races even as officers walked past on patrol.

Some may have questioned how such a police force could handle a double murder. However, the Windsor police did have one advantage: their special relationship with local prostitutes. As one officer recalled, "Hookers: I could not say a bad word against them, and most policemen couldn't, because they were informants. They were mostly from out of town, and I guess a policeman was their only friend."[10] If the killer came from a local gang or even the Detroit mob, then the prostitutes might well lead the detectives to their man.

On Friday, August 17, Police Chief Renaud made a public appeal for any information on the murders. William Davies's killer might have been injured, as it appeared that the watchman had fought back. Someone must have seen the injured man on Windsor's streets. While the chief was prepared to concede that there were no leads in either case, he added ominously, "Our detectives are working hard to unravel these two crimes. We know that if such lawlessness goes unpunished we can expect more of it."[11]

———————

Sergeant Hugh Blackwood Price had been among the returning soldiers to arrive at the Canadian National Station on August 7. Like the other repatriated men, he had received a welcome-home basket and an embrace from a young Red Cross nurse. But unlike most of his comrades, Price had no wife or family at the station to greet him. His first night home, he had joined the horn-blasting crowd up on Ouellette Avenue but finished the night alone at the Active Service Club.

In addition to having no family, at age forty-five, Price was one of the oldest men in the contingent. Born in Belfast, Northern Ireland, he had served in the Ulster Volunteers during the First World War. Later, he immigrated to Canada and lived for a time in Winnipeg. During the thirties, he had moved to Windsor, where he had achieved some local notoriety with an astrology act. Dressed in the turban and flowing gowns of "Professor Cosmo," Price had entertained restaurant crowds by gazing into a crystal ball and telling fortunes. From time to time, he had also written an astrology column for the *Star*.

In May 1940, Price packed away his gowns and crystal ball to join the Essex Scottish Regiment. All in all, he had had a good war. Considered too old for the infantry, he was transferred to the Service Corps, where his wartime experiences were limited to the mess tent. This assignment still gave him ample time to socialize with the younger soldiers, and it was reported that among his young friends were men who owed him a total of about fifty dollars in outstanding loans. Army life seemed to agree with Sgt. Price, for he had volunteered to stay in the service as part of the Far East Force. Despite what he claimed was a substantial inheritance from his father, he intended to resume his career as an astrologer once the war was finally over. He had joked with friends that it would be no easy task, as he would have to get new robes and needed about four months to get the planets back into their correct order.[12]

In the meantime, Price spent his free time socializing with other veterans or servicemen-in-transit at the Active Service Club. Even though he was on leave, he got a job hefting barrels in a cold-storage warehouse, as "He felt he could not live without working." Physically, Price was a bluff man, about five feet eight inches tall and 180 pounds. He rented a room on Church Street, and his landlady noted that although he neither smoke nor drank, he kept liquor in his room. In her statement to police, she also stated that Price "stayed out late" and "prowled about all hours of the night." On Friday night, August 17, she said that Sgt. Price returned home from work and then left the rooming house at about 8:30 p.m. The landlady never saw him again.

If Government Park was only fitfully maintained, the vacant lands over the abandoned salt mine on either side of the Canadian Pacific Railway yard were an urban wilderness containing a few scraggly trees and masses of burdock, wild carrot, and grass. A hideous line of utility poles along Sandwich Street bordered all this untidy foliage. It was an ominous landscape, but where the ground was level, children had worn out impromptu baseball diamonds, and the plots were crisscrossed by a number of trails used as shortcuts by office workers or shoppers heading downtown. Shortly after 1:15 in the early morning of Saturday, August 18, Ernest White was returning to his house on Crawford Avenue on one of these trails when a glint of light caught his eye. White had passed along the same route between 9:30 or 10:00 p.m. and had not noticed anything unusual. Now he looked over and saw a man lying on the ground, his wristwatch glinting in the dim light of the streetlamps. White's first thought was that someone had merely fallen asleep in the open air. Thinking again, he decided not to disturb the person and instead hurried home and used a neighbor's telephone to summon the police.[13]

Detectives Sam Royan and Jim Hill arrived quickly on the scene and, with the help of flashlights, were soon trampling through the weeds searching for clues. This time, they easily established the victim's identity, since the killer had not bothered to remove his wallet, which carried the military identification of Sgt. Hugh Blackwood Price. There had obviously been a struggle, for in the morning light, the detectives could see that blood flecked the leaves of the undergrowth. They speculated that the sergeant had been running toward Sandwich Street to escape when the killer had caught up to him and delivered the fatal stab wounds. The trail of blood suggested that the killer had then dragged his victim some twenty or thirty feet deeper into the brush. There was a pool of blood about seven feet from the body, indicating that the killer had paused a moment to catch his breath. To have killed a man Price's size and then dragged the body that distance told the police that the killer was a man of formidable size.

Yet it was the sheer violence of Price's death that most startled the police and would shock the public. First, Price had sustained two major stab wounds in the back—one, at the base of the right shoulder blade, had penetrated the chest wall, and the other went through a lung. While both caused extensive bleeding, neither severed any major blood vessels. Additionally, there were nine stab wounds to the chest, none of which were deep, but all of which would also have caused additional blood loss. The cumulative effect of these stab wounds was that the sergeant had bled to death, and, as the coroner concluded, the killer must have "watched the man die over a period of possibly four or five minutes." Still not satisfied, the killer had stabbed Price yet again. One thrust crashed through a rib and penetrated his heart, while another slit his throat. There was no bleeding from this last flurry of attacks, for the sergeant's heart had already stopped beating. The killer had stabbed and kept on stabbing, even when the victim lay lifeless on the ground.

Detectives Royan and Hill had no doubt that whoever had killed Sgt. Price had also killed Frank Sciegliski. Indeed, there was an eerie similarity between the two homicides. Both men had been loners with few connections in the community. Both had been stabbed repeatedly, and many of the wounds had been administered postmortem. Perhaps most chilling was the fact that the bodies had been discovered less than 150 yards from each other. The detectives did, however, quickly rule out any connection between the Price-Sciegliski murders and the Easton Garage case, since the murder of the night watchman gave every indication of being a robbery gone wrong.

Other than Price's hideously disfigured body, police had little to work with. It was apparent that robbery was not the motive, for the killer had not bothered to remove Price's money or his wristwatch. Ernest White said that he had seen a car near the area around 9:30 or 10:00 that night, and tire tracks were clearly visible leaving the vacant lands. The detectives thought that White might be on to something, for the tracks appeared to be fresh, and they conjectured that there was a possibility Price had been murdered elsewhere and his body dumped on the abandoned salt-mine lands.

The following day, Saturday, August 18, 1945, the police investigated Sgt. Price's background; however, a search of his room produced little information. He had been writing a curious piece in which he revealed that Adolph Hitler was a reincarnation of Attila the Hun. Other than this unfinished manuscript, his room contained only necessities, along with a few pictures. Although he had mentioned to several people that he had relatives in Northern Ireland and that he was engaged to a Miss Mabel Gulliver of Winnipeg, there were no family photos or pictures of Miss Gulliver in the room. There were, however, several snapshots of other servicemen.

Once again, every detail of the police investigation would be reported in full in the next day's news stories, from the position of the body to how much money was left at the murder scene. One reporter quoted the detectives speculating that perhaps this was the case of a maniac "who kills perhaps for the thrill of it."[14] Inspector MacNab was candid—perhaps too candid—with the press. To a Toronto reporter he commented, "This is the worst outbreak of crime we ever had in Windsor—We are apparently dealing with a sadist of the worst type, a maniac." He went on to speculate that the killer must be similar to Jack the Ripper, who "found a sadistic pleasure in the deeds. Relieved of his frustrated emotions for a time, he would lie low until a morbid feeling overcame him and he would strike again."[15] Such philosophizing was probably the worst thing a jittery public could hear.

Bold headlines in the Saturday *Star,* such as "Believe Maniac is on Rampage," fed the panic. Most citizens did believe it, and they wondered who would be next. Rumors flew that there had been more atrocities unreported to the public, and calls flooded the police switchboard. It was said that a girl had been murdered in Jackson Park and that a radio announcer had been abducted and killed. One woman called police dispatch saying that her husband was on a hunting trip up north and pleading, "Can you send a policeman to watch the house tonight? I'm frightened."

And so it went, the *Star* noted, "A nightmarish sort of weekend for many. Home after home called the *Windsor Star* last night to inquire about more murders." Police interrupted a dance at Jackson Park and told the youngsters to go home as soon as it was dark. Detroit reporters found that "After dark Windsorites no longer were going out alone. Even on the downtown streets they moved in twos and threes." A prominent business executive left his car on the street, as he was afraid to move it into his own garage. The panic was hardly restricted to the faint of heart. Murray Rossell was an Essex Scottish combat veteran wounded in Europe. He arrived home one evening after the panic began, sweating and out of breath. When his mother asked him what was the matter, he explained that a man had just chased him down the street with a knife. However, a peek outside the door showed that no one was there.[16]

The lead editorial in the *Star* the Monday after the Price murder summed up the prevailing sense of panic: "This Fiend Must Be Caught." The "fiend" now had a nickname; he had become the Slasher, a sadistic phantom who killed at random for his own pleasure. The *Star* editorial described his impact: "Never before has Windsor been so deeply stirred by a crime wave. People have begun to go in actual fear of their lives, and with some justification. The nature of the crimes perpetrated leaves no doubt that mere senseless blood-lust is the sole motive."[17] Here, as in the public perception, the Slasher was characterized as a degenerate, one of the frightening characters from the Saturday matinee B movies. The *Star* editorial went on to pontificate that "experts in psychology" agree that "the murders are the work of someone with a perverted mind." These conclusions—based on nothing more than editorial-room gossip and augmented by photos of Price lying in a weed patch and graphic descriptions of his slow death—would inevitably lead to communal terror.

"It caused everyone to . . . live in fear," recalled one Windsor resident. The tenor of the news stories and the photos of the victims only fed the panic, for "the description of the remains would indicate the horror of the event." Terrifying rumors began to circulate, for instance that the Slasher had sliced off his victims' penises. A policeman recalled that "Everyone was fearful. . . . Everybody, woman and child thought 'I could be next.'"[18] This hysteria seemed odd in a community in which death was no stranger. After the Dieppe raid, for example, pages of photographs appeared in the newspaper of men who were lost or killed. In the final days of the war, it was rare for a day to go by without the *Star* reporting another local boy killed in Europe. But the Slasher killings were different. They were not happening in far off Europe but down the street. The victims were not servicemen who knew that death was a possible result of their duty, but seemingly random citizens. As the police officer recalled, the Slasher hysteria was different because "everyone was fearful."

The terror intensified when someone calling himself "Slasher Evans" scrawled a message in the washroom on the Canadian side of the Detroit-Windsor Tunnel that read

I'm the slasher. I've stood and talked to cops at the scene of my last killing before this. I killed a German in a camp for that I was dishonorably discharged from the U.S. Army. I'll kill until I'm ready to stop. I can never be caught—to all cops.

On the washroom door, the following message was written, "I am slasher Evans—they will never get me" and "Civilian—sergent—sergent—girl next."[19] Without hesitation, Chief Renaud dismissed the writing as the work of a crank, for it seemed too melodramatic by far to be authentic. Nevertheless, the note fed popular hysteria and led many citizens to believe that a woman would be the next victim. One young man recalled that many people accepted the warning at face value, saying, "The writing on the wall said that a woman would be next. . . . That really threw all the women and families into terror because this guy was portrayed as a maniac, and I am sure he was."[20]

This level of hysteria created a sociological event called a moral panic, a brief episode during which a community is intensely concerned about a perceived threat that, upon later examination, turns out not to have been especially dangerous. In this case, a single killer had become "the Slasher," a menacing phantom, a folk-devil incarnate. He was an evil presence who could attack at random and who posed a special threat to vulnerable women. The creation of a moral panic relies upon exaggeration and distortion.[21] Much of the misinformation in Windsor was fed by the hysteria itself, and the rest was supplied by the press, who reported numerous nonexistent Slasher attacks.

Even before the Slasher incident, the *Star* had stressed deviance heavily in its stories. Reporters regularly followed the Morality Squad and wrote exposés revealing the evils of brothels and their inmates. The Slasher showcased deviance of a different order but still of an eminently newsworthy nature. This was a "bloodlusting maniac," a person outside of normal society. As sociologist Stanley Cohen observes, "The media have long operated as agents of moral indignation in their own right . . . Their very reporting of certain 'facts' can be sufficient to generate concern, anxiety, indignation or panic."[22] The *Star*'s editorial page best captured this chimera when it featured the image of a black, sinister Slasher confronting a vulnerable group of men, women, and children.

The Windsor panic of 1945 met most of the criteria for a classic moral panic: There was a heightened level of public concern, a consensus that the threat was serious, and a determination that something be done. The level of anxiety was out of proportion to the actual threat, and the folk devil, in the form of the Slasher, assumed a menacing figure far beyond any possible reality.[23] The Windsor panic differed from a classic panic in only one element: precise focus on a responsible individual or group. The best the citizens of Windsor could do was to categorize the Slasher as an "outsider," for no normal person could have performed such acts. Normal members of society steered clear of the fringe elements, the drifters and alcoholics who populated the flophouses and fought weekend battles downtown. Therefore, it was widely believed that the folk devil was likely to be found among these interlopers. The fever created by the moral panic justified ending the terror by any means possible. The Windsor police force immediately began to make mass arrests of anyone behaving suspiciously who did not fit the criteria of normalcy, including drifters, bums, and other outsiders.

Slasher reports poured into police dispatch and were filed, along with follow-up reports, in the police investigation file. Due to the unprecedented nature of the Slasher case, these files were preserved even after almost all other contemporary files were eventually destroyed. The Slasher investigation was subdivided into nine files based on each victim and two general files. These files are structured so that each one contains all relevant material, which could be used by the Crown Attorney's office in a later prosecution. These files give a glimpse of the frantic activity that engulfed the Windsor police in August 1945 in response to reports of suspicious activity. On August 8, two men working a night shift stopped for lunch at the Tea Garden Restaurant on Ouellette Avenue at 3:20 a.m.

They saw a man with bloody clothing enter the restaurant and go directly to the washroom. He was a heavy-set man "who looked like a foreigner." Another man was taken to Hotel Dieu Hospital, and, although he was bleeding profusely, he would not say what had caused his injuries. On August 18, at 2:10 a.m.—shortly after Price's murder—a witness reported a man entering the Belmont Café downtown wearing army trousers covered with blood. The operator of Quality Dry Cleaners reported that a bloody suit of clothes had been brought in for cleaning. Most of these reports described the man in the bloody clothes as an apparent foreigner in his thirties or forties.[24] Two-man teams of detectives were assigned to each lead. Predictably, none of these clues concerning a murderer who visited public places while wearing gory pants or who sent incriminating clothes to a dry cleaner yielded any results. They all contributed to the general misinformation and hysteria of the panic.

Windsor's mayor, Arthur Reaume, responded forcefully to the Slasher hysteria. Arguably one of the most flamboyant politicians ever to lead a Canadian city, Reaume was a tall, dapper figure who, despite a persistent stutter, was a seductive charmer. As the boy mayor of Sandwich at the age of twenty-six, he had become prominent as a result of his compassion for those on relief. In advocating for the poor, he had become increasingly identified with left-wing causes, and after the war, it would be insinuated that he had communist connections. But during the war, he had led bond drives and secured hundreds of government-sponsored houses for war workers. Also, in a deeply racist society in which blacks were denied access to hotels, restaurants, and job opportunities, Reaume had insisted that blacks be hired by and promoted at City Hall as equals.[25]

But there was another side to Arthur Reaume. No one liked a good time better than he did, and those who knew him recalled that he was a constant womanizer who, when not entertaining off-duty nurses from the municipally operated Metropolitan Hospital, could be found socializing at the Blue Water or the British American Hotel. It was rumored that the gambling halls and illegal beverage rooms made regular payouts to the mayor. The free and easy attitude the mayor took toward sex, drinking, and gambling was another signal to the police on the street that in Windsor, anything goes.

Even before Price's body had been discovered, Mayor Reaume had met with Police Chief Renaud and Deputy Chief W. H. Neale to discuss the crisis created by the Davies and Sciegliski murders. All police leaves were cancelled, and Windsor officers were put on twelve-hour shifts. Additionally, since the situation was obviously beyond the capacity of Windsor's limited force, officers from the Ontario Provincial Police and the Royal Canadian Mounted Police were brought into the investigation. Furthermore, the Windsor Board of Control, the municipality's executive, offered a two-thousand-dollar reward (the *Star* had already offered one thousand) for valid information on the case. "We will spare neither time, money nor energy in our efforts to rid the city of this fiendish menace," the mayor grandly pronounced. Somewhat more cagily, he added that civic and police officials had decided on a course of action, saying, "I am not at liberty to divulge the details of this action—but I can say that it was put into effect an hour after the meeting closed."[26]

For his part, Chief Renaud urged calm and asked citizens for their help. Price had been in uniform when last seen downtown, and someone must have noticed him. "We feel that somewhere there must be some information that will be of considerable value in our work," Renaud told the *Star*, "and the idea of the rewards is to spur the people towards disclosing that information." Just below the surface of the chief's plea was an admission that the police had no evidence or leads to work with and no idea who the Slasher might be.

3

"WHEN IN DOUBT THROW HIM IN"

What Arthur Reaume meant by "a course of action" became apparent by August 20, the Monday after the Price slaying. The largest manhunt in Windsor's history had gotten underway over the weekend, and the jails were rapidly filling up.

But filling up with whom? The *Star* had already circulated the opinion that the Slasher had to be a "blood-lusting maniac" with a "perverted mind." That narrowed things down considerably, for at least the authorities would not need to search for the Slasher among the members of ordinary society. A perverted individual would surely stand out. The *Star* editorialists advised the police to apprehend those derelicts who could be found among "the too large numbers of unsavory characters that haunt [Windsor's] parks and alleys," for they were confident that the Slasher "is to be found among the riff-raff that congregate in certain undesirable sections of the community." Taking an almost hygienic approach to the problem, the editorialists noted that "Perhaps a clean-up earlier would not have prevented the killings, but it would have avoided a number of unsavory incidents." In this cleansing process, upright citizens were beyond suspicion and should be left alone. Instead, the police "dragnet should be thrown out and every man rounded up who cannot prove that he is respectable and self-supporting."[1]

Obligingly, the Windsor police seemed to take their cue from the *Star*. Chief Renaud agreed that the killer "was not likely to be a family man" but must live among the flotsam and jetsam that populated Windsor's rooming houses. These rooming houses and cheap apartments sheltered an ever-changing clientele of drifters, men seeking short-term employment or men just trying to get away from someone or something. Most of the rooming houses were located downtown, only a block or so from the bordellos and beer halls of Pitt Street. On Saturday and Sunday, August 18 and 19, the Windsor police, with reinforcements from the OPP and the RCMP, swept furiously through the rooming houses, interrogating the occupants and ransacking their rooms. Anyone who appeared the least bit suspicious was taken in. Many men were arrested for possession of concealed weapons, even though the rooming houses were notoriously violent, and it was only prudent to carry some kind of weapon.

By Monday morning, the jail was packed with over thirty suspects. As the *Toronto Globe and Mail* reported, "the dragnet is out for all 'loose, idle persons.'"[2] On Monday, Magistrate Angus MacMillan remanded three men to jail for possessing concealed weapons. "The three accused, all shabbily dressed, heard a warning from Magistrate A. W. MacMillan: 'In dangerous times like these it's certainly not advisable to be found with weapons on you.'"[3] Throughout the manhunt, the city's magistrates compliantly detained whomever the police found suspicious.

Within the context of similar moral panics, police have responded much as the Windsor force did, by initiating a violent campaign that promises decisive results. In fact, the police "form part of the circle out of which 'moral panics' develop. It is part of the paradox that they also, advertently and inadvertently, *amplify* the deviancy they seem so absolutely committed to controlling."[4] The police respond to a moral panic in much the same way as the media and the government. Something extraordinary happens, and, as a result, something forceful must be done. It would have been unthinkable for the Windsor police force to have treated the sudden spate of killings as simply another string of crimes to be investigated.

The public also responded in a predictably extreme manner. In addition to summoning police for false alarms, during the first week of Slasher hysteria, many citizens used the opportunity to inform on anyone they disliked. A man with a pocket full of newspaper clippings seemingly re-lated to the Slasher was taken in. The detainees also included one Ernie Evans, who had an unregistered gun and the misfortune to possess the same surname as the individual who had supposedly written on the tunnel washroom wall. Perhaps it was a measure of the hysteria that a man with a gun rather than a knife should become a suspect in a series of stabbings. Scores of accusatory letters poured in to police headquarters. It seemed that the wartime camaraderie was breaking down into angry circles of denunciation and mistrust.

One of the most bizarre stories concerned a black woman who had reportedly been going door-to-door collecting money to buy shoes for Ethiopian children. She allegedly told a Windsor woman that "colored people did not get any consideration" and that, consequently, a secret soci-ety of black men in Detroit was planning to kill whites. This bloodletting would happen as soon as the war was over. Every dead white man, she said, would open up a job for a black. "How would you like to find some of your men folks lying on your front doorstep stabbed to death?" she supposedly asked, adding that this secret society had a branch in Amherstburg and that they "are going to do business."[5] It is difficult to know how seriously the police took such racist accusations, but every credible tip had to be investigated. In another report, a passerby informed the police that next door to a house where the police had found bloodstains lived a Japanese couple. "Did the police investigate these Japanese?" the passerby inquired. They did, and detectives Paget and Carter concluded, "Nothing to it."[6]

Suspicion even fell on returning soldiers. The wounds the Slasher had inflicted were so deep that the murder weapon was described as "a com-mando knife," as it was felt that only someone trained in "commando tac-tics" could have carried out such assaults. After all, many of the returned men had seen and done terrible things overseas. While that had all been for a patriotic cause, it was possible that some of these men could not turn off their wartime bloodlust. One call to the Windsor police concerned a veteran who raged that his brother had died at Dieppe and that he was going to have his vengeance on society.[7] Another referred to a discharged man who said that he had gotten syphilis from a prostitute and that he was going to kill all the prostitutes he could find. Sgt. Price had spent most of his spare time at the Active Service Club, and a number of ser-vicemen were called in for questioning to determine if anyone had held a grudge against him. Indeed, the last persons to see Price alive were two soldiers. Lance Corporal Eugene Doe had last seen Price in the company of a youthful serviceman of eighteen or nineteen walking the downtown streets at about eight o'clock that night.[8]

In an unnerving counterpoint to the panic, a macabre fascination with the Slasher phenomenon began to grow. Scores of curious people flocked to the vacant lots near the train embankment to walk over the sites where Frank Sciegliski and Hugh Price had died. Some "even dipped their fingers in the earth that had been soaked with the slain men's blood."[9] Children in the west end began to play Slasher instead of cowboys and Indians. One child would be designated as the Slasher while the others ran and hid, and if "the Slasher was able to catch you, you were dead."[10] Gawkers milled about the vacant salt mine lands snooping about for clues the detectives had overlooked. One individual announced that he intended to sleep in the vacant lands until he came face to face with the Slasher. A knife-wielding youngster from Detroit appeared and said that he intended to patrol the park until he solved the mystery. Another man was apprehended in the weed patch at four in the morning and explained to police that "he had gone out there on a hunch that a little investigation would clear up the whole affair."[11] To some extent, this private zeal may have been fed by the offers of reward money or by altruism. However, the end result was to distract the investigators from the task at hand.

That task appeared to be to arrest every vagrant in sight. As the week progressed, more and more suspects were hauled in, and the courts "cooperated with police by remanding in custody any prisoners who have appeared to be worth further investigation." By the end of the week more than one hundred arrests had been made in the Slasher case. Any rooming house inmate who could not offer a satisfactory account of himself faced being locked up in Windsor's Sandwich Jail. "'When in doubt throw him in' has been the motto of the Windsor police since their intensive manhunt began last Saturday," the *Star* reported.[12]

In addition to the massive but ultimately futile roundup, some police work was being done covertly. Charles Weston, a junior constable recently discharged from the army, was given an undercover assignment as "bait" in the parks. Weston had actually known Price when the latter was still in the Essex Scottish. Now in civilian clothes, Weston was paired with another undercover officer, Jack Adlington, to walk the downtown parks and frequent public restrooms. Chosen because of their training in unarmed combat, Weston and Adlington also carried blackjacks and handguns. "We were nervous," Weston later admitted. "We didn't want to get in a position where he could use that knife of his on us—but between the two of us we thought we could take on the world."[13] Despite their best efforts, however, they never encountered the Slasher.

Soon enough, George Mannie found himself interrogated by police once again. By Wednesday, August 22, the detectives had finally made a connection between the Price-Sciegliski slayings and the assault on Mannie. The manner of the attack, a surprise knife thrust in the back, was almost identical to that used on the other victims. Even the site of the assault on Mannie at the foot of California Street was only about a quarter of a mile from Government Park. When Mannie was called in to police headquarters, he was again unable or unwilling to give up the true story. He suggested to the detectives, "Such murders could be perpetrated by persons crazed by dope or from smoking marihuana cigarettes."[14]

Police did follow up on Mannie's repeated assertion that the attacker was black. Philip Wilson, nicknamed "Kinger," was a local black man who had been connected to a number of crimes. In February 1945, he had testified at the inquest into the deaths of four children in a house fire on Howard Avenue. Since that time, he had been living in Hamilton, Ontario. Wilson was brought back to Windsor, and on August 27, he was interrogated at length by Chief Renaud and the lead detective in the Slasher killings, John Mahoney. Apparently, the fact that Wilson had not been living in Windsor at the time of the Slasher killings was not enough to eliminate him from suspicion.

Other suspects came from as far away as Detroit, which was not immune to the Slasher hysteria. On the day after Price's body was discovered, a Detroiter boasted that he had killed three people and planned to kill more. He was promptly arrested. Justine Merlin of Detroit received a call from a man who said that he was the "Windsor killer" and that he was going to ambush her. Detroit police posted a guard at her house.[15] Some of the letters pouring in to Windsor police headquarters came from Detroit, one written by a woman who suspected that her former physics teacher at Eastern High School might be the Slasher. After all, she wrote, he was an odd individual suspected of being "addicted to dope."[16]

Detroiters were particularly intrigued when the first "hot" suspect in the Slasher case was an American. Richard Rowe, a veteran of the First World War and an itinerant tinsmith, was arrested in a flophouse, the Windsor Hotel, and found to be in possession of a commando-style knife.[17] There was no doubt that Rowe was a suspicious character who fit the *Star*'s profile of a dangerous drifter. Although he had graduated from Tri-State University in Angola, Indiana, he had never held down a job, and for over two decades, he had meandered across the United States and Canada. Two Detroit detectives, Lieutenants Harry O'Brien and Gene Kinney, had interrogated Rowe regarding the Benny Evangelista slaying in Detroit in 1929. In this horrific unsolved case, seven members of the same family had been murdered. He was also questioned by Sergeant R. W. Eaton of the Michigan State Police about the stabbing death of a seven-year-old boy in Ypsilanti, Michigan, in 1935. After a thorough interrogation, Michigan police were satisfied that Rowe had had no involvement in either case.

However, Windsor detectives still considered Rowe a prime suspect. When a knife was found in his room, and police asked him about what appeared to be bloodstains on the blade, he unwisely responded that was not possible, as he had just thoroughly washed it. Although he told officers that he did not read newspapers and was unaware that the war was over, his wallet was stuffed with newspaper clippings. One concerned a moonlight celebration for the Women's Volunteer Reserve Corps. The clipping seemed to police to be related to the washroom threats, which had indicated that a girl was to be the Slasher's next victim. When asked about the clippings, Rowe had responded casually, "Well, what's wrong with that? Can't a fellow start a scrap book?"

Foreshadowing future police tactics, Windsor detectives interrogated Rowe for nine straight hours. While he denied any involvement in the Slasher killings, he did confess to being "a believer in cosmic rays and that he holds they can make him do things he doesn't want to do." That was enough for the detectives. Rowe was charged with possession of an illegal weapon, the commando knife, and remanded into custody. The detectives who interrogated Rowe were likely the source of the *Star*'s report that "The finger of suspicion was again directed to Richard Rowe, chief suspect in Windsor's murder wave."[18]

In addition to consulting with *Star* reporters, the Windsor police turned to self-styled experts such as Royal Baker, a former Detroit police lieutenant and movie censor, who shortly after the panic began was acknowledged as their top advisor. Baker had developed a theory on "maniacal murders" in the United States that he thought could likely be applied to the Windsor situation. First of all, these kinds of murders were committed near cemeteries or railroads and occurred at times of celebration (such as V-E Day), when the public was distracted. The cutting of the throat, according to Baker, most definitely indicated "the work of a sexual pervert." Early on, Baker warned that this kind of killer, the "holiday ripper" might strike again around Labor Day. Later in the week, Baker refined his hypothesis to suggest that the killings were likely the work of a sixty-three-year-old black man who was responsible for many atrocities across the United States. He concluded that the Price-Sciegliski slayings, as well as the murder of the watchman, William Davies, were all "the kind of crime which one might expect from a homicidal maniac."[19] In the end, Baker's theories were proven not only incorrect but laughably absurd.

The implausibility of Baker's theory did not stop the Windsor police from soliciting his opinion or the *Star* from publishing his ramblings in detail. Not only did the Slasher hysteria make for good press, it gave the *Star*'s editorial staff a chance to crusade for a purification of the streets of Windsor. In an editorial published on Thursday, August 23, titled "Let's Have a Real Cleanup," the newspaper called for a war on the real cancer the citizens faced: "There is the failure to clean the bums and drifters out of the community. On the streets and in the parks and alleys these unsavory characters have for months been making things unpleasant for the law abiding citizens." According to the *Star*, these vagrants were the root cause of the problem, and when they disappeared, so would the Slasher problem. Not only were there three unsolved murders, but the city was facing "an epidemic of robberies, assaults and drunken brawls." The sooner these drifters were dealt with, the sooner this epidemic of crime would be cured. The fact that "the majority of them have committed no crime" should not have, in the *Star*'s view, stood in the way of a police crackdown. If vagrants could not be jailed, then they "could at least be ordered out of town."

It is unclear to what extent the general public shared the *Star*'s Gestapo-like enthusiasm to apprehend and punish those whose most serious crime was being down and out. However, the police seem to have adopted it with a passion. On Saturday, August 25, twenty more vagrants were taken in, and of those, six were remanded for further questioning. These detentions brought to more than 125 the number of "investigation arrests" made in the week since the Price murder.

But if the public was temporarily comforted by these police actions, its terror only intensified with the discovery, on the evening of August 30, of yet another message on the Detroit-Windsor tunnel washroom wall:

"IM SLASHER YOU MAY THINK I'M THROUGH BUT I WILL STRIKE AGAIN TWICE—FAST—VERY DAM SOON—[20]

Despite this commotion, by the second week after Sgt. Price's murder, it was apparent that the police were not about to lay any charges. Even the hottest suspect, Richard Rowe, had been a disappointment. Inspector MacNab clung to a futile hope that Rowe was a suspect even when confronted with a streetcar ticket that put him in Toronto on the day of the Sciegliski killing and with results from the fingerprint test on the Easton Garage that also exonerated him. At the beginning of September, Rowe was committed for sixty days to the Ontario Hospital in London for psychiatric evaluation and at that point could no longer be considered a plausible suspect in the Slasher case.

Meanwhile, the two-man detective teams were attempting to sort out every lead—a tedious and futile process. A businessman walking downtown saw a suspicious man trimming tree branches with a knife and assumed that he was the Slasher. A young lady was suddenly grabbed by a man in a car who called out, "Come here baby, you know the score." Perhaps this would-be lothario was the Slasher. Inevitably, there was a comic dimension to some of the incoming calls. An amorous couple near the bridge in Ambassador Park discovered a man creeping up to watch their tryst. Even when a barrage of rocks forced him to retreat, they assumed that this harmless Peeping Tom was intent on murder.

Detectives Alf Carter and Bill Blair were one of the teams assigned to investigate reports from the public. One of their tips concerned a Mrs. Little, who insisted that her boy had been assaulted by a Slasher-like person. Carter and Blair soon learned, however, that Mrs. Little had no son. Similarly, they were called upon to check out a suspicious character named Verity, who lived at the Coronation Hotel, yet they found that no such person had ever registered at that hotel. Another informer led them to a black man on McDougall Street named Johnson, whom the detectives did not find suspicious in the least. Carter and Blair reported on September 2 that every one of the tips they had pursued had been useless.[21] The last note in the investigating officer's file for the Slasher killings is dated September 6, 1945. Within three weeks of Price's murder, the trail was dead cold.

Many people in Windsor were becoming impatient at the failure to get any results, and sniping at the police began to appear in the *Star*'s Letters to the Editor section. "When is the attorney general in Toronto going to step in and clean up our inefficient police department?" one citizen asked. "Three murders in ten days; two in the same place! Windsor is wide open for murders, safe-robberies, prostitution and gambling."[22] Instead of protecting the public, another wrote, "The Windsor Police are very good at tagging cars and insulting the public." Two days later, another pundit speculated that instead of solving these murders, the police were

(1) Issuing parking tickets to poor suckers who have parked their cars outside of Fords
(2) Raiding handbooks and bringing in load on load of poor saps whose only crime is betting two megs on "Spark Plug" in the third.[23]

Even an editorial in the *Star* commented that the unsolved murders did not "speak well for the type of law enforcement we have been getting."[24]

With all the furor over the killer on the loose and the police department's failure to make any headway in the cases, little attention was paid to the Slasher victims. On Tuesday morning, August 21, Sgt. Hugh Blackwood Price was buried in the soldiers' plot at Windsor Grove Cemetery. The burial service and the playing of "The Last Post" were forced to compete with the clatter of the scrap yard on the other side of the alley. Few people were in attendance. Only two officers from the Essex Scottish Regiment and the bugler were in uniform, and one of the men from the funeral home had to fill in as a pallbearer. The newspaper had reported comments from Price's friends and acquaintances in Windsor. Perhaps not wanting to draw attention to themselves, none of them attended.

4

THE ROOT OF THE PANIC

Maureen Crone, an attractive eighteen-year-old, was working at the counter of the handkerchief department at C. H. Smith's department store on August 22, the Wednesday following the Price murder, when a man approached her and asked: "Are you afraid?" Miss Crone looked at him and asked what she should be afraid of. "Afraid to die," he responded. She said no. The man leaned toward her and said, "Well, you ought to." He abruptly turned and left the store. The Smith's management reported the incident to the police but begged them not to publicize it.[1]

This instance was only one of several accounts of women being threatened during the weeks after the Slasher attacks. The same day as the Price murder, a woman walking down Tecumseh Road was suddenly pulled into a field by a man who called out, "Come on, Sister." The shaken victim suggested to the police, "He is a sex manic."[2] Although the Slasher's victims had so far been men, the Slasher had been categorized as a "sex pervert," and the writing in the Detroit-Windsor tunnel washroom had forewarned of a Slasher attack on a woman. These factors, intensified by the writing of *Star* reporters, heightened the sense of danger for the women and girls of Windsor.

In the second week of the Slasher hysteria, the *Star* published two articles about how society had lost its way, enabling sex deviants to roam at large. Titled "Many Sex Crimes Still Unsolved" and "Prosecutions Few for Sex Crimes," the articles implied that there was a sudden epidemic of sexually motivated attacks against women and children.[3] The author, Weston Gaul, began by graphically describing the unsolved rape of a young woman. The woman had woken to find a stranger in her apartment. After bludgeoning her, "He criminally assaulted her twice, after which he tied her legs together and went about ransacking the apartment."

In addition to this horror, Gaul had discovered that there were forty-eight sex complaints (the natures of which were not stated) that remained unsolved in "police sex files." The attackers were "sex prowlers" and "moral wrecks" who victimized single females. Gaul went on to recount how children, "the majority under the age of 12," were also the victims of sex perverts. While there was seemingly no connection between the Slasher killings and the molestation of women and children, the juxtaposition of these articles with reports of the Slasher attacks made it appear as if it was all one vast contagion of crime.

The *Star* editorial on Thursday, August 23, titled "Let's Have a Real Cleanup," also linked the Slasher to the sex-crime problem. If the *Star* was to be believed, the city was undergoing an epidemic of crime for which there was no cure: "No one convicted of such a [sex-related] offence should be let off with a brief prison sentence. The law should recognize that the guilty person is a continuous menace to society who should be put away permanently. Release after a short term simply lets him loose to prey on innocent victims again and again."

A follow-up report by Gaul recounted the case of a convicted child molester who had relied on a previously unblemished criminal record and an honorable discharge from the military to get a suspended sentence. Not soon after, he reoffended, and his second offense was "disgusting almost to the point of being nauseating.... This able-bodied chap had lured a nine year old girl to an isolated spot and there had taken more than the usual type of indecent liberties with her." This time he was sentenced to six months definite and three months indefinite in the reformatory.

This and other *Star* articles gave the public the impression that sex-related attacks were frequent occurrences and that law enforcement was doing little to curb them. Yet the criminal statistics in the Chief Constable's Annual Reports indicated exactly the opposite. For the years 1941 to 1944, the number of indecent assaults (which meant any complaint filed regarding a sexual advance on a woman) averaged seven a year. In 1945, this number increased to twelve but was only a fraction of the 350 common assaults that year. From 1941 to 1944, the total number of assaults per year averaged 206, meaning that sex-related attacks counted for between two and three percent of the total. Rape was also an infrequent offense in Windsor. For the years 1941 and 1942, there was only one attempted rape reported. In 1945 there was one rape charge.

In addition to common assaults, the most frequent crimes reported involved bawdy and gaming houses—misconduct in which women featured prominently as participants, not victims. Between 1941 and 1943, an average of seven women a year were prosecuted for being inmates of bawdy houses. This figure jumped to thirty in 1944 to reflect the Morality Squad's crackdown in support of the military's campaign against venereal disease.[4] Given a city of Windsor's size—over 100,000 persons—the number of violent offenses against women seemed statistically small.

It was not until near the end of his exposé that Gaul conceded, "The total number [of sex-related offences] for the year is pitifully few. In fact, a reporter of the *Star* was able to find only 12 prosecutions for the year." None of these were for rape, and two were merely Peeping Toms. Gaul's report on rampant sex crimes also included cases where men had exposed themselves. One man convicted of indecent exposure was given six months fixed and six months indefinite imprisonment. A man convicted of being a "window peeper" received thirty days in jail. The reality was that few sex offenses against either women or children came before the courts. When such cases were prosecuted and the perpetrators convicted, they were harshly punished. Nevertheless, Gaul's reports were an important element in fostering a climate conducive to moral panic. Despite the hyperbole, the press was fulfilling a function it relished, that of casting itself "in the role of moral guardian, ever alert to new possibilities for concern and indignation."[5]

Readers of the *Star* reports had likely already been conditioned to believe that a wave of sex crimes was imminent. From 1937 to 1940, the American press had regularly warned that an army of sex fiends threatened decent society, and there was widespread media coverage of sensational cases involving child molestation and rape. Drifters, unemployed men, and other Depression-era vagabonds like Richard Rowe who did not live within the bounds of regular society were often portrayed as psychopaths. In 1937, FBI Director J. Edgar Hoover called for a war on the sex criminal and proclaimed, "the sex fiend, most loathsome of all the vast army of crime, has become a sinister threat to the safety of American childhood and womanhood."[6]

The alarm was raised against this threat at a time when there was no statistical indication that the incidence of child molestation or the rape of women was increasing. Nevertheless, "In response to the sex crime panic, police roundups of 'perverts' became common, especially in the wake of highly publicized assaults on children. The targets of the crackdowns were often minor offenders, such as male homosexuals."[7] The sex-crime panic justified increased police surveillance of all deviant behavior. Concern with aggressive sexual conduct by males, whether it came from a predatory homosexual, a sexual psychopath, or a child molester (the terms were often used interchangeably) may even have begun as early as the 1920s. Official concern with ending prostitution and "white slavery" (inducing women into prostitution) seems to have declined about the time of the First World War and was supplanted by steady increases in arrests for crimes of male aggression, including rape, child molestation, and sodomy. Evolving attitudes about sexuality focused on the predatory homosexual, and even by the 1920s, "the child molester, and especially the homosexual one, was a momentous social danger."[8]

The targeting of sexually aggressive males was a relatively recent phenomenon, for in the late nineteenth century, Canadian society was still primarily concerned with deviations from correct female conduct. Women were supposed to be pure, and therefore the worst form of female deviancy was prostitution. This "social evil" was harshly condemned, for "The prostitute, who was entrepreneurial, sexual and public, was the antithesis of true womanhood."[9] While in the early twentieth century, the term psychopath "remained synonymous with female immorality,"[10] by the 1930s, concern with sexual deviancy fell heavily on the aggressive male. In larger American cities, arrest rates for prostitution fell while arrests for rape and sodomy increased. By the 1930s, there was increased concern on the threat of male aggression to minors' sexuality.

Larger Canadian cities had similar problems with an active sex trade between men and between men and boys. Theaters attracted them to the "dark recesses of galleries and balconies" and offered a modicum of privacy for sexual encounters. Frequently, if not most often, boys engaged in sex with men and expected payment from their older companions. Working-class boys were expected to contribute to family income, and sex with men was often one of the safer and easier ways to make money.[11] Still, when such liaisons became public, they were harshly condemned, and a particularly heinous case could spark a panic. Such was the case in Oshawa, Ontario, in 1927, when H. W. Elliott, the superintendent of the Children's Aid Society, was charged with the sexual molestation of boys in his care. When his conviction was appealed, the Crown Attorney wrote to the Deputy Attorney General, "I do certainly hope that you will be successful in this appeal, as the public opinion in the City and locality is very much riled."[12]

In both the United States and Canada, such incidents could instill a fear that deviants were at large and threatening the innocent. Crime statistics for Windsor during the 1930s indicate that there was no sex-crime problem and that, if anything, these crimes were relatively insignificant. Nevertheless, demands for action from the media and the political establishment drowned out criminologists who asserted that there had been no significant rise in sex crimes. As a result of public hysteria, between 1935 and 1937, five American states passed sexual psychopath laws. During the war years, the panic abated, and the media focused on the real drama of the international armed struggle. Reports of outrages against children dwindled, even though the level of arrests for sex offenses remained similar to the 1930s. When the war was over, however, the press began to look again at stories that stirred local passions. In the postwar period, the dread of a crime wave reemerged, giving the often false impression that delinquency and crime were everywhere on the increase.

The series of articles by Weston Gaul seemed to herald a new sex-crime panic—one that even the author conceded had no basis in crime statistics. What made the situation seem all the more desperate to the public was that the authorities were doing so little. On September 1, on the heels of the Gaul articles, an editorial entitled "Sex Crime Treatment" appeared in the *Star* on the error of mercy: "Records of the disposition of sex criminals in the local Magistrate's Court for the past six months, as assembled by the Star, do not augur well for the suppression of such practices here. In too many cases, offenders have been treated with leniency that does virtually nothing to protect society. The fact that the victims in such cases are little girls makes the situation all the more serious."

In the troubled summer of 1945, the *Star* editorialists saw this misplaced mercy as the source of societal rot, claiming, "Sex perverts can serve a comparatively short sentence, and then be let loose to prey again at will on the young and innocent." The *Star* criticized the judicial system's "complete failure to recognize that the sex pervert is a psychopathic case who cannot be cured by any number of prison sentences. . . . In the hopeless cases, which are in the majority, there should be permanent incarceration."

Yet, in an odd contradiction, the editorialists were willing to consider that the Slasher (whoever he might be) was probably suffering from a mental disability—that he was a "psychopathic case" who "should be placed in an institution for study and treatment rather than in a jail cell." Even without the chance to analyze the subject, the editorialists suspected that the killer must be psychotic, based on the nature of his actions. However, their reaction was not retributive; they held out hope that modern medical science could affect a cure. Sex dangers might be controlled, not by the penal system, the *Star* argued, but by public health authorities. This line of reasoning marked a significant change from preceding decades, when incarceration or execution was considered the only appropriate response to sexual assaults.

It is difficult to gauge exactly how much influence the *Star's* articles and editorials had over the average Windsorite. The newspaper was the principle source for local information, so it is likely that the vast majority of people accepted that such a threat against women and children existed. Leon Paroian, the younger brother of several older sisters, recalled that "admonitions went out to my three sisters that they were not to be out at night."[13] The reality of the multiple killings seemed to fulfill the editorial warnings that a public menace was on the loose. Despite the fact that all of the victims to date had been men, it seemed as if vulnerable women were also at risk. Parks patrols, consisting of either uniformed police officers or groups of concerned citizens, were all on the lookout for child molesters or the Slasher—who in all likelihood could be one and the same.

No one expressed concern, however, at the mass roundup of men whose only crime was that they were unemployed or shabbily dressed. Two weeks after the Slasher hysteria began, a citizen wrote to the *Star* wondering why the wave of arrests had taken so long. After all, the persons swept up in the dragnet were all "unsavory characters," some "not fit to be at large among the citizens of this city. . . . But the clean-up has only started. It should not be stopped." A leading alderman, Thomas Brannagan, pushed to increase the number of police officers and to more strictly enforce the curfew laws. He also wanted police to watch the flophouses more closely, saying, "Some of the hotels in this municipality are incubators of crime." Another alderman, J. Al Kennedy, seconded the idea that such steps were essential, for "serious crime is taking an upswing."[14] On the whole, the public seemed to accept that the city was in the grip of a new crime wave, one in which sexual deviants were playing a leading role.

Yet just what connection, if any, was there between the Slasher killings and the sex crime panic? All of the victims had been men between the ages of forty-five and fifty-six. The stabbings had been brutal, but they did not appear to be sexual in nature. What rational link existed, then, between the facts of these crimes and the calls for a crusade on misfits? Although ignored by the *Star*, there was one connecting detail that had appeared in the Detroit and Toronto newspapers: Frank Sciegliski had spent time in jail in 1943 for attacks on fifteen-year-old boys. It was a detail that *Star* reporters had either found unimportant or too distasteful to print. The fact that at least one of the victims was a sexual deviant—a pedophile and a homosexual—was something that was not publicly disclosed and therefore could not affect how the public perceived the crisis. Had this detail been widely known, the panic of 1945 might have taken a different turn and focused on a very different target.

Barely a week after the discovery of Sgt. Price's mutilated body, a mass rally of Ford workers took place at the Windsor Market. By the fall of 1945, the majority of Ford workers were seized by a new sense of militancy and had demanded that the company recognize the union and grant mandatory check-off of union dues. Vegetable stalls in the Windsor Market were shoved aside to accommodate the men who heard their leadership report on the recommendations of Justice S.E. Richards, who had been appointed to conciliate the dispute. For many years, Ford management, led by the feisty Wallace Campbell, had resisted union organization of the United Auto Workers. During the war, the government had sought to avoid disruptions (not always successfully) by mandating a system of compulsory conciliation. However, even with peace around the corner, the company still refused to deal with the key issue of union seniority. The rally at the Windsor Market, attended by hundreds of men, many of whom were wearing their best suits and ties, led to overwhelming approval for a strike.

Just as public attention had been diverted from the Slasher attacks by the victories in Europe and the Pacific, the growing storm at the Ford plants began to edge the Slasher panic off the front pages. On September 12, 1945, the workforce at Ford went out on strike. It was by far the most dramatic labor confrontation that Windsor had ever seen, and it would have implications felt across the country.

Investigation of the Slasher case was suspended, as all police resources were dedicated to keeping the peace on the picket line. As the strike ground on and the union closed the power plant that kept the assembly machinery from freezing, matters became increasingly desperate. On November 2, 1945, a small detachment of fifteen Windsor police officers backed up by a similar number of Ford guards tried to force entry into the main company offices. Charles Weston, the same rookie police officer who had been used as "bait" in the parks after the Slasher murders, witnessed the assault: "Chief Renaud led the procession through the lines of strikers, and there were many of them at that particular time . . . and I know there were some punches thrown. . . . It seems to me our fellas backed off and didn't try again."[15] As the police squad retreated, a union loudspeaker called out for "a big hand for the Windsor Police Department," and amid catcalls and boos, the officers left the scene. As Windsor convulsed with labor unrest, local police were reduced to ineffective bystanders. Three days after the failed assault, the union leadership decided to commandeer vehicles and blockade the streets leading to the Ford plants. It was a dramatic escalation but did little to resolve the underlying issues. Windsor police stood back and let events take their course.

The police could at least claim that they had made two arrests in the Slasher case. Stanley Sokoloski and Eugene Senyk were convicted of public mischief for writing the Slasher notes on the washroom walls in the Detroit-Windsor tunnel. The two young men sheepishly explained that they had written the warnings as a joke. Magistrate Angus MacMillan was not amused, and he scolded them for compelling the police to follow up on specious leads. They were remanded to custody for a week with the prospect of more jail time.[16]

When the Slasher failed to strike over the Labor Day weekend, it seemed to put to rest Royal Baker's theory that the police were dealing with a "holiday ripper" who only struck when the public was preoccupied. For whatever reason, the killings had stopped, and the police had an opportunity to consider the situation. Even though the Ford strike had disrupted the investigation and all leads so far had proven futile, the Windsor Police had not completely given up. Perhaps they were even on the verge of establishing a plausible motive for the killings.

5

INTERESTING PERSONS

"Sex men" were the Slasher's targets—at least according to Margo Hind. Miss Hind ran a small beauty parlor in the Alexander Building just off of Ouellette Avenue, and she called the police on August 23 to give them an important statement. She explained to Detectives Sam Royan and Jim Hill that these sex men, or perverts, gathered together at the Ambassador Hotel, a seedy riverfront inn at the foot of Goyeau and Sandwich streets. Miss Hind had developed an interest in homosexuals. She had "made a considerable Study of this type of Person and according to her there is nothing to be done as the persons are this way by Nature." As well, she disclosed to the police officers the prominent role these homosexuals played in society, for according to her, "eighty-five Per cent of big men in Detroit who hold jobs managers Etc, carry on this Sort of Practice."

In Windsor, Miss Hind's brother, a "returned man" (a serviceman returned from overseas), had seen homosexuals frequenting the Ambassador Hotel. Hind volunteered that she knew a "very nice young chap" from Detroit who could accompany her to the Ambassador Hotel. He was the kind of fellow "[homosexuals] all fall for." At the Ambassador, he could "put on his Act, Then follow and search any who took up along with him," thereby entrapping the Slasher. She had concluded that all the victims to date were also homosexuals and therefore that the murders were acts of jealousy. She "suggested that [the Slasher] might have been in Love with the Victim or enraged because he was not taken."

The detectives did not take Miss Hind seriously. For one thing, "She had on a suit of Pyjamis or lounging suit and not dressed in Girls dresses. Her nails are painted." This was not the way a respectable lady presented herself, at least not while she was talking to police detectives. Moreover, she seemed a trifle too interested in the homosexual lifestyle. Royan and Hill concluded that her unorthodox dress and conversation indicated that she was likely a lesbian. They did concede that "She is rather an interesting Person and seems to know a lot about this kind of Person, and we have been thinking that she may be one herself."[1] Margo Hind had made a critical link—one the police had yet to make—that all the victims were homosexuals, but the statement made by this putative lesbian was simply filed away. No attempt was made to mount a watch on the Ambassador Hotel.

Detective Sergeant John Mahoney, the lead detective on the Slasher killings, was a tall, soft-spoken man, "a nice guy, not a ruffian. . . . He was one of the few that had a little intelligence."[2] But he did not have any credible suspects in custody. What he did have were three victims and three crime scenes, and at the very least he could review the available evidence and investigate in greater detail the backgrounds of the deceased. In December 1945, Mahoney filed a detailed report on the Mannie attack and the two murders. There seemed to be little to go on in the Mannie case, as the victim had given only a general description of his attacker. However, the Scielgliski killing was unusual in a number of respects. What impressed Mahoney was how little disturbance there was at the scene. The victim was still wearing his eyeglasses, and, amazingly, his straw boater was still on his head. The attack must have been sudden and come as a complete surprise, for the area had hardly been disturbed. But with six stab wounds in the deceased's back and "the trousers . . . almost cut away from the body" there was no denying the ferocity of the attack. Then there was the final, gratuitous stab wound in the left buttock. What had motivated it?

Turning his attention to the habits of the victims, Mahoney learned that Sciegliski "was a sexual-pervert, that he was convicted in our Courts, of gross indecency, with another Male person." He was also a pedophile who had "committed acts of gross indecency with boys of the age of 15 years." Mahoney also checked with military authorities and discovered that Sgt. Price "was somewhat of a sexual pervert in the Army, and no doubt was associating with persons, of known character, while in this City." Having concluded that Price and Sciegliski were homosexuals (Mannie's sexual inclinations remained unknown), Mahoney inferred that Price and Sciegliski's killer had to be "a person of a sexual pervert nature."³ Mahoney offered no explanation in his report as to how he made this connection. He apparently assumed that since two of the victims belonged to the homosexual subculture, the culprit was bound to know that subculture intimately as well.

Making the connection between the victims and homosexuality enabled the police to have a better idea of what may have happened during the summer of 1945. The victims and their killer had sought isolated areas where they could be alone and undisturbed, for what they were about to do was not only socially unacceptable, it was also illegal. Church law had always harshly condemned sexual acts between men, and in 1533, the Parliament of Henry VIII made "the detestable and abominable vice of buggery committed with mankind or beast punishable by death." When early Canadians came to write their own criminal laws, they abolished many anachronisms and substantially reduced the number of capital offenses. However, Upper Canada's (Ontario) reform statute of 1833 specifically provided that "every person convicted of the abominable crime of buggery, committed either with mankind or with an animal shall suffer death as a felon." Under this statute, at least one man convicted of buggery was sentenced to die, even though the jury had recommended mercy. The trial judge felt it "proper," "considering the horrid nature of the crime . . . to pass sentence of death."⁴ The first post-Confederation criminal statute also outlawed buggery as an "unnatural offence," but whether buggery and sodomy were considered the same act was not clear.

"Gross indecency" was made an indictable offense in 1890, but what exactly this term meant was also questionable. When it was incorporated into Canada's Criminal Code in 1892, Justice Minister John Thompson was asked to define the term, and he haltingly suggested, "We only punish [gross indecencies] as crimes when they are offensive to people, or set a bad example. . . . It is impossible to define these cases by any form of words."⁵ Subsequent cases would indicate that an "indecent act" might include masturbation, exposing oneself, or even suggesting an indecent act. Gross indecency probably included all of these things, as well as actual male-to-male contact, from fellatio to fondling the penis. The result of the 1892 Criminal Code was that "the new legal definitions moved beyond 'sodomy' and 'buggery,' which were retained as well, grouping together various kinds of non-reproductive sex and instructing the police to clamp down on emerging homosexual networks."⁶

And clamp down they did. During the first decades of the twentieth century, arrests for buggery and gross indecency steadily increased. In 1923, the Toronto chief constable noted in his annual report that gross indecency was one of the "abominable offences [that] seem to be on the increase." If the original laws proscribing homosexuality had a biblical basis, the modern restrictions were based on scientific theories that considered homosexuals "biological freaks of nature" to be set apart from healthy society. Homosexuality was considered so loathsome that some medical experts considered lobotomy or electric shock therapy the only cure.⁷

As their encounters were thus proscribed both socially and legally, gay men had to be exceedingly discreet in choosing their meeting places. In Toronto during the 1920s and '30s, darkened theaters and public washrooms became regular meeting places. However, the public nature of such venues also made them subject to regular police surveillance. During the summer months, parks offered the best opportunities to meet, and places as isolated as Government Park and the abandoned salt-mine lands made ideal sites for trysts in the weeds. In many American cities of this period, gay men would gravitate to a particular park that became a designated meeting place. In Portland, Oregon, for example, the main meeting place became known as simply "the park," "a name that denoted its centrality to their world." In New York City, Central Park, with its unsupervised wooded grounds, "was especially renowned within the gay world both as a social center and as a cruising ground." In Toronto, social spaces such as Memorial Square or Allan Gardens likewise enabled men to meet other men to solicit sex. The park "figured most prominently in the sexual struggle over urban spaces."⁸ In this struggle, municipal authorities fought to control who used these social spaces and to squeeze out homosexual couples. Advances in electric lighting assisted the police in monitoring washrooms and other meeting places, and enabling them to witness illegal acts.

Understandably, unlighted and isolated areas such as Government Park and the abandoned salt-mine lands would have a strong attraction for gay couples. Especially for lower- and working-class men such as Mannie, Sciegliski, and Price, the parks were a democratic gathering area where status was unimportant. For middle-class or professional homosexuals, crawling through the grass and thistles of Government Park was probably unacceptable, and it is likely they used the services of male prostitutes or attended bathhouses. But Government Park offered the advantage that it could be used by any group of men or boys with same-sex interests. From the park, it was only a few blocks back to downtown and the "normal" world.

Being hemmed in by criminal laws and compelled to meet in unlikely places may have been particularly irksome to returning gay servicemen like Sgt. Price. For men interested in same-sex relationships, the war years had been relatively liberating. While many gay men were victimized as a result of the official antihomosexual policies of the military, to many others it was a time of sexual self-discovery. Young men of the time were expected to respond sexually to women and to eventually marry, so "some queer men saw the military as an opportunity to escape communities in which they felt socially constricted." Mobilization required thousands of young men to leave smaller areas and join the large, single-sex institution of the military. Indeed, "the tension of living in the all-male world of the military, the comradeship that came from fighting a common enemy and the loneliness of being away from home in strange cities looking for companionship all helped to create a kind of 'gay ambience.'"[9]

For young or inexperienced gay men, close confinement with experienced gay men often served as "a training ground in love."[10] While overseas, some young Canadian soldiers may have realized their sexual orientation for the first time and discovered as well that other societies did not have the same strictures against same-sex relationships as Canada did. In 1944, Herbert Sutcliffe, a young Canadian soldier, earned the Member of the Order of the British Empire during the fighting in France. He also learned about his own homosexuality and the existence of a gay world "I didn't know about until I went overseas."[11]

Gay soldiers may also have been encouraged to learn that there was far more homosexual behavior in the service than they had previously thought. One Canadian, who before the war had never even heard of homosexual expressions, found himself drawn into "the Community of gays during the war." An airman recalled, "By the time I got back to Canada, gay life was just about natural to me." One airman from the Windsor area was posted to an English base where of the fifty men in administration he estimated that about half were "queer," the word gay men commonly used to describe themselves at the time. This base was hardly the only friendly haven, as London had a vibrant gay nightlife. The relationships this airman had established in the Air Force continued after the war. When he returned to Canada, he boarded in Toronto with five of the gay men he had served with in the RCAF.[12] A new generation of Canadians was experiencing pleasures previously kept hidden away in private networks.

It seems likely that Sgt. Price was an active homosexual before the war. However, army service had given him the opportunity to live in a freewheeling all-male environment, and he seems to have relished it. His "loans" to younger soldiers were likely intended to buy favors and establish contacts. In investigating Sgt. Price's personal life, Detective Mahoney had discovered that Price's superiors knew of his inclinations but did not move to discharge him. In fact, he had even been accepted for future service. Unlike the U.S. military, Canadian medical officers labeled gay men and lesbians as "psychic disorders" as opposed to "sex deviants." According to this viewpoint, homosexuals needed help, not discipline or confinement. While some formations were intolerant of any queers, there were instances of unit cohesion being considered more important than gay conduct. In one case, an infantry company sought to protect a popular officer, for "although he made no pretensions towards heterosexuality, he had upheld his part of the bargain by being discreetly queer."[13]

The stigmatization of homosexuals affected the Slasher investigation in that it compelled gay men to live a subterranean life that had to remain a secret from the police. As it was, homosexuals were already likely prey to blackmailers who could threaten to reveal their secret sexuality. In order to preserve their jobs and families, gay men living in mainstream culture had to be exceedingly discreet. Thus Slasher victims or potential victims had every reason to fear investigators and to keep whatever they knew about the Slasher to themselves. It is likely that George Mannie had been so uncooperative, if not downright misleading, during his interrogations by the police because he was hiding a secret identity.

By December 1945, people in Windsor had greater things to worry about than a stalled police investigation. In addition to the thousands of men idled by the Ford strike, hundreds of veterans were returning to the city. For many of them, there were no jobs and no housing. Finally, in mid-December, under intense pressure from Ford leadership, auto workers accepted a contract that referred the seniority issue to an impartial judge. The eventual result, determined by Judge Ivan C. Rand, provided essentially what the strikers wanted: union protection for all workers and mandatory union dues. The "Rand Formula" became a template for labor agreements across Canada. On December 18, the ratification vote began, the picket lines dissolved, and Ford went back into production.

If most of the Windsor police force had been assigned to the Ford strike, lead detective John Mahoney had managed to stay with the Slasher case. On December 18, the same day that the Ford strike ended, Mahoney submitted his report to the Inspector of Detectives in which he reviewed each of the Slasher attacks. In the report, Mahoney noted that Sciegliski and Price were homosexuals and that a thread of homosexuality bound the incidents together. In his view, it was likely that Sciegliski had been murdered by "sexual perverts like himself."[14] Of course, this conclusion was based on pure speculation, for there was no evidence to support the idea that the Slasher was a homosexual.

Even after Mahoney's report confirmed that the Slasher's victims were homosexual, Windsor police seemed to take very little interest in understanding the size or activity of the local gay community. As has been noted, the police were aware of illicit heterosexual activity—specifically prostitution—in downtown Windsor, but they deferred to it. In contrast, the police do not appear to have been particularly concerned with or knowledgeable about homosexuals. In the chief constable's reports for the late 1930s, there were few charges laid for indecent acts. Charges for public exposure or being caught in flagrante with another man numbered about four a year.[15] Undoubtedly the police monitored the public washrooms, but the low level of arrests (which increased to about eight a year during the war years) does not indicate any measure of grave concern.

Considering the indisputable fact that a gay subculture existed in Windsor, it is surprising how little contact Windsor police had with homosexuals. At a later trial, acting-detective James McLauchlan, who had previously served in the Morality Squad, was questioned about his knowledge of homosexuals:

> Q. And in the morality squad, I suppose, in your duties, in the course of your experience, you ran into a number of cases of [gross indecency]?
>
> A. No sir.
>
> Q. In a year's time, you would not?
>
> A. No sir.
>
> Q. I mean, men who have been guilty of acts of gross indecency, or things of that sort?
>
> A. No—twice only previously in my own experience—twice before.
>
> Q. And I suppose you know something about that type of man, do you?
>
> A. Well, very little to be honest.[16]

Perhaps the police were unaware of their presence, but queers knew where to go and which beverage rooms catered to them. A gay man living in Windsor in the 1930s recalled that the British American Hotel at the foot of Ouellette Avenue was the place to be, even though, he said, "It wasn't one of the best hotels in this city. If that's all you wanted was sex then why waste your time in a good bar?" The same man recollected that queers had to be exceedingly discreet in their personal lives, and that it was only in a place such as the British American that the "nellies" could gather freely and discuss sex. In addition to the British American, it was possible to meet a companion at the Ritz Hotel downtown and at the steam baths on Wyandotte Street. But the same gay man noted that in the working-class beverage houses, a gay man had to be especially careful, for, he said, "You're dealing with labouring people who worked hard for their money and a lot of them went in there just to get drunk, period. . . . I played it very cool when I went into that kind of bar. I knew what I wanted, but I didn't make any advances." Outside a familiar bar, gay men drank, smoke, and swore like "good straight people."[17] Pretending to be what they were not was crucial to their survival.

Yet even a smaller city such as Windsor had its cruising areas in the 1930s and 1940s. In addition to the riverfront, where George Mannie had been attacked, Jackson Park at Tecumseh and Ouellette was a place men went to get acquainted after dark. In such a park, there was always the spark of excitement that accompanied not knowing whom you might pick up or what pleasure might result from a casual conversation. Gay men were also constantly aware that hustlers and rollers also worked the cruising areas and that their lifestyle carried a constant risk.

Windsor police officers on active duty during that period later doubted that there was any one location in Windsor that overtly catered to a homosexual crowd. However, confirming Margo Hind's observations, these officers knew that there was a much larger and well-organized gay community in Detroit, where there were several notorious gay bars, including the "Gay Paris." From time to time, Windsor officers might go on a spree in Detroit and end up in one of these establishments. One Detroit police officer recalled that the 509 Club at the foot of Woodward Avenue was a convenient place for gay men from Windsor to meet gay Detroiters.[18] On one occasion in the late 1940s, a man from Windsor who was cruising the Detroit bars was picked up by an undercover police officer. After the arrest, the man recalled, "We got talking. I like fishing. I like camping and this kind of thing and so did he . . . so he never did press charges." Even after this incident, the man still felt that for queers, Detroit was the place to be, since "Windsor was quite a small city compared to Detroit . . . everything hung out over there . . . [In Detroit there was] a lot more freedom."[19]

Leading a second life seemed almost a necessity to those who cruised Government Park or frequented the British American Hotel, and society wanted it that way. After Oscar Wilde's conviction for gross indecency in 1895, the *Montreal Gazette* warned all homosexuals to be "more careful in their criminality."[20] They were told to remain out of sight and out of mind or face the consequences. A 1950s medical textbook noted, "If known for what he is sexually, [the homosexual] is at once an object of ridicule, derision, and contempt on the part of the normal population. The slightest error of judgment may bring immediate physical attack or jail."[21] If the Slasher did come from this milieu, elusiveness would be second nature to him.

It was not until mid-1946 that two low-level officers, Constable P. MacLaren and Acting-Detective E. Patterson carried out an investigation of the gay community in Windsor. Using an informant, Alexander Voligny, a homosexual who was already facing charges for indecent assault and who hoped to curry some favor, the two officers tried to assemble a snapshot of local gay life. It was no easy task, given the need for gay men to mask their activities and appear harmlessly conventional on the outside. The gay presence blended into the larger street culture of Windsor, especially in the freewheeling atmosphere downtown.

The informant had come to Windsor from Montreal in 1943. According to MacLaren and Patterson's report, it was on a walk through Government Park in 1944 that he "first became acquainted with a number of Sex Perverts 'Queers.'" The centrality of Government Park in the Windsor gay community is apparent right from the start. As the English sexologist Havelock Ellis noted as early as 1915, "The world of sexual inverts . . . is a community distinctly organized—words, customs, traditions of its own; and every city has its numerous meeting places."[22] It was on the informant's first visit to the park that he encountered "Harry," a man who lived at the YMCA, and it was through Harry that he was introduced to other gay men. Harry had no apparent means of support but was nonetheless the director of the group. The report listed a number of homosexuals, for the most part men who worked at various factories, including the Hiram Walker's Bottling Room, a shoe repair shop, and the post office. One member of this "group of 'Queers'" lived in Detroit and "was in the habit of coming to Windsor every Saturday night and meeting at the Government Park."[23]

One member of the group allegedly told the informant that "after the two murders in the summer of 1945 . . . he was scared to go near the Park. He did not give any reason for his Fear." The reason should have been obvious. A study of gay gathering places in Philadelphia in the 1940s revealed that one of the risks gay men took in trolling for partners was retributive violence—that straight men would come to the park and "beat people up and terrorize people."[24] Once hostile individuals or groups found out where gays gathered, they could ambush them at any time. After the Slasher attacks, there seemed to be a stubborn unwillingness on the part of the Windsor police to acknowledge that gay men were the prey and not the hunters. The MacLaren-Patterson report found that the informant had gone out drinking with the group and learned that Harry or another gay man was with Sgt. Price about two hours before he was murdered. The implication was that one of these men had to have been involved in the crime. Still, after unapologetically prying into the lives of these vulnerable men, neither officer followed up on the lead or made any arrests.

In his report of December 18 of the previous year, John Mahoney had mentioned yet another area of investigation. Perhaps, he speculated, Windsor was harboring a serial killer who operated in more than one city. In the preceding five months, Chicago had experienced a spasm of multiple murders that seemed strangely similar to the Windsor homicides. Much like Windsor, Chicago had been undergoing a traumatic transition to peacetime with labor unrest and rising crime rates. In the first ten days of December 1945, there had been four rapes and eight murders. But a strange and terrifying phenomenon had also occurred in Chicago. In June 1945, Josephine Ross was butchered in her apartment. The following December, Frances Brown died in a frenzied knife attack in her home. Using the victim's own lipstick, the killer had written on the living room wall: "For heaven's sake catch me before I kill more. I cannot control myself." Chicago police had no idea who the Lipstick Killer might be.[25] Mahoney noted the similar method of attack used in the killings. In his view, "the person or persons who committed these murders may be one and the same." He suggested an exchange of information with the Chicago police department to investigate any link between the murders. It is not known if the Chicago police department responded to Mahoney's communication. In any event, worse was in store for both Chicago and Windsor.

Police departments across North America had few ideas about where to start when looking for these kinds of killers. The phenomenon of multiple murders was relatively new, for it was not until the late nineteenth century that maniacal killers began to appear in the industrialized world. There had been ample violence and mayhem before then, but the anonymous killer who struck again and again motivated by some strong sexual or antisocial urge was a modern and terrifying phenomenon. The first and most infamous of them all was Jack the Ripper, who held late-Victorian London in thrall as he silently stalked the night streets to kill and then dissect prostitutes. Significantly, the Ripper chose as his victims the most despised group in society. In one of his few recognized notes, he confessed, "I am down on whores." So was the rest of society. Prostitutes were held in such contempt that a British act of 1864 made it compulsory for prostitutes to submit to medical examinations, and if they were found to suffer from a venereal disease, they were to be incarcerated.

The same animus against prostitutes and women seeking abortions motivated Dr. Thomas Neill Cream. Between 1877 and 1892, Cream poisoned seven women. Before he was hanged, Cream even boasted of having eliminated prostitutes. "I have killed lots of that cattle," he said, "all of that class are to be killed." Prostitutes were invariably described as "unfortunates" and a "menace to society," because they spread disease. Not only were prostitutes the lowest of the low, the murderer could in his own mind consider that he was performing a commendable act by ridding the streets of these "guilty" women.[26]

In the early twentieth century, the United States experienced a murder wave containing several instances of multiple homicide. Between 1900 and 1940, there were more than one hundred serial killings reported in the United States. In the six years between 1935 and 1941, there were at least ten cases that attracted national attention.[27] Many more probably went unreported. The public was so accustomed to reports about serial killers that one of the most popular films in the year before the Slasher incident was *Arsenic and Old Lace,* a comedy that featured two groups of serial killers—a psychotic madman on the loose and two elderly ladies who poisoned their gentlemen callers. The two ladies had the higher number of victims. The movie also underscored another aspect of the serial killer, that he or she frequently came in the guise of the most innocent individual. Albert Fish, described as a "meek and innocuous little old man," murdered at least fifteen children during the 1920s. This was one of the least noted aspects of multiple murderers—that they had a chameleon-like quality that allowed them to blend in with regular society. While serial killers may be psychotic, psychopaths have been known to be "secretive, clever, often charmingly seductive."[28] Police profilers have noted that certain criminals may for years lead normal lives, possessing the ability to pull down a curtain over the monster within. As a result, such killers might escape detection for lengthy periods, perhaps forever if they never made a mistake. Throughout 1945, the Windsor Slasher had blended in perfectly and had not made the slightest slipup.

One of the few recorded serial killers in Canada before 1945 seemed to have a similar ability. Earle Nelson, an American, had crisscrossed the United States in the mid-1920s and killed about twenty women, most of them his landladies. Yet to all outward appearances, he appeared to be a decent, devoutly religious man. He arrived in Winnipeg in the summer of 1927 and proceeded to kill two more women before he was caught. There was little direct evidence against him, and it took a nine-hour grilling by

Winnipeg police before he gave enough information to implicate himself. Nelson's case generated a near-hysteria in Winnipeg, and there were rumors that he might be lynched.[29] As it was, he was speedily convicted and executed in January 1928. At the time, Canadians were likely to dismiss the "Dark Strangler," as the press dubbed him, as a foreign killer who had invaded Canada's peaceable kingdom.

By the late twentieth century, police forces in major cities would take a disciplined approach in any serial-killer investigation. The investigation would focus on three factors: physical evidence, the description of the offender, and crime-scene behavior. Modern investigators have learned that serial murders are unlike family homicides or street crimes, whose victims are not isolated by their killers. Most murders are random and spontaneous, and the perpetrators leave plenty of clues and witnesses at the scene. In contrast, sociopaths take time to formulate their crimes. They carefully plan the entrapment and "choose isolated spots where they can act out their fantasies in private."[30] Ritualistic behavior is often a characteristic of these killings, creating an observable pattern to each event that is so distinct that even the killer cannot alter it.

Yet even when investigators today have ample physical evidence, a description of the killer, and a pattern of ritualistic behavior, serial-killer investigations are still the most time-consuming and expensive police undertakings. They can require all of the computer organization, forensic skills, and DNA analysis of a modern police force. In spite of such technological support, serial-murder investigations are often futile. This reality frustrates the officers involved, dampens morale, and leads to public accusations that the police are ineffective.[31] In 1945, the Windsor police lacked not only rudimentary forensic tools, they were even denied the three major factors for success. There was George Mannie's faulty, if not misleading, description of the killer; there was only a sketchy idea of what had happened at the crime scenes; and other than the bodies, there was practically no evidence left behind. It is therefore no surprise that by December 1945, the search for the Windsor Slasher had all but petered out.

Over and above these difficulties, the search for the Windsor serial killer was unique in its time. Whereas previous multiple killers, from Jack the Ripper to Earle Nelson, had targeted prostitutes or vulnerable women, the Slasher was targeting male homosexuals. It was almost unheard of for a serial killer to stalk and murder men, particularly men of a particular sexual orientation. Under the circumstances, the Windsor police might be forgiven for being stymied by the unprecedented nature of these crimes. For the time being, the public remained unaware that the Slasher was seeking out and murdering homosexuals. This information was known only to a few Windsor detectives, and they gave no notice to those they now knew to be at risk.

As time passed without another murder, the public appeared to lose interest in the Slasher. Perhaps the Detroit expert Royal Baker was right and the killer had moved on to fresher fields. There were a few residual ripples from the Slasher hysteria. For example, in early December 1945, an eighteen-year-old girl was accosted by a man who "grabbed her and ruffled her clothing with his hands." The suspect was described as having a "foreign appearance." Sexual attackers rarely appeared to be native-born.

The *Star* had also moved on to other, more pressing problems, including the growing menace of "reefers" on Windsor streets. Shrill editorials proclaimed that these insidious cigarettes were now readily available in Windsor and that a reefer was a "despoiler of the young" that "deadens the whole moral sense."[32] With the *Star* on the watch, the moral guard would never be let down.

As of January 1946, a better world appeared to be in view for the majority of Windsorites when a new master plan, prepared by Dr. E. G. Faludi, was unveiled containing ideas to turn Windsor into a unified city instead of a hasty amalgamation of border towns. If implemented, the plan would provide more parks, clean up the unsightly mess on the riverfront, and move toward opening the river lands for public enjoyment. By early 1946, however, much of the riverfront was jammed with shanties occupied not by the poor but by workers with good jobs. Mayor Reaume responded to pleas to level these shanties as unfit for human habitation with the question, "What would we do with these people?"[33] The housing shortage was so acute, there was simply no other place for people to live. But as winter began to ebb, building supplies and developers began to appear. There was work in the city, and as construction workers began to erect house frames, the smell of freshly sawn lumber prevailed.

In March 1946, when the Slasher hysteria of the previous summer was a distant memory, a peculiar letter, postmarked March 20, 1946, arrived at the Windsor police station. Whoever had mailed it had only bothered to use a one-cent stamp, and a dutiful postal clerk had noted on the envelope, "4 Cents Due." The letter was addressed to "Police Headquarters In Connection of Murders." The note itself was brief and began with a formal "Dear Sirs" followed by a message printed in red pencil:

> This is a challenge to you. "I" will strike in the near future. I can not disclose this to you of course. My avenge of these people are great. Nothing shall stand in my way. I will use only the knife on my supposed enemies. I am not a returned soldier. This is no prank.
>
> THE SLASHER

On the back of the page, the message continued:

> Please forgive me but these people have destroyed my whole life.

The written text was followed by a crude sketch of a bloody knife.[34]

One of the first things that leapt out from the note was the writer's air of deference. He seemed to respect authority and was nothing if not gracious to the police. Solicitously, he advised them that the Slasher was not a veteran and thereby eliminated one pool of suspects, perhaps intending to relieve returned servicemen from police harassment and roundups. In some respects, the letter supplemented Mahoney's report from the previous December. If it had indeed been written by the Slasher, he was, as Mahoney had thought, taking vengeance on "these people," his "enemies"—meaning homosexuals. While the police now believed they had conclusive proof that the Slasher was specifically stalking and killing gay men, the reason he was targeting them remained unclear. According to the letter, homosexuals had "destroyed" the Slasher's life, but he declined to say how.

Unlike most criminals, who would do anything to escape detection, the Slasher—by announcing that he would strike again and that he would use a knife—was dropping hints that might result in his arrest. He had written, "This is a challenge to you," but did that mean he was making this series of homicides into a game between him and the police? The action was most peculiar, for law enforcement experts have noted that serial killers rarely talk about their crimes, tending "not to confide in relatives, spouses, friends or strangers."[35] In fact, one mark of a serial killer is psychological isolation. Nevertheless, there have been occasions when killers want to communicate anonymously with law enforcement or the press. Only a few weeks before the Slasher letter arrived in Windsor, the Lipstick Killer had scribbled another plea to the Chicago police to catch him before he killed again.

The question was how seriously the Windsor police should take the Slasher letter. The printing and spelling were infantile, and the crudely drawn knife did not appear to be the product of a mature mind. Should the warning be dismissed as just another high-school prank, in the same vein as the tunnel-washroom notes? Above all, the note was suffused with an air of high drama. The language—that the writer was seeking his "avenge" on his "supposed enemies"—seemed the kind of B-movie dialogue appropriate to some comic-book hero. There is no record of how the police assessed the note. Other than dusting it for fingerprints, they made no attempt to glean any further information from it. They made no attempt to track down the location in Windsor from which it had been posted, and the letter would play no role in later events.

Still, the letter's timing was most curious and should have put the police department on alert. The panic had subsided, the days of the prankster had passed, and the letter had come out of the blue with no prompting. The police should also have found the tone of the letter disturbing. It seemed to chide them for their failures and dare them to intensify their efforts to catch the killer. It should have been a warning to the detectives that the Slasher was still out there and bolder than ever.

6

RETURN OF THE SLASHER

Even though the summer of 1946 was hotter than usual, some things seemed to be timeless: A bitter longshoreman's strike had closed down the Windsor harbor, and other strikes were imminent at several auto plants. A new government initiative promised to construct 104 one-story dwellings with priority given to veterans. Three-fifty-nine Brant Street was raided yet again (the eighth time since 1943), and the current operator, Miss Thelma Roy (who gave her occupation to Magistrate MacMillan as "housewife") was given two months in jail (a month *less* than the minimum sentence) and a small fine. On Wednesday, June 12, the weather forecast called for a cool break in the heat over the weekend.[1]

Around six o'clock on the following Monday evening, June 17, a dark green cloud swept across the river from Detroit, and the ominous funnel of a tornado appeared just south of Windsor at Brighton Beach. Cottage dwellers were bombarded by debris from the U.S. side of the river: "They said the river seemed to boil under the tornado's lash, sending a huge wave that threatened their cottages." Skirting the southern fringe of the city, the funnel veered northward, hit Sandwich West Township and turned closer to Windsor. It crossed Walker Road and left the Pillette-Clemenceau area looking like a war zone, with houses smashed and vehicles strewn everywhere. The tornado had cut an erratic path, destroying some houses completely while leaving adjacent ones untouched. Jim Ure, a young man trying to reach home in the wake of the storm, recalled, "I got out of the bus at Walker and Tecumseh, and I could see the tail end of [the tornado] disappearing in the east. Houses were out on the road, all the power lines were down." Hospitals operated on the desperately injured by candlelight. The death toll for the storm, the worst natural disaster to strike the Windsor area, was seventeen dead, including five members of one family.²

Within days, the oppressive heat was back.

It was late on Saturday night, June 22, less than a week after the tornado, that Constable Gordon Preston was on duty at the central police station. The station itself was an old, fortress-like structure with little ventilation. During the summer months, when the humidity could make it oppressively hot, the large wooden doors facing Park Street were left open to let in some air. At 11:20, a thin, pale man staggered through the doors into the station. It took only an instant for Preston to notice the ice pick protruding from the man's back.

Another man accompanying this bizarre specter told Preston that he had been driving on Sandwich Street near Government Park when he saw this man come running up the embankment waving his arms and saying that he had been stabbed. He managed to get the victim into his car and drive to the police station. Preston, assisted by Constable George Souchuk, drove the victim to Hotel Dieu Hospital. Dr. Frank DeMarco carefully removed the ice pick and noted that the man's survival seemed just short of a miracle, for the spike had narrowly missed his heart. Had it been on target, he would have died in a matter of seconds.

Constable Preston stayed at the hospital, and as soon as Dr. DeMarco permitted, he talked with the victim. His name was Alexander Voligny, and he was a twenty-nine-year-old French-Canadian who lived with his brothers and sister in the east end and worked at Canadian Industries Limited in the paint and varnish plant. Saturday night was to be a night on the town, and Voligny had intended to go to a dance at the Windsor Arena. But instead he went to the Lido Venice Hotel on the far west side. After a few drinks, Voligny took a bus downtown and had a coffee at the bus terminal. Then he decided to take a walk along the riverfront "to get cooled off." Sitting down at a bench in Government Park, he was joined by a young man. After a while, the men lay down together on the grass, and the stranger asked Voligny to lie on his stomach. As Voligny began to turn over, the young man stabbed him twice and then ran off toward Sandwich Street.[3] Voligny, sensing that something was stuck in his back, ran up the embankment and flagged down a car.

Finally the Windsor police had a break in the Slasher case, for Voligny was able to give them a detailed description of his attacker. He was white, about eighteen years old, well dressed, five feet seven or eight, slight in build, and he spoke good English. That is, he was neither a foreigner, a black man, a mental case, nor a man in his sixties, as had been so often predicted. The young man's description was distributed to all police units, and the following order was posted to all officers: "We have reason to believe that this is the same person who stabbed and murdered two persons in August 1945 and wish to draw attention to every police officer of the need for a sharp lookout for this man around Government Park and the river front."

The following Monday, the *Star* reported Voligny's dramatic appearance at the police station. This time the floodlights shone directly on the Windsor police department. "The stabbing season is here again," R. M. Harrison announced in his "Now" column. There seemed to be little question that the gory mayhem from the previous summer and this latest attack "are all of a piece, the work of the same perverted killer." Harrison called on the police to employ every resource to succeed this time. He wrote, "We can't go through another summer in which Windsor's streets and parks are unsafe for those who use them. The challenge is to the police." The *Star*'s main editorial the following day was even blunter in its admonition: "Failure to capture the man who some months ago committed two, and perhaps three brutal murders in Windsor caused deep concern here. As time went by, however, and no more such crimes occurred, the people adopted the secure theory that the criminal, though not detected, had probably left the area." Now it was apparent that he was back, and, according to the editorialists: "It is not in the Canadian tradition that murders should remain unsolved. The challenge faces all the law-enforcement agencies of this district to prove their ability as Canadian police officers.... It calls for a man-hunt on an unprecedented scale, continued until this fiend is brought to justice. The public is not in the mood to listen to excuses."[4]

This time, the police adopted a more restrained attitude toward notifying the public on their progress. Inspector Duncan MacNab had died a few months previously and had been replaced by James P. Campbell. Campbell was not about to raise any false hopes in the press, and he told reporters that there was "nothing new" on the case. The ice pick (which actually turned out to be a harness maker's awl) contained no fingerprints. The description of the Slasher could have fit several hundred young men. Still, the unnervingly familiar method of the attack had to be the work of the Slasher. At least this time the police had a live victim and one who seemed willing to give a candid account of what had happened on the riverbank.

On the day after the assault, Acting-Detectives Brand and Anderson interviewed Voligny in his hospital room. Retracing his steps of the previous night, he recounted how he had met a young man a little after ten o'clock. As they began to walk, Voligny tested him, asking, "You be a cop and he said I don't bother with the law." Assured that his companion was not an undercover officer, Voligny suggested that they walk westward toward the Ambassador Bridge. The couple passed by some striking dockworkers and turned down the walkway that ended at the isolated riverbank. Once they were alone, the young man seized the initiative: "He started to monkey around with me, he pulled my penis out, then he took his out and we both started playing with one another. Then we layed down on a slope underneath a tree," he admitted with stubborn candor. Whether he knew it or not, Voligny was admitting to acts of gross indecency that could get him several months in prison. Naively, he seemed to be unaware of how dangerous his admissions could be.

As they lay underneath the tree, the men began to undress each other. They took down each other's suspenders and then slid their trousers down. The young man wanted Voligny to roll over and lie on his face, for "he wanted to put it up my back side, but I did not go for that." Still, the young man insisted, and he tried to push Voligny over. Once Voligny's back was turned, the young man suddenly stabbed him and then "laughed and ran away along the beach towards the Ambassador Bridge." After that, Voligny recalled fighting his way up the embankment and flagging down a passing car.[5]

Although it had been less than twenty-four hours since the incident, the detectives had learned a great deal about Voligny. In December 1944, he had been arrested in Detroit for soliciting a man for homosexual purposes. While he lay in his hospital bed at Hotel Dieu, the police had gone through his wallet, discovered several obscene pictures, and concluded that, like the other victims, Voligny was an active homosexual. Three weeks later, when the police questioned him again, he gave an even more detailed account of the sexual bargain struck between himself and the stranger. As they had gone down the stairway to the river, his companion had taken Voligny's arm and solicitously told him to take care not to fall. Once they had partially undressed, the young man asked if he could "cornhole" or have anal sex with Voligny. "I said I didn't like that I would rather 'Frenchie' meaning that we would both put each others penis in each others mouth. He said let me corn hole you and I will frenchie you after."[6] He then described how the stranger had persisted, kept trying to turn him over and had suddenly attacked him from behind. After he had been stabbed, Voligny yelled after the figure "You dirty bastard."

The stranger's suggestion that they have anal sex seems to conform to prevailing working-class notions of male-male sexual contact. A study of homosexual conduct in the Pacific Northwest for this period indicates that "the most common form of sex, whether between adult males or between men and youths, was anal and interfemoral penetration." For the most part, working-class men tended to avoid oral eroticism. The reduced frequency of oral sex among lower-class men in relation to other classes was later confirmed by the Kinsey studies, where it was noted that, unlike their middle-class counterparts, working-class men were "relatively sexually liberated, probably because beginning early in life [they] had easy access to sexual intercourse."[7] Oral sex to them was "filthy" and a "source of disease." In that context, Voligny's suggestion that he would prefer to "frenchie" was unusual, so it was not surprising that the young stranger declined.

The Voligny incident was unusual in other ways. The police had made no attempt to reconcile Voligny's early attempt that evening to find a female companion at the dance and at the Lido-Venice. When he failed to get one, he turned to trolling the riverfront in search of a man. Voligny may well have been bisexual, an orientation that was even more invisible than homosexuality in the 1940s. Well into the 1950s, medical authorities doubted that a condition such as bisexuality even existed.[8] As a result of this denial, persons with Voligny's sexual identity must have been confused and were probably isolated.

Once the details of the attack on Voligny were made public, the fears of the previous summer—that there was a mad killer on the loose who could strike at random—were revived, but with a remarkably different tone and target. Moral panics can vary in tone and style, and there was a distinct difference between the events of 1945 and those of 1946. In 1945, there had been an intense feeling of imminent danger, that a woman or child would be the next victim. The Slasher's presence was palpable, and no one knew when, where, or who he would strike next. As a result, the *Star* had called for all drifters and misfits of any kind to be hauled in on suspicion. But in 1946, the whipping boy would not be vagrants but an ill-defined yet dangerous group of "sexual perverts," who had engineered their own downfall through their immoral behavior.

It was a period during which people carelessly tossed pejoratives at nonconformist groups. The term "perverts" could describe rapists, pedophiles, or persons who engaged in consensual same-sex relations. The change in the public perception of the Slasher harkened back to the prewar period when deviants were considered a danger to children, and all homosexuals were deemed to be psychopaths. The second Slasher hysteria would take place in a community in which the notion that all homosexuals were a threat to children was very much alive.

In spite of this threat, there was a general sense of relief in mainstream society, for the folk devil had taken on a more definitive shape—the shape of a sexual deviant who attacked only other sexual deviants—so normal people were now safe. One young Windsor man recalled that 1945 was "complete terror," but that 1946 was different. "This one didn't bother us," he said, "because by that time we knew or we had been told that he was not looking for people like us . . . he wasn't looking for straight guys. Women were no longer afraid."[9] Nevertheless, the Slasher and deviants like him could not be ignored. Led by editorialists such as Harrison and Clark, the public came to recognize that this subculture had to be dealt with, "that serious steps must be taken to control the behaviour, punish the perpetrators, and repair the damage."[10]

The second panic occurred just as the postwar return to normalcy was starting to take hold. In January 1946, Mayor Reaume had publicly commended women for their war service and then "urged that whenever their husbands returned to their employment that they vacate their jobs to provide employment for veterans."[11] This and other official proclamations made it clear that women were supposed to leave the factories and return to their normal sphere, the kitchen. Women were also supposed to cover up. One writer to the *Star* abhorred the fashions that had crept in during the war, decrying "the shocking spectacle of women striding about the streets in varying states of nudity."[12] Sex was everywhere, and it was a danger. In Riverside, a town adjacent to Windsor, police seized comic books in which "skimpily dressed women were rampant." Some authorities came to view comic books as sinister propaganda filled with thinly veiled elements of homoeroticism and sadomasichism.[13] The summer of 1946 had already seen an epidemic of "curb cruising," when young men in cars slowed down to chat with young women. These seemingly harmless attempts at flirtation were harshly condemned, and the cruisers spent several days in jail.[14]

In this postwar world, women were supposed to retreat to their proper sphere, heterosexual relations should once again be conducted with propriety and decorum, and homosexual conduct—which was abhorrent—should be eradicated. From magazines and movies, teenagers in the 1940s knew that "While heterosexual desire, on its own, wasn't enough to guarantee one's station as normal, it was essential." Teens were also taught that if same-sex relations existed at all, they "existed as that place in the books where discussions of abnormality were up front and explicit. . . . Homosexuals were other people—not, certainly, teens themselves." Homosexuality was portrayed as an adult maladjustment, and youngsters were trained to protect themselves from deviants.[15]

In this era of comfortable simplicities, the *Star* recommended that the gathering places of the "sex perverts," the city's parks, be cleaned out. Harrison's "Now" column related an incident in which a man had performed a "disgusting act" before a six-year-old girl. A soldier had intervened and captured the culprit, who spent a mere thirty days in jail. This brief incarceration left him free, in Harrison's view, "to roam the streets and molest," when he should have been sent away till cured. Yet the problem, according to the *Star*, was deeper than a lax justice system. In his "As We See It" column, W. L. Clark was far more shrill about what needed to be done:

PERVERTS A MENACE

How about gathering in the sex perverts in Windsor as one definite step toward ending these crimes of violence? If that were done, people could feel more at ease. As long as these perverts are allowed to run free, they are a menace to everyone. . . . With so many persons being slashed, Windsor will have another couple of murders on the sheet before long. To save human life, it would be advisable to round up all the perverts and hold them for observation.[16]

In this remarkable editorial, Clark suggests that there be a general inquisition against not only child molesters but also against all nonheterosexuals. As the Slasher had to be a pervert, it was simply a matter of arresting all of them and letting the police sort them out until they came to the killer. Besides which, all perverts were a menace, and it was imperative that even if they had committed no crime they be removed from society, and especially from contact with children. This corrosive rhetoric ignored the reality that the vast majority of child molesters are not homosexuals. Most sexual attacks on children are committed by heterosexual men on girls, usually their daughters. Nevertheless, in the postwar period, the "mythology of homosexual 'seduction' and 'corruption' of young people was organized and took root."[17] The *Star's* lead editorial for July 8, 1946, noted that the root of the evil could be found in the municipal parks, which were "becoming hot beds of sex perversion" when "they should be healthful, pleasant places" for decent people. The parks were described as the favored site for "the stabbings which have come to be part of the habitual pastimes of certain of the degenerates."[18] Child molesters and queers were the enemy, and the city's parks were their nests. It was the responsibility of the Windsor authorities to eliminate the former and clean up the latter. Only then would the Slasher attacks come to an end.

Viewed from an historical perspective, this outpouring of venom is consistent with the interpretation of Christian law since medieval times that resulted in an intense hostility toward homosexuality.[19] It was apparent from the furor in the Windsor press that the scriptural ferocity against homosexuals was an enduring reality even in twentieth-century North America. And yet, the second Slasher hysteria does not seem to have been as shrill or as widespread as that of 1945. For one thing, people in Windsor were still dazed by the impact of the tornado and distracted by other events. The latest attack also had been overshadowed by a visit to Windsor from the Governor General. Only a few days after the Voligny stabbing, Viscount Alexander paid a formal visit to the city and decorated several veterans at Jackson Park. The vice regal occasion was muted out of respect for the lives recently lost to the natural disaster. These events conspired to distract the public from the reality that the Slasher menace had not gone away.

Less than two weeks after the Voligny stabbing, the Slasher struck again. This time he returned to his old haunts. Shortly after midnight on Saturday, July 6, 1946, a man was seen staggering across the street at the foot of Bridge Avenue where it intersected with Sandwich Street, not far from where George Mannie had been stabbed in July 1945. A passing soldier and a young woman helped the man into a cab. The driver, Lloyd Lauzon, noticed that the victim was holding a bloody butcher knife. Lauzon held onto the knife until the victim was in emergency care at Grace Hospital and the police arrived to examine the weapon.

Detectives identified the victim as Joseph Gelencser, a forty-eight-year-old married man who held a steady factory job. As he came out of the operating room, Gelencser told the police that he had gone for a walk after work down to the river to see the cruise ship *Noronic* leave the harbor. He had continued walking east to the bridge and was trying to cross Sandwich Street when he suddenly felt a pain in his back and fell to his knees. After pulling a knife out of his back, he had tried to flag down a car. He had not seen the attacker and did not even know if it was a man or a woman.[20] While it appeared that he would survive, Gelencser had to be given plasma to replace lost blood and fourteen stitches to close his wounds. The doctors forbade the detectives from interviewing the victim further until he recovered.

Two constables, Gordon Preston and Gilbert Ouellette were dispatched to the scene, and when they arrived, it became apparent that Gelencser's story made no sense. The area close to the bridge was a popular place for parking couples, and a survey of young people in the area showed that none of them had heard any disturbance that night. It was significant that the foot of Askin Avenue, close to the Ambassador Bridge, was a heterosexual gathering place where boys and girls would meet to "watch the submarine races." Clearly Gelencser had not been attacked there, for he had been picked up near Bridge Street. The only blood stain the investigators could find was on the sidewalk at Campbell Avenue Park, a significant distance from the bridge and in the vicinity of what the police should now have suspected was one of the principal gay meeting places in the city.

Their next stop was Gelencser's home, where his wife confirmed that her husband had left the house at eight o'clock the previous night. Perhaps she had some idea of his destination, for she had warned him "not to go down to the Government Park because he might get stabbed."[21] The *Star* reported Gelencser's police statement almost verbatim, explaining that, as he stood waiting to cross Sandwich Street, a man had suddenly attacked him and plunged a butcher knife into his back: "He saw no one, heard no one. He knew nothing of the stabbing until he felt the pain in his back."[22]

Once Gelencser was sufficiently recovered, his hospital room was invaded by detectives, and suddenly his memory showed a remarkable transformation. Now he recalled that he had met a young man on Sandwich Street and that together they had walked in the direction of the bridge. The stranger had begun to talk about sex, and Gelencser instantly interrupted him. "I told him I was not interested in sex talks that I was married and that I had a wife to take care of," he allegedly said. The young man wanted to sit down, but Gelencser moved away, and suddenly, "I felt something sharp in my back."[23] He dropped to his knees and felt blood running down his back. Reaching behind, he pulled a knife out of his back and then began to climb the dirt path up to Sandwich Street. Upon reaching street level, he found a soldier and a woman and begged them to flag down a car. This story was significantly at odds with the one Gelencser had previously given, but he offered no explanation for the many discrepancies.

This latest version, featuring a sudden and completely unprovoked attack, still did not ring true. Detectives Paget and Tellier interviewed Mrs. Gelencser and a man who had roomed with the couple for the past ten years. They also examined a book Gelencser kept, which contained the names and addresses of several men. The information they found in that book would be kept in a separate file, set apart from the Crown prosecution file. One of the men noted in the book, Hailey Friend, was in Mrs. Gelencser's description, "a young fellow who her husband kept company with." Friend was brought to police headquarters from his home in Remington Park for questioning, and he gave a revealing portrait of Joseph Gelencser. They knew each other from work, and on one occasion, Gelencser had lent him money. One evening, when Mrs. Gelencser was out, Friend had come over for a visit that evolved into a sexual encounter.

After a brief chat on a chesterfield, Gelencser had stimulated Friend's penis, performed oral sex on him, and given him three dollars. Thereafter, Friend would go over to his house two or three times a week, where they would engage in oral sex and Friend would be paid for his services.

Male prostitution was certainly not uncommon in an era when homosexuality was so proscribed. Moreover it could be quite lucrative, for the payment per session was only part of Friend's compensation. He was conscious that he held enormous power over Gelencser, and when he asked for a "loan" of $150, a substantial amount of money, Gelencser borrowed the funds to give to him. There were other loans as well, all no doubt intended to keep Friend quiet about their relationship. None of the money was ever paid back, and in total he had received about a thousand dollars from Gelencser. Friend was likely a "hoodlum homosexual," an individual who was not gay but who knew that he could exploit queer men by prostituting himself. As a means of protecting their own heterosexuality, male prostitutes often threaten and abuse their patrons.[24] About two months before the attack, Friend had told Gelencser that they were finished and that he would not see him any more.[25]

Outwardly, Joseph Gelencser had a conventional heterosexual lifestyle. His wife told the police, "He acts like any other married man and did not act like a maniac." But in reality, his sexual desires had to be deeply buried, and his only available outlet was a male prostitute. He lived in a society in which those who accepted him at face value, his wife and co-workers, would likely reject him instantly if they knew who he really was. To avoid their finding out, he lived a double life, an existence based on secrecy and fraught with peril. A gay man who lived in Windsor during this period recalled just how selective he had to be, saying, "I was quite careful who I picked up. I never experienced any blackmail."[26]

For Gelencser, this double life, having sex with Friend on those occasions when his wife was out, had probably become an essential part of his life. But there was a price to be paid for this duplicity: it meant being at the mercy of an increasingly greedy and fickle prostitute. This dynamic was another aspect of the postwar homosexual existence that was not covered in the police reports. Because he was married and living a fully closeted life, Gelencser could not afford to be found among the "group of queers" who gathered at the YMCA or who trolled Government Park looking for partners. Maintaining a heterosexual facade meant being excluded from the society of those men who would suit his natural inclinations and living a life "replete with alienation, isolation, dissonance, emotional pain and uninterrupted vigilance."[27] In Gelencser's case, masquerading as a heterosexual was his way of internalizing the shame that resulted from the pervasive homophobia of the culture in which he lived, reflected almost daily in the *Star*. However, once Friend abandoned him, Gelencser had, in desperation, resorted to the risky prospect of seeking out a companion on the street.

Detectives Tellier and Paget returned to Grace Hospital and confronted Gelencser with Friend's story. Predictably, he denied that he had ever committed any acts of gross indecency with Friend. He did admit that, for no apparent reason, he had advanced Friend substantial amounts of money.[28] By this point, the police must have begun to appreciate that the Slasher's victims had a great deal to hide and that their accounts were invariably suspect. At least Gelencser had given a description of his attacker. The young man was about twenty to twenty-two years old, 5 feet 8 1/2 inches tall, and about 155 pounds. It was a description that was generally consistent with Voligny's. The Slasher was also getting careless. Not only had he failed to kill his last two victims, in each case he had left his weapon behind. In Gelencser's case, the blade of the weapon, a typical butcher knife, was designed to be attached to its wooden handle by three rivets.

One of the rivets was missing.

7

ARREST AND REDEMPTION

Like Windsor, Chicago had been going through a period of profound turmoil. On January 6, 1946, Suzanne Degnan, a cherubic six-year-old, was abducted from her parent's home. The kidnapper left a ransom note, but within hours, police found parts of the dismembered body in sewers. The brutal murder of the child shocked Chicago, leading Mayor Edward Kelly to term the crime "the most horrible thing that anyone can imagine." The evidence indicated that the Lipstick Killer was back, and Chicago police were under intense pressure to make an arrest. A janitor became the prime suspect, and he was subsequently tortured by investigators for two days with his handcuffed hands stretched behind his back until his shoulders dislocated. After the suspect was released for lack of evidence, there were mass roundups of homosexuals. One gay man wrote to a friend that the police thought "perhaps a pervert had done it and they rounded up all the females [i.e., male homosexuals] they blame us for everything and incidentally it is more and more in the limelight every day—why they don't round us all up and kill us I don't know."[1]

Eventually, a young college student with no known homosexual proclivities was arrested in Chicago. Strapped to a hospital bed and interrogated around the clock by shifts of detectives, with threats made to himself and his mother, ether administered to his genitals, and forced injections of sodium pentothal, William Heirens admitted to killing Suzanne Degnan. While accusations of police misconduct tainted his confession, at least Chicago police had someone in custody.[2] Windsor police had a serial killer in their midst and had yet to arrest a credible suspect.

In an effort to help police catch the Slasher, the *Star* reporter who had covered the riverfront attack of Joseph Gelencser (no byline was permitted) had a suggestion for the layout editor. The reporter knew that the knife used to stab Gelencser had been recovered and that the *Star* invariably wanted photographs to illustrate a story. Approaching police inspector Jim Yokum, the reporter asked, "Why can't I have a picture of that?" Yokum had no objection. When the reporter saw the knife, he told his editor, "Look, this knife has got a rivet missing. We should carry a picture of it. It might be recognized." When the editor agreed, the reporter telephoned for the city desk to send a cameraman. He asked them to hurry, as it was urgent that the photo make the Saturday edition, the last run until Monday. A photographer, Cecil "Cec" Southward, was dispatched to the police station.

Southward had covered the war as a combat photographer, and once he returned to Windsor, a friend had arranged a job for him with the *Star*. Southward quickly learned that at Hugh Graybiel's nonunion newspaper you worked night or day, whenever required, and got your facts right the first time. If you did not, you quickly found yourself out of a job. Inspector Yokum took a personal interest in the photo shoot, and he advised Southward to "take the picture with the missing rivet side of the handle in view." The reporter had a final suggestion, to "have an arrow pointing at the missing rivet." But it was too late. The deadline for the afternoon run had passed. The big presses began to roll, and by two o'clock, newspapers were being printed that featured a photograph of a worried-looking Joseph Gelencser, his beaming nurse, and an inset of the peculiar butcher knife. The afternoon edition of the *Star* was being distributed house to house by about three o'clock. The Slasher mystery had ground on for a year with no prospect of a resolution. Now, in a sudden rush of events, matters were to be resolved within minutes.

At 4:40 that afternoon, a man described only as "the informer" came into the detectives' office at the Windsor police department. He said that he recognized the knife and that it was missing from a house on Cameron Avenue. The informer's step-daughter was living in this house, and she could identify the knife's owner, a very peculiar young man, whom the informer "suspected . . . may have stabbed one Joseph Gelencser." The informer was eventually identified as Isaac Taylor, the stepfather of a young bride named Dorothy Sears. As housing in Windsor was so limited, she, her husband, Donald Sears, and their newborn child had been forced to live with Donald's parents and their grown children. In the tiny house on Cameron Avenue, Dorothy could not help but observe some odd behavior. Her husband's twin brother had a fascination with knives, and one night in August 1945, she had seen him arrive home with blood on his clothes. His mother had instantly washed everything off. On another occasion, he had even talked about the men he had killed.[3]

The young man's name was Ronald Sears.

By 5:15, a five-man squad of detectives headed by Detective-Sergeant John Mahoney arrived at 261 Cameron Avenue. They walked up the steps of the prim frame house and were let in by Mrs. Sears, Ronald's mother. Mahoney asked if Ronald was in, and his mother responded that he was just upstairs getting ready to go out to a party. She would call him down. Mahoney nodded to Acting-Detective William Brand to cover the back door in case their man made a break for it. The precaution was unnecessary, however, for when Ronald Sears came down the stairs, he appeared calm and unruffled. He was average height—5 foot 7 inches tall—with a slim, athletic frame. Wearing a casual suit and with his chestnut hair slicked back, he gave every appearance of being the boy next door.

"We want you, Ronald," Mahoney said to him.

The sergeant motioned for detectives James Hill and James McLauchlan to put on the handcuffs and take Sears out to the waiting squad car. A distraught Mrs. Sears asked what all this was about, and Mahoney responded that it was in connection with the previous night's stabbing. Mahoney asked if he and Brand could have a look at Ronald's room. After a perfunctory search, the detectives found nothing. As they searched, Ronald was squeezed in the backseat of the squad car between Hill and McLauchlan. The young man asked how long they might be, as he had a wiener roast to attend. McLauchlan replied that he did not know. Detective Hill recalled that Sears asked, "What do you want me for, have I done anything?" and then added wistfully, "Mother will be worried." When they were joined by the other detectives, the five police officers and their captive drove in silence to headquarters.

Once there, Sears was taken to the Inspector of Detectives' office to be interrogated. The office was a tiny space in which two men could barely sit. Now Brand and Sears were jammed into the room while McLauchlan brought in a typewriter and set it up on a desk. Outside, it had been a typically hot and humid summer's day in Windsor; in the close confines of the Inspector's office, it was stifling. Mahoney had left instructions that Brand and McLauchlan would conduct this interrogation, focusing on the most recent stabbings of Voligny and Gelencser.

"Scotty" Brand was, as his nickname and pronounced burr suggested, of Scottish origin. By reputation, he was a bit of a plodder. McLauchlan, on the other hand, was known to move quickly to the heart of an issue. Small in stature for a police officer, McLauchlan had a pencil mustache and a weakness for fine suits. He was remembered as "an A-plus personality. He never walked anywhere; he half ran." As an interrogator, "he would go at an interrogation fast and heavy and maybe not brutally hard but really pound a person, while Scotty would be more laid back and try and use psychology on a person."[4] Neither man was a full detective, and Brand had only been back in police work for less than a year after service with the RCAF. It seems odd that Mahoney chose two of his most junior investigators to handle what would become one of the most important interrogations ever conducted by the Windsor police department. But perhaps he knew who he was dealing with. Brand and McLauchlan were not large, intimidating men, and a fellow officer recalled, "They had patience, and they got the accused to feel that they were on his side."

According to Mahoney's instructions, McLauchlan would ask all the questions and type both the questions and Sears's responses. As McLauchlan was, by his own admission, a one-fingered typist, this promised to be a tedious process. For the most part, Brand would simply act as a witness. Before they began, Brand did lean over and ask a few preliminary questions. For the record, he got Sears's statement that he was eighteen years old and had quit school two years previously. Curiously enough, Brand asked him if he had a girlfriend. Sears replied that he did. By 6:10 that evening, they were ready to begin the formal interview. McLauchlan read out the caution that was printed at the top of each examination sheet, which advised Sears that he was charged with "Stabbing with intent to

Murder," that he was not obliged to say anything, and that anything he did say could be used as evidence. Sears was asked if he understood the caution. When he said that he did, they proceeded.

The young man seemed to have no trouble telling the police what he had been up to on the night of June 22. *The Return of the Shadow* had been the feature at the Palace. After the show, he had walked to the Capital Theatre and bought a *Detroit Times*. From there he went home. He denied any knowledge of Alexander Voligny, of owning an ice pick or being anywhere near Bridge Avenue that night. On the previous night, July 5, that of the Gelencser stabbing, Sears had attended the Empire Theatre on Pitt Street to see *House of Dracula*. This show got out at nine o'clock, at which time he caught a bus to Pillette and Tecumseh Road. This intersection was at the edge of the city and the end of the bus line. It was also one of the areas devastated by the tornado. Sears intended to meet a friend, Herb Chatwin, who was helping Sears's brother repair his badly damaged house. He waited for a while in a restaurant and had a pop, but he did not connect with Chatwin. He took another bus back downtown and was home by eleven o'clock. He had neither been near the river nor stabbed anyone.[5] When they were finished (each statement was barely a page and a half long), McLauchlan read back the questions and answers and asked Sears to read them and sign each page. He did so.

In the hour that it had taken the detectives to obtain these statements, they had learned little else other than the fact that the suspect had a penchant for horror movies. He had flatly denied any involvement in the recent attacks, and there was not a shred of direct evidence such as fingerprints, clothing, or witnesses to connect him to any crimes. The detectives must have been wondering if Ronald Sears was another Richard Rowe. At 7:15 they were finished questioning him, and he was transferred to the custody of the desk sergeant to be formally booked and put in a holding cell. Brand and McLauchlan went out for dinner. No one appears to have thought to ask Sears if he wanted anything to eat.

Ronald Sears was not the only member of his family to be questioned at police headquarters that night. After the information supplied by her stepfather, Isaac Taylor, had proven so interesting, the police wanted to talk directly with Dorothy Sears. Here was a person who lived in the Sears household and who proved more than willing to talk about what was going on at 261 Cameron. She provided a handwritten note to the effect that her brother-in-law Ronald regularly went to see the Dracula movies and had developed such a fascination with knives that he had used one to carve up an old mattress. A German bayonet had been stolen from the Taylor's house at such a time that it could have been used for the Slasher killings in the summer of 1945. Later in the year, Dorothy's brother had found it in Ronald's possession and demanded its return. The Taylors had since turned it over to the police. As a result of the stabbings, Dorothy had become "very worried about him." In the past week, the Sears children had found the butcher knife with the missing rivet outside, and it had been placed in a kitchen drawer. On Friday night when Dorothy went to the drawer to get a spoon to feed her baby, she noticed that the knife was gone. About two weeks before, Ronald's sister had had an ice pick stolen.

As incriminating as this information was, Dorothy Sears's next comments were bound to catch the detectives' attention. During the past winter, Ronald had told Dorothy and her husband that he had killed men during the previous summer; he described how many times he had stabbed each one and how he had dragged the bodies through the fields. He even wrote it all down but later destroyed the paper. "I couldn't believe him, it didn't sound right," Dorothy Sears said, but there was no concealing her concern over Ronald's unusual behavior. "I think there is something wrong with his mind," she wrote. "He walks around talking to the cat and stays up in his bedroom all day." There was also no hiding the thin element of panic in her disclosure: "I have been afraid to say anything about this because of the baby. I have found knife slits in the pillow."[6]

Dorothy finished her statement at 7:30 p.m., about the same time Ronald was being booked and led to his cell. The detectives now had some breathing space to consider their next move. Even though Sears had denied everything, Dorothy's statement must have convinced them that their prisoner was holding back and that there was far more to the story than he was letting on. Throughout that Saturday night, various members of the Sears family would pass through police headquarters without ever seeing each other. Ronald's father, Edward Sears, had learned of his son's arrest around seven o'clock, when he had arrived home after work. He immediately rushed to the station but was told by the officer in charge, Sergeant Alf Carter, that he had no record that Ronald was there. Edward Sears came back two hours later, at which time Carter was able to confirm that Ronald was a prisoner but that Edward would not be allowed to see him, as "an investigation is ongoing."

What happened between the time Ronald Sears was booked at 7:30 and the time his questioning resumed at nine o'clock is one of the most intractable mysteries of the Slasher story. He did not talk to any police officers. Various cells officers peeked in and saw him sitting passively in his cell, his head bowed and his hands clasped. No one thought to bring him any dinner. No one knows what thoughts went through his mind as he contemplated the events of the previous two hours. But whatever happened during that ninety-minute interval would irretrievably alter the course of the Slasher investigation.

Although Dorothy Sears's statement indicated to the police that they were on the right track, they did not share her statement with their suspect. Neither did they immediately show him the brown envelope that Mahoney had retrieved from the evidence locker, which held the ice pick and the butcher knife. At nine o'clock that night, Ronald Sears was moved from his cell back to the inspector's office, and the questioning began anew. The detectives employed some classic interrogation techniques. The cramped office containing only three chairs, a desk, and a typewriter was presumably far removed from anything in Ronald Sears's previous experience, and for a typical person, it might have been a frightening and intimidating environment. During the interrogation, the police worked to keep Sears's focus on the questions and answers, in order to minimize sensory stimulation. It was also crucial to the success of such an interrogation that "the accused be denied communicative access to friends and family." Sergeant Carter had seen to that by denying Sears's father access to his son. Lastly, the cramped office was the perfect place for, as a later police manual would advise, "invading the suspect's personal space," which would serve to "increase his or her level of anxiety from which the only means of escape is confession." Later studies would show that as a means of extracting information, simple methods work best. Keeping a suspect confined in a small room, for example, is often more effective than physical violence.[7] Moreover, as a result of the information they had received from Dorothy Sears, the police now had several narrative strands around which to build their questions. It has been suggested that "the interrogative process, drawing upon specific police schemas and theories of suspect culpability, is designed to persuade a suspect to accept a particular, pre-determined rendition of events."[8]

McLauchlan began the second interrogation by asking Sears about the Gelencser stabbing. Sears responded with much the same story he had given earlier about going to the Empire Theatre and seeing a horror show. However, this time, instead of taking a bus to Pillette and Tecumseh after the show, he said that he had walked down to the government dock. A man came and sat down next to him:

Q. Then what was said?

A. His conversation was dirty that he was talking about jacking off and wanted to know if I would let him suck me off.

Q. What did you do or say?

A. I was shocked at first and had in the inside pocket of my grey suit coat a short bread knife that I had taken out of my brother's car.

Surprisingly, Sears confessed that it was the same knife that he later hid under the front steps and that subsequently had been discovered by the children and thrown into a kitchen drawer. Getting back to the incident, he explained:

I agreed to let him suck me off at first. I told him I didn't think anyone would do a thing like that. He said to come on down here and took me down to the dock near the water's edge at the government dock. When we got there I told him I knew a darker spot and a better spot.

Q. Then what did you do?

A. From the long walk we both instinctively sat down. He was getting ready to take his pants off. While he was taking his pants down I took the knife from my inside pocket. At first I wanted to scare him with it. He was startled at first and it looked like he was getting ready to run and I was afraid he would squeal on me and Had the knife in my right hand and as his back was toward me I plunged the knife into his back.

If McLauchlan and Brand were surprised by Sears's sudden admissions, there is no record of it in their report. At this point, they produced the brown evidence envelope that contained the knives and withdrew both of them for Sears's inspection. With a display of theatricality, McLauchlan announced: "I, acting-detective McLauchlan and he acting-detective Brand, in the Inspector of Detectives Office at Police Headquarters show you these. Do you recognize any of them?"

Ronald Sears seemed remarkably willing to play his part in the production, for the typed transcript recorded his reply as: "Yes I was shown a knife by acting Detectives McLauchlan and Brand, in the Inspector of Detectives Office at Police Headquarters, and I recognized it as being the same knife."[9]

The fact that Sears's answer was recorded in this format—exactly the format and phrasing that the police required—seems quite convenient— so convenient, in fact, that one is left to wonder if these were really Ronald Sears's exact words or if had they were tailored by the detectives for the occasion. For a young man who had not graduated from high school, it was suspiciously sophisticated wording. The sudden display of the weapons may have, in actuality, served another purpose, for their appearance implied that the police knew a good deal more about Sears's role in the Slasher killings than they actually did. Still, they had done nothing to deliberately mislead him.

It was not clear from Sears's narrative whether or not he had actually planned to kill Gelencser. According to him, he only wanted to "scare" him with the knife and then attacked him when he feared that Gelencser would go to the police. The detectives did not follow up on this detail to determine if Sears intended to commit murder. Perhaps the most unusual aspect of his statement was Sears's assertion of shock at Gelencser's suggestion of oral sex. If in fact he was the Slasher, then it was likely that Sears would have been approached by several men with similar suggestions over the course of the past year.

By 10:15, an hour and a quarter after they had begun, the police had Sears's signed statement, which ran slightly more than two pages. During that time, there must have been much more give and take between the officers and their subject than appears in the report. But none of that conversation was recorded, and no clues exist as to why Sears changed his story so dramatically between the first and second interrogations.

With the Gelencser confession in hand, the detectives returned to the Voligny case. This time, Sears said that he had not gone to the show at all but instead had dropped by the bus depot and then headed to Government Park. A man came by and asked for a match, a common enough way to start a homosexual pickup. Sears replied that he did not smoke. Together they went to the Arizona Lunch for something to eat, and thereafter Sears's companion suggested that they return to the river and stroll around. Sears recommended a "nice spot" down by the river:

Q. What was said or done there?

A. He asked me if I felt like getting hot and pulled out his cock and began to feel mine. I pushed his hand away and started to leave. He held onto me and tried to persuade me not to go I told him that I didn't feel like doing anything like that.

Q. Did you or he jack off?

A. No we didn't. He mentioned he wanted to go back on the grass and lay down. He became a little angry because I wouldn't let him suck me off.

Q. Then what happened?

A. He went to remove his suit coat and I plunged an ice pick into his back, once is all I remember.[10]

Sears's account of the incident differed from Voligny's in many significant respects. Voligny, for example, had never mentioned the detour to the Arizona Lunch. According to Voligny, it was Sears who was the sexual aggressor, who suggested the walk by the river, and who first initiated sexual contact. It was Sears who first took out his penis and suggested that they have sex. In Voligny's account, they were on the verge of engaging in anal sex when the Slasher stabbed him. However, Sears maintained that he was the passive one throughout the encounter and that he rebuffed all of Voligny's advances. By his account, Sears did not take part in any indecent activities and had struck out almost in self-defense.

Sandwiches and coffee were brought in at 11:45, and they all took a break. Brand and McLauchlan appreciated the fact that cross-examining a witness does not necessarily mean browbeating and intimidation. It can be most successful when "conducted on a relatively businesslike basis"[11] when all concerned are working toward a common goal, the establishment of a factual record of what happened during these incidents. If anything, Ronald Sears seemed to appreciate the opportunity to give his side of what happened during these encounters.

Just before midnight, the interrogation resumed. Once again, McLauchlan read out the caution, but this time it simply said that Sears was charged with "Murder." For the first time, Sears interrupted McLauchlan and asked, "Do you think because I stabbed these other two men that I killed [Sergeant Price]? McLauchlan looked over at him, said, "I don't think anything," and completed reading the warning. Once again, Sears seemed to have no difficulty recalling the incident down to the smallest detail, and once again he cast himself as the passive victim of the piece. About 11:30 on a Friday evening in August of the previous year he had been sitting on a bench in Government Park when a soldier sat down beside him. The soldier suggested that they go to a darker spot behind the silos, and as they strolled in that direction, "He started talking dirty."

Q. What did he say?

A. On the way down behind the silos he said I would like to suck you off. Right then it came to me he was a sex pervert and I was planning to kill him. I said it was too busy here, there were too many people walking around, and I held him by the arm and led him into a field right along the pathway on the south side of Sandwich St. between the railway and Crawford Ave. just off the bridge over the C.P.R. Railway.

Finally, Sears had made an admission that was missing from his other two statements—that even as he gently led the Sergeant by the arm to the place of slaughter, his intention was murder. It would have been the easiest thing in the world for Sears simply to have avoided these men, to have refused to talk to them or walked away. But he did not, for it was his purpose to seek out homosexuals, lead them to a convenient place, and kill them. In the case of Sergeant Price, he had taken his victim to the exact place in the killing field to accomplish this task without detection:

Q. Did [Price] go willingly?

A. Yes he went along willingly. We lay down in the weeds together and he had unfastened his pants and began to jack me off. I told him to roll over on his stomach and I was going to put my cock up his rectum.

Q. Did he lay on his stomach?

A. Yes he layed on his stomach and I had on a topcoat and in the right hand pocket I had a hunting knife . . . and raised it as far as I could and had it poised ready to bring down where I thought his heart would be on the left side. I stabbed him once and he tried to get up groaning slightly and I stabbed him again through fright on the right side.

Sears began to run toward the darkest part of the field but looked back and to his horror, saw that he had not killed his victim:

He was up on his feet wobbling and shaking from side to side and appeared to be trying to run after me when he fell backwards.

Q. Then what did you do?

A. I retraced my steps and went back to see if he was still alive and I wanted to make sure he was dead because I was so frightened he might give information about me. I stabbed him again repeatedly and saw a car coming and tried to conceal him.

The young man then gave a detailed description of how he had fled from the field, ran behind the nurses' residence at Grace Hospital, and arrived home to wash off the blood.

But why? For a year, everyone had speculated on who the Slasher might be. Now he was revealed as the polite young man sitting across from the detectives. McLauchlan had to ask:

Q. Why did you want to kill this man?

A. Because when I was about 9 years of age a man came to our place and he was a stranger to me. He took me into the garage at the rear of the house and started to feel around me and make love to me as if I was a female. He had me jack him off and tried to put his cock in my mouth. But I wouldn't let him. I heard my mother call and didn't say anything about it because at that time I didn't think it was very bad. But as I grew older it seemed to grow on me.[12]

By his own admission, the incident in his youth had not seemed very bad at the time. However, in his early adolescence, he had come to understand more about homosexual acts, and now he realized how abhorrent and unnatural they were. It had been a learning process during which he had discovered the evil of anything homosexual. At no time had Sears attempted to make any distinction between the pedophilia attack he had endured and homosexual acts between consenting adults. To Sears, and to society in general, they were all depraved and culpable acts. By his understanding, he was implicated in them, and it was a matter that had to be put to right.

As for the murder weapon, it was an aluminum-handled blade, which had gone missing. When the detective showed him an aluminum-handled knife taken from the Sears home, Ronald did not think that it was the one, for the weapon he had used had a nicked blade where it had struck bone. Once again, he had a remarkably specific recollection of details.

It was now almost 1:00 Sunday morning, July 7. The interrogation had been an exhausting process for all concerned. McLauchlan's one-fingered typing must have seemed endless to the young man who had long ago abandoned any hopes of getting to the wiener roast. But there were still two more cases to discuss, and the process of reading cautions and questions began yet again. As in so many other cases, the incident concerning Frank Sciegliski began on a bench in Government Park. "Lovely evening," said a man approaching Sears's bench. "Would you like me to sit down and talk to you?" Sit down he did, and the conversation between the two quickly came to sex. The man asked if Sears went around with girls very much, to which he replied, "I told him no I don't very much." The man asked if Sears wanted a ride in his car, but as soon as they got in he started to feel Ronald and "I repeled for a minute and knew he was a sex pervert."

At that point, Sears recounted the ritual that would be replayed in the Price killing, the same tactics that would be used on Voligny:

> I asked him if he would like to go for a walk down to the water's edge. He said he would go along.
>
> Q. Did you go to the water's edge?
>
> A. We went behind the silos at the west end of the Government Park and he started to feel me up again. People were coming down There and I told him where there was a grassy field and led him into the field on the West side of Caron Ave, near the embankment of the C.P.R. Tracks.
>
> Q. Then what did you do?
>
> A. We layed down together and he started to unfasten his pants. I played along with him and told him to lay over on his stomach. I had on a topcoat and had a hunting knife in the right hand pocket and when he layed over on his stomach I struck him with the knife on the left side of his back where I thought the heart would be. He got up to his feet, stumbled and fell down. I had ran a little ways and returned to him and stabbed him repeatedly. I went through his clothing and took some money maybe two dollars that was in his wallet, and some keys and change.[13]

Ritual is a vital element in any serial killer's method, and Ronald Sears certainly seemed to prefer a set pattern each time he attacked. First, he would identify the victim as a homosexual or a "sex pervert" and then lure him under the promise of sex to a secluded area. Once there, he would engage in limited sex play and cajole his victim into lying face down preparatory to having anal sex. In that vulnerable position, the target would not notice Sears draw the knife from his coat. With Sears, as with most serial killers, "this ritual is a repeated observable pattern, so that there is a fundamental sameness from crime to crime that even the killer can't alter. It forms the basis of the serial killer's personality." Ritual provides a framework for serial killers, "an architecture for their fantasies and a structure to the violence that informs their conscious existence." As one profiler has noted, "To the killer during the act of the crime, the rituals are a form of morality play."[14] Ronald Sears, confident in his own righteousness, explained to the detectives that he was justified in killing Sciegliski, because "I knew he was a sex pervert and I knew he would probably try to get some other young boy and ruin his life." It was a vital step in the process for Sears to dissociate the victim from the rest of humanity and make the killing an acceptable, even meritorious act.

In the course of these morality plays, Sears disengaged from his victims emotionally. Once he had identified a man as a "sex pervert," that man instantly became a worthy target. If part of the interrogation process is to separate deviant criminals from normal members of society, Sears was placing himself on the side of decency. Ronald Sears and people like him are not outlaws; if anything, they are "oversocialized" and consider themselves "simply carrying out sentences that society at large leveled."[15] Perhaps he felt that he and the detectives were kindred spirits. There is no record in the transcripts of any responses by McLauchlan or Brand, but it is not likely that they had any sympathy for the homosexuals who were trolling city parks hoping to commit acts of gross indecency. Sears could easily have perceived himself and the detectives as part of the same process of cleaning up the parks and ridding Windsor of a menace.

By the time Sears read over and signed the Sciegliski statement, it was 1:30 a.m. McLauchlan would later recall, "It was possible up to this time that the boy was exhausted after the Sciegliski statement had been taken." He had noticed that the young man was sweating profusely, and after the signing, he appeared to be completely done in: "It was visibly evident without going further that the boy was exhausted and becoming ill."[16] After a pause, Sears fainted, fell to the floor, and began to vomit. Brand and McLauchlan quickly carried him into the Deputy Chief's office where they hoped he might get more air. Emergency medical help was summoned, and Dr. William Markkanen arrived at 2:00 a.m. to find a pale young man stretched out on the floor of the police office, having interludes of nausea. His pulse was rapid, and he was sweating heavily. The doctor gave him a sedative, but almost instantly, he vomited that up as well. However, Markkanen felt that he was in no immediate danger, and Sears was removed to a cell in the women's section—the quietest part of the cellblock.

Prior to the fainting incident and just after Sears had given the statement on Price, there had been a quiet moment between the prisoner and his interrogators. By this point, the detectives seemed to have earned Sears's trust. They had been working for quite some time in a collegial effort to piece together what Ronald remembered of the Slasher attacks. They had even taken a break together and shared food and drink. Perceptive interrogators try and foster a sense of rapport between themselves and the suspects they question, since a subject is more likely to confide in a friend than in a stranger or an adversary. As Scotty Brand recalled, "We were all sitting there and no one was talking to my knowledge and he said, 'I am glad I was caught before I killed someone else.'" Up until this time, the police officers had directed the flow of information. Now, for the first time, Ronald Sears was speaking his own mind. The detectives were so taken aback that they did not record the comments till later that morning. One of the detectives noted that at least two of the stabbings had occurred on weekends. Had Ronald had any plans for that weekend? "Yes I intended to go out to-night," he responded. Again they all paused for a few minutes. "I know I'll die for this," he added.

McLauchlan tried to assure him that this was not the case. "Don't cross any bridges until you come to them," he said. Sears then asked if the detectives would see him through the case, and in a spirit of generosity, they promised that they would.

"It will be good to know that somebody is on my side," Sears replied. The police officers noticed that there were tears in his eyes.

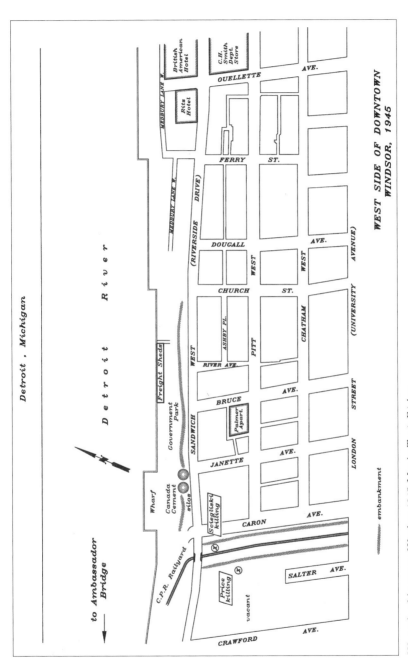

West side of downtown Windsor, 1945. Map by Travis Frickey.

Police photo of automobile tire tracks leaving site of Price killing, August 1945. Windsor Police Service.

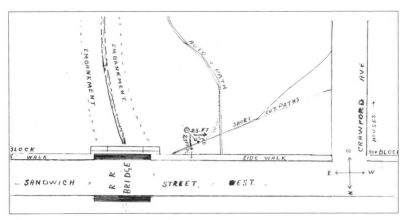

Sketch of Price murder site. Windsor Police Service.

Windsor detective at the east side of abandoned salt lands, the site where Frank Scegliski's body was found, August 8, 1945. Windsor Police Service.

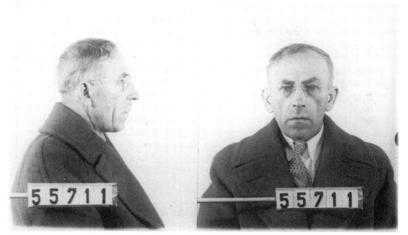

Mug shot of Frank Sciegliski. Windsor Police Service.

Deputy Chief J. J.
Mahoney. Windsor
Police Service.

Police photo taken July 14, 1946, showing wooden steps going down to the Detroit River. Windsor Police Service.

Police photo of Caron Ave. leading down to the river, taken July 14, 1946. Windsor Police Service.

Ronald and Donald Sears during the war years. Sears family collection.

Ronald Sears with parents Florence and Edward Sears. Sears family collection.

Ronald Sears in Woodstock sanitarium, 1950s. Sears family collection.

From left: Detroit detectives Harry O'Brien and Eugene Kinney, Windsor inspector Duncan MacNab. *Windsor Daily Star,* August 22, 1945.

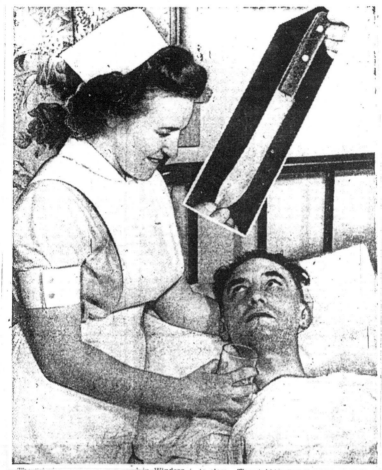

Slasher's Latest Victim and Knife He Used

From the *Windsor Daily Star,* July 6, 1946.

From left: Victims Frank Sciegliski, Sgt. Price, Alexander Voligny, and Joseph Gelencser. *Windsor Daily Star,* July 8, 1946.

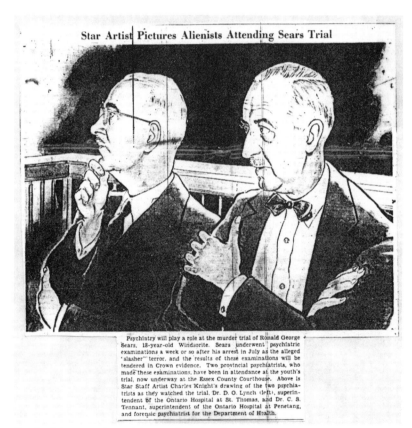

Sketch of alienists at the trial, *Windsor Daily Star,* September 13, 1946.

Star Artist Sketches Counsel Talking to Sears in Prisoner's Box

This sketch was made during Saturday's sittings of the Sears murder trial by Star Staff Artist Charles Knight. Mr. Knight's remarkable drawing has caught almost perfect likenesses of Major James H. Clark, K.C., defense counsel, and Ronald George Sears, 18. The sketch was made shortly before the confession of the youthful alleged "slasher" was read into the court's record by Crown Attorney E. C. Awrey, K.C. The trial is expected to last until Wednesday.

Sketch of James Clark and Ronald Sears from the trial, *Windsor Daily Star*, September 16, 1946.

Exhibits Entered By Crown in Sears Case

The Crown entered 10 exhibits, including photographs, in the Sears' murder trial. The vital exhibit, of course, was the youth's confession to police dealing with the knife murder, of "a soldier." This picture shows Miss Margaret Whalen, of the Essex County Supreme Court offices, checking the exhibits. She is holding the aluminum-handled knife. Sears told police was identical to the one he used in the "soldier's murder." Another knife exhibit lies on top of a trench coat. The trench coat, on which a bloodstain was found, also was an exhibit.

(Star Staff Photo.)

Photo of exhibit items, *Windsor Daily Star*, September 19, 1946.

Letter from Ronald Sears, June 16, 1947. Record Group 4-32, Ontario Archives. A few of the cursive letters seem to match the cursive that appears on the address of the "Slasher" letter.

The "Slasher" letter received by Windsor Police, postmarked March 20, 1946. The identity of the sender was never established.

Dear -Sirs

This is x challenge
To you. I will strike
in The near future. I
can not DISCLOSE this to
you of course. My avenge
of These people are great,
Nothing shall stand in
my way. I will use only
The Knife on my vic...
...   I'm not a reLimed

TRUE / This / the
Proph / he

SLASHER

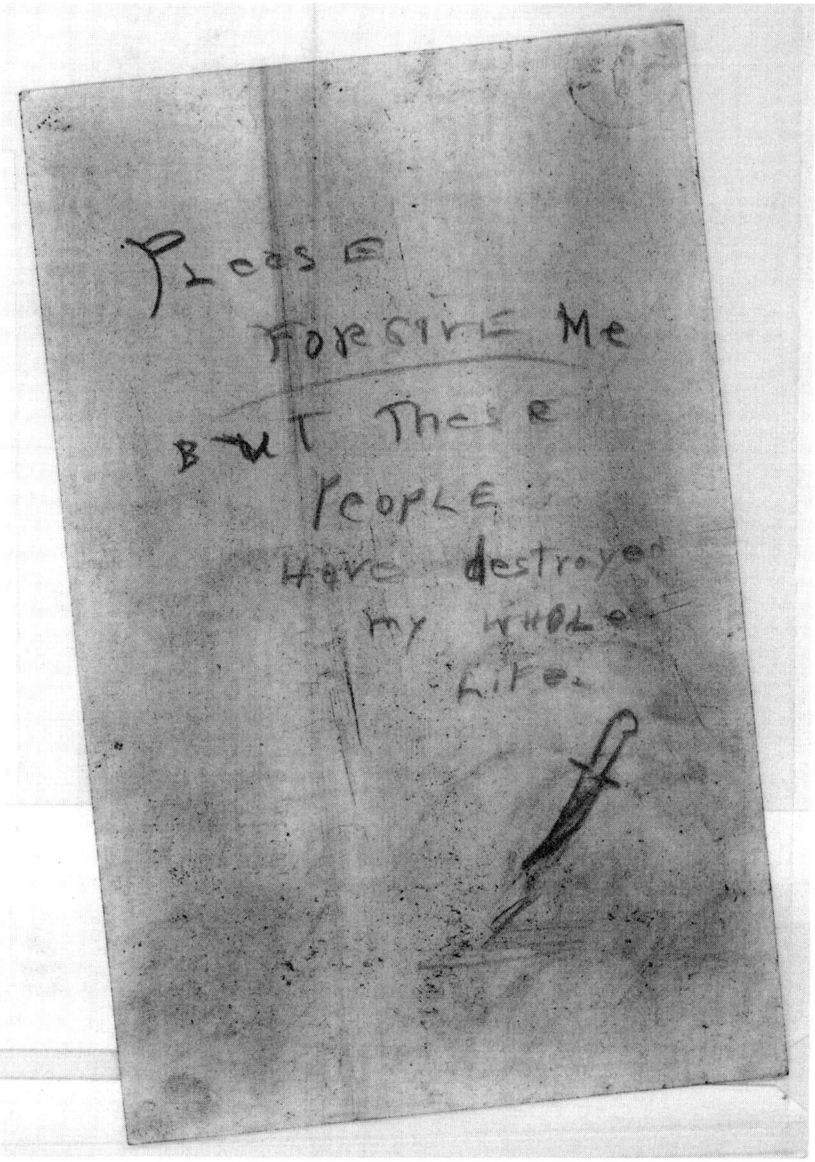

Please
Forgive Me
But These
People
Have destroyed
my whole
Life.

8

AN AVENGING FORCE

So this was the *Star*'s "blood-lusting maniac" who had terrorized a city, murdered two men, and stabbed three others. This thin boy stretched out on the floor of the police station, gasping for breath, vomit drooling from his mouth, was the infamous "Windsor Slasher."

To those who knew him, Ronald Sears was the last person they would have suspected of being the Slasher. A schoolmate remembered him as being so quiet "you didn't hardly know he was in class." Her reaction to Ronald's arrest was typical: "Are you sure they had the right person?"[1] Detectives spent the week following Sears's arrest combing the west side of Windsor, seeking out any of the boys who knew him. Most thought him reserved, but pleasant enough. On occasions when he went with a gang of friends to the movies, he would sometimes get up in the middle of a film and walk out. He never gave any explanation. When younger boys met in the vacant lot by the train embankment to play Slasher, Ronald would join in. One companion, Ronald Robinson, told the police that Sears would roughhouse, and although he was deceptively strong for his size, he would not bully other boys. Whenever a boy showed signs of weakening, Ronald would let up. "He always had lots of life," Robinson recalled, "but during the last year he appeared to have something on his mind and looked worried, he would wander off by himself and that is the last you would see of him for awhile."[2] The identification of this quiet, unassuming young man as the Slasher must have been disquieting to those in the press. They had provided a shape and form for the Slasher, characterized him as a monster, and now he was revealed as nothing at all like that image.

One topic that was raised in every interview was Ronald's fascination with knives. He avidly traded or bought knives, and among his prize acquisitions was an aluminum-handled navy knife. A friend remembered that Ronald had up to six knives in his possession at one time and that he would practice throwing them at trees. Herb Chatwin, the boy Sears was supposed to meet on the night of the Gelencser attack, recalled a German bayonet that he had once shown to Sears. Two days later it went missing. Chatwin suspected that Sears had stolen it, and when he confronted him, Sears sheepishly returned the weapon.

In addition to his love affair with knives, Ronald Sears seemed to be a commando in training. One evening, a group of boys lounging on the steps of Ascension Church caught glimpses of Ronald flitting through the bushes. Sometimes he would sneak up behind some of his pals and tap them on the head or shoulder. Other times, he would play a game where he would pull back a boy's head and give him a "vampire bite" on the neck. While some of his chums felt that "he seemed like a good fellow to go around with," others thought that his behavior was becoming noticeably eccentric: "Sometimes at night he would go out into the alley and meow like cats and one night his brother Donald was in their yard when Ronald was doing this and Donald said he thought his brother was going a little crazy and when he does that sometimes he thinks he is head of the cat band."[3]

A *Star* reporter who combed the neighborhood looking for comments about Sears found that most people held Ronald in high regard. A typical comment from a west-side woman was "He is such a nice boy, so polite and courteous it seems impossible that he would do such a hideous thing."[4] If the *Star* was deferential, the Detroit newspapers took a more inflammatory approach to the Slasher story. Rex G. White of the *Detroit News* wrote that Ronald had been the victim of a sexual attack at the age of nine (amazingly enough, the most intimate details of the police interrogation were available to the press) and that the memory of that attack had grown and festered in his memory until it ultimately resulted in this "tragedy and horror."

White's research uncovered new details of Ronald's bizarre behavior, for example, how he had been hearing "voices." "He heard them often and was annoyed that his family did not hear them," White wrote. "'Can't you hear him?' he would cry angrily. 'He's talking loud and plain.'" Ronald would find comfort in his daydreams and his voices, and when not in his room, he would be in the alley stabbing the shapeless form of an old mattress, "a practice ground for the more dreadful stabbings that were to follow." Recently, he had become even more reclusive than usual, spending hours in his room with his cat, "a brown, dingy animal which he loved extravagantly." Sometimes, when Ronald was alone in his room, the family could hear animated conversations between Ronald and his voices. At night, he would pace about the darkened house and "listen to the voices of the unseen."

Ronald confided some of his deepest thoughts to his sister-in-law Dorothy Sears. He was closer in age to Dorothy than to most of his siblings and had known her throughout grade school. To Dorothy, he expressed his horror at having being molested while still a child. He told her, "The police were lax in their efforts to find sex perverts who, he insisted, were many." Oddly, Ronald Sears's comments reflected the opinions of Weston Gaul, in his series of articles addressing the serious sex-crime problem in Windsor. According to Gaul, the authorities were doing nothing to stop this type of crime. Similarly, the *Star* was constantly harping on the inadequacy of the justice system, as when R. M. Harrison decried the "polecats accused and found guilty of molesting little boys and girls," the same men who were the undeserving recipients of "judicial leniency." Perhaps, these articles suggested, someone should take direct action. Was Sears led, or at least encouraged, by the local press to do what he did? To Dorothy, "He declared that if the police could not do their duty he would constitute an avenging force."[5]

Sunday morning, July 7, 1946, Edward Sears was back at police headquarters, and again he was turned away with the excuse that the investigation was ongoing. Shortly before nine o'clock, McLauchlan and Brand once again resumed their interrogation. Ronald could not have had a very long or comfortable sleep, nor was he given much of an opportunity to have breakfast, but the detectives were eager to finish their deposition. McLauchlan began that day by questioning Sears about the Mannie case. In the same manner as the previous night, he read the warning—this time that Ronald was charged with "stabbing with intent to kill" and that he need not talk. Once again, as he had throughout the previous night, Ronald appeared to be the soul of accommodation. Yes, he had met Mannie (who appeared to be a little drunk) at the water's edge by the foot of California Street. This interrogation would prove particularly interesting, for it was the only record of Ronald's first attempt to take the law into his own hands. According to Ronald, Mannie initiated the conversation and told Ronald "that he sucked other boys off. I was really shocked because this was the first time I had met someone that would do a thing like that. . . . I hated him for the filthy suggestion, he wanted to suck me off. Really he did. I found out he was one of these guys."

Having identified Mannie as "one of these guys," Sears's account of what happened next was predictable. The only variation from the scenarios he had already described to the detectives was that in this case, Sears alleged that Mannie had threatened him:

Q. Did anything happen between you and he?

A. He got a little violent and grabbed a hold of me around the waist. I was lying down and started to get up and he got up with me. At first I thought he was going to do something.

Q. What do you mean by that?

A. He started to take down his pants and I thought he was going to make me suck him off? I had a hunting knife on me that I had just got that day. I came down there to cut up, that is there are a lot of trees down there. I got angry with him and started to wrestle with him and I instinctively went for my knife.

The scenario Sears was describing was later termed the "homosexual advance defense," where straight men would take such affront at a proposal to engage in homosexual conduct that they would lash out. Juries would be invited to conclude that this was a normal reaction from any decent man and should not incur any criminal liability.[6]

Yet, by Sears's own admission, Mannie posed no threat to him, for once Mannie saw the knife, he retreated up the embankment toward Sandwich Street. Instead of letting him go, Sears pursued him and "leaped on his back, we both fell to the ground and at the same time I brought the knife down plunging it into his back twice." In a blind panic, Sears fled the scene. As he ran away, he could see Mannie stumbling to his feet. After this, Sears's first attempt to eradicate a sex pervert, he said it seemed simple enough to accompany a gay man to an isolated place and attack him. What he needed to practice was how to cajole the victim into assuming a vulnerable position so that he could then administer the fatal blow. There was no question that the hunting knife was up to the job, and Sears would use it again to kill Sciegliski and Price. When the police asked where it was, Sears said that he had lost it. When Brand pulled out the aluminum-handled knife found in his room, Sears denied that it was the one. He distinctly recalled that the blade of the knife he had used to kill had been nicked by bone and had lost its sharp edge.[7] While the police did not have the murder weapon, they had yet another remarkably detailed story. That Sunday, the police conducted a more thorough search of the Sears house and removed several pieces of Ronald's clothing, including a fingertip (knee-length) raincoat that had spots of blood on the inside collar and on the left-hand pocket.

On Sunday afternoon, the detectives and their prisoner drove out along Sandwich Street to inspect the sites of the attacks. Sears pointed out the places near the train embankment where he had killed Price and Sciegliski and then the spots by the river's edge where he had tried to kill the other three. He had no trouble recalling the places, and the sites all matched with the police reports. An official photographer had come along to take pictures of the sites as Ronald pointed them out.[8] After another full day of police questioning, the boy seemed utterly exhausted. Undoubtedly, he also felt isolated from his family, unaware that they were being prevented from seeing him. At 6:30 that evening, the cells officer noted that Sears was gasping for breath. A doctor was called in, who diagnosed him as suffering from heat prostration and prescribed a sedative. Thereafter, Sears managed to go to sleep.

The following day, Monday, July 8, the early edition of the *Star* proclaimed that the days of anxiety were over at last: "The 'slasher' terror that chilled the hearts of Windsorites last summer, and broke out anew this month, is believed to have ended with his dramatic arrest over the weekend." There was no question of the suspect's guilt, for the *Star*'s lead article announced that Sears "stood today self-indicted as the notorious knife wielder."⁹ Two days later, the *Star* headline read "Police Sigh in Relief—Slasher Terror Ended."¹⁰ Displaying an alarming awareness of what the police had discovered, the *Star* reported in detail the evidence obtained in each of the confessions and even Sears's comments that he had intended to go out that weekend searching for a new victim. The newspaper had all the inside information on the informant who had broken the case and how the police had pieced together a solution from what Dorothy Sears had told them. Someone was obviously feeding the press the very latest—and what should have been the most confidential—information. While it was not unusual for the *Star* and the Windsor police department to share information, within the context of a murder trial, the leaks were wildly inappropriate.

On Monday, July 8, Edward and Florence Sears were at last permitted to see their son. Together with his brother Donald, they were led to the crown attorney's office, where Ronald sat leaning against a wall. "I could hardly stand to look at him," his father recalled. "He was in a very weak state. He was in a terrible condition." His mother fell to her knees and wrapped her arms around him. He whispered to her, "Mom, mom, take me home with you; I didn't do anything." The most his father could do was pat his shoulder and say, "Cheer up, cheer up Ron, be brave."¹¹

Looking pale and wan, Ronald Sears had been taken from his cell to be arraigned on two charges of murder and three of attempted murder. John Mahoney, described by the *Star* as the "sleuth in charge of the case," was the first one in the courtroom. Scotty Brand had one arm hooked around Sears to support him, while McLauchlan offered support from behind. While the charges were read out by Magistrate Arthur Hanrahan, "the youth slumped a bit, his hands gripping hard at the rails. He looked completely dazed. A *Toronto Globe and Mail* reporter noted that Sears "was in a state of semi-collapse and was half-carried to the dock. Here he stood drooping, supporting himself by the front railing of the box while the police remained close by."¹² Crown Attorney E. C. Awrey asked that he be remanded, and with the help of the two detectives, the prisoner shuffled back to the cellblock.

If the general public was prepared to accept that the terror was over and that the Slasher was in custody, it was a verdict that the Sears family was not prepared to acknowledge. They dismissed the portrayal of Ronald in the Detroit papers as a demented lad who talked to his cat as laughably absurd. He was just another boy from the neighborhood with an overactive imagination. Florence Sears blamed her son's eccentric behavior on his horror-film-addled mind—for he had seen the Dracula movie at least three times, and as a result, he was "terribly excited. It seemed to affect his behaviour at home. . . . He was moody and restless." A reporter asked her about Ronald's late hours, and rather injudiciously she replied that yes, he was regularly out late at night and always told her that he had been to a double feature.

In contrast to Florence, Edward Sears's initial reaction to his son's arrest reflected his strict moral compass. If Ronald did these things as the police said, then there were consequences. To a Detroit reporter, he confessed, "I can't believe it, but if he did it, he'll have to pay. I don't know what to believe." Life had not been easy for the older Sears. Born in Brantford, he had come to Windsor for a better life and made money to support his wife and eight children by building houses. During the Great Depression he lost everything and was now working as a laborer at the Ford plant. In his spare time, he did house repairs and frequently hired Ronald to assist him.

Once he learned more about the circumstances of the attacks, Edward changed his view on his son's culpability. If he had committed these stabbings to resist the advances of homosexuals, to prevent them from polluting other young boys, then he must have been justified. Under the headline "Asserts Son Robin Hood," the father tearfully explained, "You can be a criminal and a Robin Hood at the same time." The implication was that ridding the parks of homosexuals was technically illegal but still an act worthy of praise. One of Ronald's sisters added, "He must have had [his sexual assault] on his mind all these years and took the law in his own hands. I hear [the victims] were all sex maniacs." A schoolmate of Ronald's recalled that public support of his crimes grew, saying, "Some people thought it was well that he did it, that his victims can't hurt any other people any more."[13] The report that a predator had victimized Sears at the age of nine only proved the existence of the deviant threat. Perverts were a menace to the helpless and ultimately a threat to the social order.

The idea that Ronald Sears may have been justified in his one-man killing spree was even picked up by the *Star*. There would never be any hint of remorse in the *Star* for its previous exposés on the alleged threat from deviants that seemed to have encouraged and sanctioned Sears's actions. Instead, it came close to praising the alleged killer. In his "Now" column, R. M. Harrison wrote, "There'll probably be plenty of sympathy for the young man who, by his confession to the police, became a 'slasher' and crusader against perverts because of a psychosis that was the outgrowth of being forced into abnormal sexual relations at the age of 9."[14] The *Star*'s editorial staff evinced no concern over Sears's victims, the innocent men whose lives had been threatened or cut short. Rather, they urged the authorities to attack the root of the problem—the existence of homosexuals or, as the *Star* invariably called them, sex perverts. News reporting is a complex process, and editors select what they deem is important for the public to know or what they feel are the most extraordinary events.[15] Focusing public anger on gays likely increased the *Star*'s circulation and underlined the role of the newspaper as a moral leader.

The views of editorialists such as R. M. Harrison carried enormous weight in the community. One avid reader of the *Star* from the 1940s recalled, "My parents read Harrison as if he was the Bible . . . everybody in the neighborhood turned to Harrison, because he seemed to encapsulate the thinking of the average guy."[16] If so, that thinking encompassed the most vitriolic homophobia. Harrison advised Windsor readers that homosexuals congregated in places such as Essex Square in New York's Greenwich Village. Fortunately, he said, the New York police freely applied their nightsticks to these perverts to good effect. In eliminating homosexuals from decent society, Harrison believed the police should not feel constrained by technicalities such as due process or presumption of innocence. Harrison urged, "The task of the authorities is far from ended. There must be a concerted drive to round up 'queer' persons of the sort who were responsible for [Sears's] plight. And we're not too ready to believe the public would object to some good old-fashioned strong arm tactics in the process."[17]

The other *Star* columnist, W. L. Clark, hastened to endorse these inquisitorial tactics. Now that the "whole sordid story of sex perversion and the rotten conditions in our parks is coming into the open," the only solution was a "cleansing of conditions in the parks and public places of the city." With tones of hushed horror, Clark advised the public that "these persons" roamed the parks of Windsor. In his July 9, 1946, editorial "Round Up the Perverts," Clark concluded that the source of the problem was a conspiracy of sexual deviants. Furthermore, he wrote, "The police have known for months that the murders involved some of these people." He was technically correct, as all of the victims were homosexual. Nevertheless, there had been no indication that the killer was homosexual. Still, gays were to blame for the crimes, and Clark concluded that "for the protection of everyone, some means should be found to curb the perverts before there is another rash of killing. Innocent people could easily suffer." Presumably, none of the victims to date had been innocent. The *Star* incessantly characterized homosexual men as a threat to children, even though no such connection existed in general or in relation to Sears's victims. His victims had not been child molesters at all but adult gay men seeking out other adult gay men.[18]

The *Star* cast homosexuals in the role of folk devils to be driven from society. Even a reader who had never met a gay man would know from the press that they were the ones responsible for the Slasher crime wave. Inevitably, this spin required multiple distortions, since the Slasher case was not really a criminal epidemic but the work of one isolated individual who, as far as anyone knew, did not identify as a homosexual. Nevertheless, the *Star* trumpeted, a crisis existed, an enemy was at large, and the "moral barricades" had been populated by "right thinking people."[19] During 1946, the tone of the panic was not nearly as shrill as it had been during the previous year, but the panic still fulfilled its purpose by stirring up the public and reasserting the values of decent society, especially the idea that all public spaces belonged exclusively to those who conformed.

In light of this sex-crime crisis, delegates from groups representing concerned citizens, women, the YMCA and YWCA, and Catholic and Protestant churches met in Mayor Reaume's office during the final week in July to draw up a plan of action. The threat, it was decided, existed not solely in homosexual behavior but in sexual perversion of all kinds. An educational campaign would be initiated to warn young women of the dangers lurking in the parks and especially the peril of "curb cruisers." These young men in cars who passed slowly by girls and tried to initiate conversations were a serious menace to safety. The delegates decided that maximum sentences should be imposed on these miscreants. One women's group advocated that "lashes . . . along with jail terms should be administered as a deterrent to such crimes in Windsor."

Shortly after this meeting, eighteen parks employees and several members of the Legion of Frontiersmen were sworn in as special constables who were given authority to patrol the parks and arrest any suspicious characters.[20] The city's parks had become a battlefield, and the enemy was a shadowy group of perverts. On July 8, 1946, under the headline "Cleanup of Parks Is Needed," the *Star* issued an unequivocal call to arms:

> The stabbings are the outgrowth of degeneracy. Our parks are becoming hot-beds of sex perversion. So bad is the condition in certain localities that decent folk are virtually debarred from the enjoyment of these outlying spots.
>
> Our parks should be places where the citizens, particularly the children, can find healthful, pleasant recreation. Instead, some of them are being monopolized by the vilest scum of humankind. With these derelicts all about, it is positively unsafe for young folk to be in the neighborhood, quite aside from the stabbings which have come to be part of the habitual pastimes of certain of the degenerates.

In this contest between the "decent folk" and the "vilest scum of human-kind," there was no question which side would eventually prevail. In the struggle for social space, the force of the police and an aroused public would compel the queer element to go even further underground.

In the meantime, gays could have no doubt how the wider public perceived them. Homosexuality was akin to an infection, and its "hotbeds" had to be eliminated before the infection spread. The newspaper's ceaseless vitriol substantiated the "conception of homosexuality as a potentially contagious disease," and characterized it as a vice "born of man's inherent lust rather than the distinguishing characteristic of a particular type of person."[21] It was, the *Star* editorial argued, a vice born of some men's darkest urges: "The kind of actions that are going on do not result from sudden whims. They are the work of psychiatrics who are a menace to the public every minute they are roaming at large. Actually, there has been no 'mystery' about the slashings. Whether they were the work of one or more of these perverts or whether the perverts were being made the victim of a person with a crusading psychosis they all stemmed from this degrading form of degeneracy."[22]

Therefore, as it was gay men who were responsible for perversion, violence, and even their own deaths, it was imperative that they be removed from society. Such a rationale could, in fact, easily justify the extermination of any undesirable subgroup. The moral panic of 1946 showed a heightened hostility toward this particular enemy, a consensus that homosexuals must be eliminated, and an assumption that they were a sizeable number.[23] This last belief illustrates the disproportionate nature of the panic of 1946. It seems a feature of every moral panic that the public believes a more sizeable number of individuals are engaged in the behavior in question than actually are. Ousting homosexuals—a group previously unknown to police—from the parks in Windsor required the raising of a small army. And yet, the *Star*'s antiqueer crusade was only part of a wider pattern of hysteria spreading across North America.

The sex-crime panic of the late 1930s seemed to have returned with a vengeance. In the United States, the FBI reported that an "orgy of crime" was overtaking the nation, led by gangs of hoodlums and prowling sexual psychopaths. Even in the face of statistics that showed that attacks against women and children were not increasing, extensive articles in periodicals such as *Colliers* focused on the imminent threat posed by social deviants. The *Saturday Evening Post*, a magazine widely read in both Canada and the United States, published articles indicating that there were over 24,200 sex crimes committed in the United States annually by men "who cannot control the dark impulses which are latent in all of us."

In the United States, in the years immediately following the war, the media "adopted a calculated, inflammatory stance out of proportion to any known facts about modern levels of crime." As a result, "the terms sexual psychopath, sex criminal, deviant, and homosexual came to be used almost interchangeably in discussing the situation."[24] Canadians were hardly immune to this renewed panic. In addition to the Slasher panic in Windsor, there had been several widely publicized child murders in other Canadian cities. In early 1945, nine-year-old John Benson of Montreal was murdered, and police immediately arrested and interrogated "1,500 previously convicted sex perverts." Winnipeg had been rocked in the late fall of 1945 by a series of assaults against children that culminated in the murder of a thirteen-year-old boy in January 1946 and another boy that September. As had the Windsor police, the Winnipeg force conducted a massive roundup of homosexual suspects, insisting that "all known and reported sex perverts are being brought to police headquarters for grilling."[25]

During the summer of 1946, the same season that witnessed the reemergence of the Windsor Slasher, western Canada was shocked by two gruesome child murders. The first occurred in Vancouver, where an eleven-year-old boy was lured away by a soldier, sexually molested, and then killed. A few weeks later, six-year-old Donnie Goss was raped and murdered in Calgary. In beginning their investigation, the police automatically "combed their files of known sex perverts." A writer for the *Calgary Herald* described the atmosphere generated by the murders, writing, "The brutal, sadistic slayings created a state of terror in Calgary and Vancouver homes ... and in both cities a general call was made for greater protection and more severe penalties for sex offenders." The same pedophile admitted to both killings, and within four months of his arrest, he was executed.[26]

During the moral panics that swept Winnipeg, Calgary, Vancouver, Montreal, and Windsor, the first reaction of the authorities was to round up homosexual suspects and to charge them with threatening children. The Canadian media, much like its American counterpart, broadcast the existence of a plague of sex criminals. In a report titled "The Truth About Sex Criminals," *Maclean's* magazine analyzed this national problem. Sex criminals were active in all cities and all provinces, and, most disturbingly, they often appeared as normal and respectable citizens. These deviants were motivated by an overpowering compulsion: "They suffer an illness just as surely as does a man with tuberculosis or a broken leg." Something had to be done, the writer argued, for "like the lunatic of 100 years ago the sex criminal today is despised, lashed and incarcerated." The writer speculated that while the young homosexual would have little difficulty forming attachments, in later years, he would have to force himself on others, especially "on the group of people least capable of resisting him— young children." An exposé in the *Toronto Globe and Mail* went even further, proclaiming, "Men as dangerous as any wild beast of the jungle are at large on the streets of Canada's cities and towns."[27] Similar to the American media, neither the *Globe and Mail* nor *Maclean's* drew any distinction between predatory crimes and consensual sexual acts.

Disregarding the media frenzy over the growing hazard of deviants and sex perverts, just how dangerous were Windsor's parks? There is no indication from their records that the Board of Commissioners of Police were concerned about any real threat. Letters to the *Star* from the period, usually a good barometer by which to gauge public concern, did not bring up the issue of park safety. In the summer of 1946, the city's manager of parks pleaded for calm and noted that there was no record of serious crime originating in the parks. That the parks in Windsor were not dangerous is corroborated by the recollections of two west-side residents of the period. While one recalls that a gay youth frequented Wilson Park, he was not considered a menace but rather "part of the park.... You just didn't go [to the public washrooms] with him. We didn't see him as much of a threat."[28] Another resident who was a youth during the same period observed that there was a queer fellow at the arena who was trying to get boys to go into washrooms with him. He was largely ignored. Similarly, regarding the Windsor crusade against curb cruisers, a group of high-school girls suggested, with a sense of logic that belied their years, that "the boys are just having fun."

There was no tangible threat to boys or girls in the city's parks or on the streets, nor were there any statistics that would indicate an increase in sexual assaults on youth. Indeed, the postwar sex-crime panic was taking place during one of the safest periods in North American history. Rates for all forms of violent crime were far lower than they would be in later decades. A New York study of a supposed wave of sex crimes showed that it simply did not exist and that such offenses were rare and not increasing.[29] An examination of the reports from chiefs of police from Ottawa, Windsor, Toronto, and Vancouver indicates that there was no official concern over sex crimes. If anything, the incidence of rape and sexual assaults on children had declined in the postwar years. In fact, statistically, the frequency of overall violent crime was declining across Canada.[30] Vancouver police chief W. H. Mulligan had seen a significant increase in crime during the war, which had gone down significantly by 1947. In Windsor as well, there seemed to be a substantial divergence between the hysteria being whipped up by the press and the peaceful reality that prevailed in the neighborhoods.

The florid coverage of the Sears case was symptomatic of the times, but that fact did not stop higher authorities outside Windsor from noticing it. Provincial Deputy Attorney General C. L. Snyder was "surprised and disturbed" at the in-depth information leaked by the Windsor police concerning Sears's alleged confession. He admonished Crown Attorney Awrey that this indiscretion could prejudice a fair trial, stating, "It is impossible for a person to secure a fair trial if announcements have been made previous to the trial that he has confessed or that he has made statements indicating his guilt." As well, Snyder ordered Awrey to make a thorough investigation, find out who was responsible for the leaks, and see that they were punished.[31] However, no action appears to have been taken. Judging from the specific information that regularly found its way from police reports to the pages of the *Star*, leaking appears to have been an ongoing procedure for the Windsor police force, and the sharing of information with friendly reporters was a normal, if obviously improper, occurrence.

Shortly after Sears's arrest, a far more embarrassing fact suddenly came to light. In the great roundup of the summer of 1945, Ronald Sears had been among those taken into custody. A Toronto youth, Kenneth Lavery, recognized Sears's name as he was reading about the Slasher case in the newspapers, and he telephoned to suggest that the Windsor police revisit their records from the previous September. That month, Lavery, then aged fifteen, had gone off on a spree and had ended up on the Windsor riverfront trying to figure out a way to cross the border to Detroit. Meeting a slightly older fellow, Lavery discussed his dilemma, and his new friend offered to sell him his National Registration Card (to prove that he was seventeen years old) for five dollars. As they walked along the Detroit River, Lavery's companion pointed to a vacant lot and said, "That's where the Slasher killed a man." Lavery's Detroit adventure lasted only a few hours before he was apprehended and his papers seized. Windsor police had no trouble tracing the conscription card back to Ronald Sears, who was charged with a breach of the National Registration Regulations Act. Without compunction, Ronald had admitted to selling the card. However, the offense was minor, and with the war over, the charge did not seem worth pursuing.[32]

If Ronald Sears had trickled unnoticed through the hands of police in 1945, he was not about to avoid a full investigation now. Police lineups were arranged and held in the Number One courtroom. Sears and a group of young men, several of them students from Assumption College, were paraded before the Slasher survivors to see if they could identify him. Alexander Voligny could not make any identification. George Mannie had mentioned that his attacker was a "light-skinned negro," so in his case the lineup had consisted mostly of black men. Even with this decided advantage, Mannie could still not identify Sears. However, Joseph

Gelencser, who had to be transported from his house by ambulance and who lay on a stretcher during the process, quickly pointed out Sears as the individual who had knifed him only a few days before.[33] In addition to the lineups, Sears was subjected to psychiatric examinations. The Crown's office was anxious that any questions about Sears's mental state be addressed as quickly as possible. Crown Attorney Awrey assured reporters that it was the "customary procedure in such cases" and did not amount to any prejudgment on Sears's mental capacity.[34]

Alexander Voligny's failure to identify Sears would have grave consequences for him. Now that he was of no real use to the police, he would face prosecution for his self-confessed act of gross indecency. In September, he pleaded guilty to conspiring to commit an indecent act with another male person. His sentencing before Magistrate Hanrahan the following October was a harsh lesson in how, during this second wave of sex-crime hysteria, society abhorred any hint of homosexual conduct. According to the magistrate, Voligny belonged to those classes of persons who were "a constant threat to decency, and particularly dangerous in their possible contamination to innocent youth."

Hanrahan (who had no professional legal training at all but owed his position to political influence) maintained that deviants could be divided into two different groups. The first were "mentally twisted" from birth, meaning they were unable to make moral distinctions and belonged under psychiatric observation. The other was the "moral pervert" who had knowingly deteriorated into degeneracy and was fully aware of what he was doing. Unfortunately for Voligny, Hanrahan assigned him to the latter category, whose members merited the harshest punishment. Therefore, although he had been stabbed in the back and nearly killed, had been waiting in jail for four months, and admittedly showed "no other criminal inclination," Voligny was sentenced to serve an additional eight months in reformatory and an indeterminate period under observation as a sex criminal.[35] These extraordinary consequences were visited upon Voligny for attempting to have consensual sex with another man in an area as private as they could find. It was also the price he paid for having given the police the only frank and accurate account of a Slasher attack. While he was not allowed to speak during his sentencing, undoubtedly he would have had some interesting comments on the price of honesty.

The Windsor police, in another attempt to acquire as much information as possible before the preliminary hearing, subjected George Mannie to another interrogation. Now that the police had a better idea from Sears as to what really had happened on July 23, 1945, McLauchlan and Brand subjected Mannie to a grueling round of questioning. Mannie stuck to his story that he was drinking rubbing alcohol with a group of vagrants and that after the others left, he slept it off by the riverbank. There he encountered the young man who he thought was black and started up a conversation with him. For no apparent reason, the youth stabbed him as Mannie attempted to walk away. McLauchlan was not buying it, and he pressed Mannie:

Q. Did you tell this fellow you had sucked off other boys?

A. No.

Q. Did you want to suck this fellow off?

A. No.

Q. Did anything happen between you and he?

A. Nothing with respect to sucking anyone off.

Q. Did you get a little violent with this fellow and grab him around the waist?

A. No.

Q. Did you start to take your pants down?

A. No.[36]

Unlike Alexander Voligny, Mannie had known all along the price of admitting to acts of gross indecency. His tight-lipped responses also implied his resentment at the detective's accusations.

If the police were putting additional touches on their case against Sears, his family was moving forcefully to his defense. Major James H. Clark was hired to defend Ronald, and one of his first moves was to counteract the adverse publicity caused by the police leaks. He told reporters, "I should like the people of this county to withhold their decision on the youth's case until they hear all the facts." In Clark's view, it seemed remarkable that a boy of seventeen could have overcome the older and bigger men who had been attacked and killed. In an artful way he was laying the groundwork for the argument that he would flesh out before a jury: that it was improbable that young Sears could be the Slasher. Undoubtedly, there was a quiet groundswell of support on behalf of the accused; the *Star* reported that unsolicited donations to defray his legal expenses were coming in. Some most likely agreed with Clark. To others, it appeared that Ronald Sears may well have been a Robin Hood and justified in what he had done.

He would certainly be well served by his defense counsel. Raised in Ingersoll, Ontario, James Clark began his legal studies in 1914 but shortly thereafter went off to serve in World War I. Not only did he survive the trenches, he advanced from private to major and finished the war as a highly decorated hero. His dynamic personality served him well in the courtroom, where one colleague recalled that he "was a no nonsense person, but I didn't see him as a threatening person. That is, he was always very civil, composed, and gentlemanly." As for his approach to litigation, he once remarked to a young lawyer that a jury trial "was 90 percent facts and 10 percent law."

Clark's considerable skill as a defense lawyer had been on public display the previous year during the murder trial of John Shemko. On the morning of September 28, 1944, Frank Scibor's burned body was found in the shell of his car in Malden Township, twenty miles south of Windsor. Suspicion soon fell on Shemko, who had been having a torrid affair with Scibor's wife. At his first trial, Shemko had been convicted and sentenced to hang. However, the Court of Appeal felt that there were errors during the trial. At the second hearing, Clark went meticulously through the evidence and pointed out that there was no proof that a brake handle the Crown alleged had been used to bludgeon Scibor had actually been used. In a brilliant but risky move, Clark asked an investigating officer to fit the brake handle into the ratchet from which the Crown alleged it had been removed. The brake did not fit, and the Crown's case collapsed.[37]

Foreshadowing an argument he would advance on behalf of Ronald Sears, Clark also attacked the way the police had conducted the interrogation. While the detectives had cautioned Shemko and used a court reporter to take down his statements, a relative had not been permitted to be in the room. It was a travesty, Clark thundered, "and will continue to happen so until the officers protect themselves with just a little bit of evidence. If they had kept his half-brother there they would not have to rely on police evidence alone as to the statement." Shemko was acquitted, and Clark's reputation as a winning counsel was secured.

Yet, there was also a very different side to Major Clark. For one thing, he loved the glare of publicity and political life. In 1934, he had been elected the Liberal Member of the Provincial Parliament from Windsor-Sandwich, and from 1939 to 1943, he had served as Speaker of Queen's Park. One of the major's old school chums from Ingersoll was the flamboyant evangelist Aimee Semple McPherson, and during her triumphal tour of the Midwest in 1929, Clark hosted her in Windsor. However, despite his association with this beautiful celebrity, there was talk about Clark's private life. He never married, and there was a steady fund of stories about his real sexual inclinations. While some regarded these stories as malicious rumors, others were convinced that Clark harbored keen homosexual tendencies. One gay man who lived in Windsor candidly recalled that he knew "some very fine businessmen in this city who were gay. I know they were very, very careful who they associated with."[38] A man in Clark's position in society and in government could never be seen prowling about Government Park or associating with the likes of the YMCA crowd. However, he was known to frequent sporting places where nearly naked boys were on display, and it was reported that he paid well for young men to visit his apartment. If this were the case, then it was perhaps one of the greatest ironies in the Slasher affair, a story already replete with ironies—from terror during a time of celebration, to the victims being blamed for causing the mayhem. Now, it appeared that the defender of a serial killer of gay men was more than likely a gay man himself, one whom Canadian society of the 1940s dictated keep his sexuality deeply buried.

9

FIRST TRIAL

"DISGUSTING DETAILS"

There was no serious question about the outcome of the preliminary hearing, for Crown Attorney E. C. Awrey was in possession of signed confessions to two murders and three knife assaults. The prosecutor had been called to the Ontario bar before the First World War and was known as a quiet, competent practitioner who did not give way to flamboyance. The only question he had to answer before Magistrate J. A. Hanrahan was whether or not there was sufficient evidence to commit the prisoner for trial. No one seriously expected this case to go anywhere but to a jury. On July 24, 1946, Awrey began his case on the preliminary hearing by putting acting-detectives McLauchlan and Brand on the stand to prove that the confessions had been made. Clark challenged the confessions on the basis of Sears's state of mind but would save his real cross-examination for the trial.

Joseph Gelencser also took the stand and gave a revealing account of what had occurred to him only three weeks before. He still bore the effects of the attack and had to be helped into the witness stand by McLauchlan. According to Gelencser, he had been minding his business and walking along the riverfront when he had heard light footsteps behind him, and a voice called out "Good evening, it is a nice night to take a walk." A young man came alongside and together they walked to a riverfront park. Once there, the youngster threw himself on the ground and suggested that they stay for a while. Looking up at Gelencser he asked, "Have you got any kind of cigars on you?" When Gelencser began to fumble in his pockets, the young man laughed and said, "I don't mean that kind." Gelencser was initially unaware that this was a way of initiating a homosexual encounter. When it dawned on him, he replied, "Look here, I'm 25 years and two months married, and I'm not going to do anything like that." When he attempted to turn his back and leave, the young man, who he identified as Ronald Sears, stabbed him. All of this was completely at odds with what the police knew about Gelencser's double life, but they were prepared to go along with this version if it bolstered the prosecution's case.

Clark did not put Awrey to the trouble of providing further evidence of the charges. However, he did use the occasion for some additional public relations, telling the Court that his client had not admitted to anything and strenuously objecting to the admission of the confessions. Predictably, the magistrate admitted the statements but consoled Clark with the comment that their final admissibility would have to be established at trial in September. Throughout the proceedings, Sears sat quietly in the prisoner's dock. A *Star* reporter wrote that he "looked pale; his eyes blinked constantly." He said nothing, and only once did his lawyer lean over to say anything to him.[1]

Justice moved quickly in 1946, and by the second week of September, barely three months after the five detectives had stormed the little house on Cameron Avenue, Sears was about to go on trial for his life. The blaring headlines identifying him as the Slasher and giving details of his confession were still fresh in the public mind. As well, Windsor was a community still reeling from the *Star*'s ongoing crusade against deviants. Six weeks before the trial began, the *Star*'s editorial "Sex Crime Drive" reminded its readers of the serious and pervasive "violations of the code of decent living." "So long as perverts escape with brief jail terms," the *Star* insisted, "there can be no hope for a permanent solution."[2] It was in this charged atmosphere, in which the facts of the Slasher case were widely known and the problem of deviants was supposedly out of control, that the trial of Ronald George Sears began on Wednesday, September 11, 1946.

The prosecution had decided to proceed only with the charge of murdering Sgt. Price and to hold the other cases in abeyance. Perhaps Awrey felt that the murder of a serviceman still in uniform would resonate with the jury. The prolonged death of the victim might also be a factor that would reflect on the killer's brutality. Yet, it was a case fraught with danger for the prosecution, for it was a case without a murder weapon, without witnesses, and without direct evidence of any kind. The Crown could only hope that the jurors would find the accused's own words sufficient to convict.

"A Pickwickian character, round-faced, pleasant, jolly person" was how one lawyer remembered the presiding judge, Dalton Courtwright Wells.[3] Despite his gnomish appearance, Wells was a formidable intellectual who had been recently chosen for the Ontario Supreme Court after only twenty years of practice. Although he had only been a judge for a few months, Wells would have little difficulty controlling the process or sorting out the legal matters at issue. The formalities of a murder trial had changed little over the centuries. The Justice of the Supreme Court of Ontario (referred to as "My Lord") was a successor to the King's justices of England. As he entered the courtroom, all stood, and the lawyers, clad in medieval gowns, bowed in respect. After the jury had been empanelled and the justice had reminded them of their duty to administer impartial justice, the Crown Attorney would bring forward evidence in an attempt to prove the prisoner's guilt. In an age of atomic weapons, it was a performance that would have been familiar in Stuart or Tudor times. Even the venue, the old Sandwich Courthouse, predated Confederation and had been designed by Canada's second Prime Minister, Alexander Mackenzie. The "aged and dingy Sandwich courthouse," as one Detroit newspaper accurately enough called it, was filled to capacity when the Sears case was called to order.

A jury of eleven farmers and one storekeeper would determine the facts. Clark had used his challenges to keep any management persons (a class of individuals he considered too sure of themselves) off of the jury. Awrey outlined the Crown's case that Sears had lured Sgt. Price to the vacant field for the express purpose of murdering him. On the way there, "[Price] made some proposals of an improper nature to have relations of an improper nature." As background, Awrey presented medical evidence to show that the sergeant had died of multiple stab wounds. The pace quickened when one of the detectives, Jim Hill, described the grue-some murder scene, and the prosecution produced a photograph showing Price's mutilated body lying on the grass. Clark ignored this display, and his cross-examination of Hill veered onto an entirely different path:

> Q. Did this deceased have a police record as a homosexual pervert?
> A. Not that I know of.
> Q. He had a police reputation as a pervert?
> A. No, not that I know of.[4]

Clark then asked about the pictures of Price that appeared in the *Star* in which he was shown wearing flowing, feminine oriental garb. Hill knew nothing of these pictures. The answers were irrelevant; Clark was trying to plant a seed in the minds of the jurors that Price was one of those notori-ous deviants who were infesting the public parks. As such, his life was not a particularly valuable one, and anyone who had killed him had rid the world of a pervert. This would be the only reference to Price's sexuality during the trial, since Clark's defense was founded on the denial that his client had stabbed Price at all. As a result, the issue of Sears defending himself against a homosexual advance was never developed. Still, a mod-est aside had been made that Price, a person who (as even the Crown conceded) made proposals of an "improper nature," may have instigated and been responsible for the attack that took his life.

Whatever this trial was about, it had little to do with the bloody events of the night of August 17, 1945, and everything to do with what had hap-pened at Windsor Police headquarters between 6:00 p.m. on the evening of Saturday July 6, 1946, and 2:00 a.m. the following morning. The heart of the prosecution's case was the confession made that night, but it could only be admitted after a voir dire—which in the Canadian legal system is a hearing within the trial during which the jury would be excused while the lawyers presented evidence on admissibility.

McLauchlan was the first on the stand. He recounted the arrest and the transportation of Sears to the Inspector of Detective's office. It had been a hot day, he recalled, "extremely warm," and together with Brand, the three men barely fit into the room. Sears had originally denied any involvement with the Voligny or Gelencser stabbings. Then, when they resumed the interrogation at nine o'clock that night, Sears suddenly admitted to the Slasher attacks and the two murders. Justice Wells looked up:

> Q. Was there any reluctance on his part to give answers?
>
> A. No sir.
>
> Q. He just answered when you asked?
>
> A. Yes.

McLauchlan described how, during a lull in the interrogation, Sears had said that he was glad it was over and that he had been caught. He also testified that Sears had shared his intentions to go out and kill again that very weekend.

James Clark designed his cross-examination to paint a picture for the Court, and his first question for McLauchlan set the tone. "When this boy was first taken down to the police station," he began, referring to Ronald Sears as "the boy," a vulnerable waif left at the mercy of the police. He would refer to Sears this way throughout the trial to help characterize his client—who was the same age as many Canadian soldiers who had fought in Europe—as a young, inexperienced victim of older men. Had Brand and McLauchlan verbally pummeled Sears into submission?

> Q. You cannot take a boy and throw questions at him hour after hour without having some effect on him?
>
> A. It had some effect.
>
> Q. But you cannot make him write out a statement unless he wants to?
>
> A. We didn't.[5]

Clark pressed the point that the detectives had to get a confession out of somebody:

> Q. There was a lot of clamour for the clearing up of these four slasher cases, was there not? The police were being castigated for not clearing up these murders?
>
> A. Public opinion; I am not prepared to say.[6]

Why, Clark asked repeatedly, had McLauchlan persisted in his one fingered typing when a court reporter could have been called in? "It is not customary," McLauchlan insisted. Clark persisted; in the Shemko case, less than a year ago, the Windsor police had called in an official reporter to take down the prisoner's statement. Why not this time? McLauchlan's answers continued to be noncommittal.

The central question during the voir dire, and the one that would most trouble Justice Wells, was why Sears had so dramatically changed his story after his respite in the cell. As the judge phrased it to Clark, "I find the reversal is very queer and I have no explanation of it so far." The judge would seek an answer from William "Scotty" Brand. As the only other person in the inspector's room, Brand should have been able to shed some light on why Sears's account had changed so dramatically. Wells asked him:

Q. Was there anything said to him when he came back from the cells about the further information that you had obtained?

A. No sir.

Q. Was any indication given to him that you had any further information?

A. No sir.

Q. I have to make sure that there is no pressure on Sears. He tells you two stories in connection with these offences and he is fed something and left alone and he is brought back again and without any preamble at all you simply sit down and warn him again about offences you warned him about two hours before and you say, "We are going to ask you some more questions," and he tells you different stories. You say nothing whatever occurred then?

A. No.

Q. You are quite certain of that?

A. No.

Q. There is nothing you are concealing from me?

A. No.

Q. You say that absolutely nothing occurred?

A. Absolutely nothing occurred.[7]

It was the defense's strategy to show the inherent unreliability of the confession by showing the incompetence, or better yet deceit, of the officers who took it. McLauchlan had stated that after he had read out the completed statement to Sears that the latter had read it over silently to himself. However, Brand swore that he had heard Sears read it out loud. How was it possible, in such a confined space, that McLauchlan heard nothing and yet Brand had heard Sears reading? There were other discrepancies between the two officer's recollections. McLauchlan stated that after reading out the standard caution he had used his own words to explain to Sears that these were serious charges. Brand could not recall this detail. Clark had winkled out two contradictions, perhaps not major ones, but ones he would use to hammer away at the detectives as best he could.

As Brand recounted the interrogation, he reached the point where they took a break and for the first time Sears began to speak his own mind, expressing his relief that the killing spree was finally over. McLauchlan mentioned that the previous killings had occurred on weekends and he asked if Sears had had any plans. Sears revealed that yes he had planned to stalk a new victim that weekend. They paused, and Sears said that he hated the impact this ordeal would have on his mother. "I don't want to see her again," he told them. According to Clark it was an "amazing statement" that should have been properly recorded by a stenographer, but McLauchlan would only remember to record the conversation later that morning. As the police officers testified, Sears sat at the extreme end of the prisoner's dock, as close as he could to Constable Norman Gibb. He "watched each witness intently, with little visible emotion." When Brand left the witness stand, Sears looked up and gave him a friendly smile and nod.[8]

As the voir dire ground on, Dr. Markkanen testified about seeing Sears at 2:00 a.m. when he was vomiting and prostrate with fatigue. Clark asked him if he was surprised at the prisoner's condition "after several hours of questioning in a state of almost complete exhaustion?" The doctor responded, "I suppose I was surprised."[9] Sgt. Mahoney swore that during the arrest no charges had been laid and that he would not permit Edward Sears to visit his son. "You were keeping this boy without charges whatever and you refused him the right to see his father?" asked an incredulous Justice Wells. "Those were my instructions," Mahoney responded.

For the defense, Clark called Edward Sears, who recounted how he had rushed down to police headquarters only to be told that as an investigation was ongoing, he could not see his son. Later that afternoon, a packed courtroom got its first glance of Ronald Sears on the witness stand. Peering at the signed confessions on the evidence table, Sears admitted that he had signed them but that he had no recollection of what it was he had signed. He did remember that the detectives told him that they had proof of his guilt and all the while he had adamantly insisted that he had nothing to do with the stabbings. Despite his denial, "They kept asking questions and I still denied everything and they kept on and on and I denied it, and I guess I got nervous and asked for my father and a lawyer to help me out of this."[10]

Sears swore he could not remember ever being cautioned by any of the officers. On the critical issue of why he had changed his story, he had little to add. After 7:15 that evening he had just sat in his cell. "I can't remember between the hours of 7:15 or whatever time it was until 9 o'clock," he said. "I woke up in the cells. That is all I remember. I must have fainted or something." Still intent on getting to the bottom of what had happened, Justice Wells asked "Did you see anybody in the interim or talk to anybody?" Sears replied that he had not. His mind was simply a blank.[11]

Yet, as the prosecutor began to lead him through the confession answer by answer, Sears's memory staged a remarkable recovery. Sears agreed that he had made the answers, but quickly retreated to the position that he remembered nothing. He could not recall what the police had said or, for that matter, where he was. As he gave his steady litany of "I don't knows" to Awrey, Sears grew increasingly nervous and upset. His eyes filled with tears, and he seemed to have difficulty in making any response. In an effort to help him regain his composure, Clark brought him a glass of water. But still, "with distraught manner Sears wiped his face nervously with his handkerchief and continually reiterated that 'I don't know' to Mr. Awrey's questions."[12] How could the officers possibly have invented such a fabulous tale, Awrey asked? The witness shrugged, stared at the courtroom floor, and said nothing. At times, Sears vacillated between remembering previous answers and denying their validity. Awrey read back one answer:

> Yes, I was sitting on a bench in the Government Park, Sandwich Street West at 11:30 p.m. and a soldier wearing short pants sat with me and talked to me and he asked me to come to a dark spot—he acted natural at first and then started talking dirty.
>
> Q. Do you remember that answer?

A. Yes.

Q. If you made that answer was it true?

A. No.[13]

So, he did remember the interrogation (or at least parts of it), and his claims to being unconscious during the proceedings became increasingly untenable. The best he could say was that the police were troubling him with endless questions when all he wanted to do was to go home. In final reply, Awrey brought in the cells officer who testified that between 7:15 and 9:00 o'clock that night Sears had sat quietly in his cell. He had not been threatened or cajoled, nor had he passed out.

With the evidence complete on the voir dire, the trial moved into the argument phase. On its face, a confession seemed to be a clear admission of guilt that no reasonable person could disregard. Sears had admitted that he had killed Sgt. Price, he had described how he had done it, and he had explained that he had done it in retribution for what had happened to him as a child. If the confession was admitted into evidence, who could possibly question Sears's guilt? The question of whether or not Ronald Sears's confession would be admitted into evidence would depend on the interpretation of the case of Private Ibrahim of the 126th Baluchistan Infantry.

During the sixteenth and seventeenth centuries, there was no limit to the use of confessions, and even when they were obtained by way of torture, they were usually considered the equivalent of a guilty plea. Perhaps that was why by the beginning of the eighteenth century, the pendulum swung violently against the admission of confessions on the premise that they were tainted. In the Ibrahim case of 1914, the Privy Council set a new legal standard on the admissibility of confessions. Private Ibrahim had been apprehended in his barracks shortly after an officer had been shot, and when confronted by a superior, he confessed to the killing. The British court laid out the rule that would be followed thereafter: "no statement by an accused is admissible in evidence against him unless it is shewn by the prosecution to have been a voluntary statement, in the sense that it has not been obtained from him either by fear of prejudice or hope of advantage exercised or held out by a person in authority."[14] His conviction was upheld, and Private Ibrahim went to the gallows.

Only three years before the Sears case, the Supreme Court of Canada had applied the Ibrahim precedent in the Gach case. In that situation, an impatient police officer had not bothered to give the accused a warning that his words could be used in court against him and had even suggested that "it would be better for him" if he cooperated. Justice Taschereau ruled that the police had created a poisoned atmosphere and that all confessions made without a proper caution were inadmissible: "This rule which is found in Canadian and British law is based on the sound principle that confessions must be free from fear, and not inspired by a hope of advantage."[15]

Awrey began his submissions by referring to the Ibrahim precedent and suggesting that the Crown had proven that Sears's confession was voluntary. He cited the Gach decision as well and noted that the caution appeared on the form the police had read aloud to Sears. All the evidence supported the conclusion that no force or threat had been used. Whether the father had been permitted to visit his son was irrelevant to the central question of whether or not his statement was voluntary. One issue Awrey could not ignore, however, was the sudden change in Sears's story. Putting his own spin on this unusual turn of events, he told the judge: "My lord, in police experience and in human experience we can bring a general knowledge. Here is a chap who, if his statements are true, had committed very serious offences, two murders and three attempts to murder, and they were on his mind and he was in custody and thinking about them during these two hours and he came to the conclusion, a sound conclusion, that he might as well tell the truth."[16]

This was pure speculation on Awrey's part, but it seemed to fit. The need to confess was fundamental, a compulsion with roots deep within human nature. Sigmund Freud had suggested in his *Civilization and Its Discontents* that modern man restrained his aggressive actions, which in turn suppressed his natural urge to act and then to confess. Therefore "there can be no doubt that, as psychoanalysts have repeatedly observed, confessions tend to relieve guilt."[17] By telling all to McLauchlan and Brand, perhaps Sears had been relieving himself of a heavy psychological burden.

James Clark would not be as generous as Awrey in his assessment of the conduct of the Windsor police. He repeatedly questioned why the detectives had not used a stenographer or permitted Edward Sears to be present. These acts would have put Sears's statement "beyond peradventure." As it was, the Court was left to depend upon admittedly fragile human recollections. Clark stressed the conflicts he had found in the evidence: that Brand said he had heard Sears read out the statement while McLauchlan was sure he read it to himself, that McLauchlan said he had explained the caution while Brand thought he had simply read from the form. Over and above these contradictions, was Sears's bizarre change in attitude between 7:00 and 9:15 that night. While Awrey thought that Sears had been overcome by conscience, Clark found it inexplicable and therefore suspect: "To me, my lord, the whole thing is too fantastic to believe, that any young boy, 18 years old, in possession of his senses, if he is normal at all, will come into a police station and voluntarily admit murdering two men and voluntarily admitting attempting to murder three others. . . . It is away out of this world."[18]

For his part, Justice Wells was looking for a rational explanation. There were some serious drawbacks to the Crown's case, for the young man "was undoubtedly handled in a high-handed manner. He was arrested without any information being given for some time after the cause of his arrest." He was particularly scathing toward the lead detective, saying, "I cannot place much faith in Sergeant Mahoney's evidence in this court." And yet, there was no evidence that any pressure had been applied to the prisoner. Before he was questioned, he was properly warned, and apparently, he had talked freely and without hesitation. As for Ronald's assertion that he had blacked out after 9 p.m., the judge "could not place much reliance on it." In the end, "the courtroom was hushed as the justice gave his ruling and all strained to catch every word." The confession was admissible as evidence, and the Crown had taken a major step in proving its case.[19]

On Saturday morning, September 14, the jury returned to the courtroom, and the prosecution and defense began the process of going over the same evidence for their benefit. It was a tedious process, especially for the non-jurors who had heard it already. But this time, the evidence from the detectives would also include the confession itself. McLauchlan began by reading the warning printed at the top of the form, which indicated Sears would be charged with the murder of Hugh Price. For once, the usually docile boy spoke up and interrupted him. McLauchlan asked him to keep quiet until the warning was finished. Then Sears asked, "Do you think because I stabbed these other two men that I killed this man?" McLauchlan replied, "I don't think anything."

Holding the original copy of the confession before him, Awrey began to read it aloud for the jury. He spoke in "an even and unemotional voice. The spectators sat in the hushed courtroom as if carved from stone."[20] The confession started with Sears reciting how he had met the soldier in Government Park. The *Star* discreetly omitted the contents of their conversation but reported that the soldier was obviously a sex pervert and that because of it Sears planned to kill him: "I said it is too busy here, there were too many people walking around, and I held him by the arm, and led him into a field."

"Did he go willingly?" McLauchlan asked.

"Yes he went along willingly," Sears replied and described how he had stabbed him in the back, on the left side where he thought the heart was. The sergeant groaned slightly and Sears stabbed him again. This time, the soldier got up and wobbled about as he tried to run but only made it part way to Sandwich Street when he collapsed on his back. Sears then stabbed him repeatedly to make sure that he was dead. After Sears's attempt to conceal the body in the bushes, it was a short run back to his house, where everyone was asleep. Once there, he washed off the blood and went to bed. He had hidden the knife under his bed, but it had since disappeared.

The *Star* referred to but refused to print Sears's allegation that he had been sexually assaulted when he was nine. During the recital of the confession, "Sears sat in the box rubbing his chin with his hand in a reflexive manner and showed no sign of emotion at all. The several women in the room dropped their eyes."[21] The nature of the evidence was so shocking that *Star* editorialists questioned why any decent woman would be in the courtroom at all. The Sears trial had already drawn a wide assortment of "morbid thrill-seekers," and it disturbed the editorial staff that a trial dealing "with the lowest kind of sex perversion" had attracted so many females, "who are manifestly drinking in all of the disgusting details with avidity." That men and women might have an equal fascination with the depraved was something the *Star* was not prepared to countenance. The display was "not an inspiring sight. It is, in fact, sickening."[22] In spite of the availability of cheap horror films, the ghoulish thrills of a real murder trial were hard to resist. The trial contained high drama and a storyline that the movies of the day were forbidden to tell. A movie plot in which a homosexual sergeant searched for a male lover in a city park and that prospective lover turned on him would never have passed the censors of the day. And yet, the taboo subjects of these proceedings, despite the *Star*'s prim disapproval, brought the general public out in droves.

Whatever its merits as drama, the trial was supposed to be a display of facts. Just how few facts the Crown possessed was about to become glaringly apparent. When the trial reconvened on Monday, September 16, a huge crowd was expecting the prosecution to present its case in full. The halls of the Sandwich Courthouse were packed, and court officials were hard-pressed to keep lanes open for jurors and lawyers to pass through. It was important for the prosecution to show that they had more evidence than just the confession. Therefore, Awrey presented the fingertip raincoat belonging to Sears that the detectives had recovered from his home. The coat had pockets large enough to carry a knife or knives, and investigators had found a sizable bloodstain on the inside lining. Verda Vincent, an analyst for the attorney general's department and the only female expert to take part in the proceedings, identified the coat. She had analyzed the stain and found it to be human blood. Clark fingered the exhibit and pointed out to Vincent that instead of a bloodstain, now there was only a hole. She explained that in order to analyze it, she had had to cut up the fabric and that the bloodstain had been consumed by the analysis. She agreed with Clark that the blood was untraceable and could have come from anyone. Rather than adding to the Crown's case, it seemed that the soiled raincoat and the ambiguous bloodstain had demonstrated its shallowness.

When Acting-Detective Brand again took the stand, it enabled Clark to add a few more brushstrokes to his picture of a grueling, interminable interrogation that had all but forced young Sears to confess. While Clark was usually gentlemanly in his cross-examinations, he could turn combative when the situation required it. Clark began,

> Q. No 18 year old boy in possession of his faculties would come in and voluntarily make two confessions of murder and three of attempted murder would they?
> A. Recently there was a case in Chicago of a 17 year old boy confessing to three murders. It was in the papers.

Clark saw an opening and went after it:

> Q. And there was a lot of truth serum used in that case according to the newspapers?

A. I don't know.

Q. You mentioned Chicago. What about the ones in Detroit where they got confessions of murder there and found out the confessions were all wrong?

Mr. Awrey: Surely, my lord, this is improper.[23]

The prosecutor wanted to put a stop to this line of questioning before Clark went on a rhetorical flight about how police forces were prone to use medieval techniques to extract confessions. Many of the jurors must have read about the Heirens case in Chicago, where it was discovered that police had dripped toxic chemicals on the genitals of a seventeen-year-old boy to get him to talk. While it was unlikely that anything remotely close to this kind of torture had occurred in Windsor, the reminder of the Heirens case was meant to instill a popular suspicion of police tactics. This suspicion was only part of the picture Clark was in the process of painting.

Next, Clark turned to John Mahoney, the tall, stern sergeant who cut such an imposing figure in the courtroom. During the trial, Clark liked nothing better than to cut Mahoney down to size and let the jury have a laugh at his expense. In an attempt to clear up some confusion that existed over whether Edward Sears had talked with Mahoney or Alfred Carter that Saturday night, Clark asked if there were other members of the staff who resembled him:

A. I expect there is a number of officers as big and tall as I am.

Q. And as good looking?

A. They resemble me.

Clark used ridicule to illustrate that the police were not as competent or as reliable as they pretended to be. When Mahoney said that Price was the only soldier murdered in 1945 in Windsor, the judge enquired, "If there had been others stabbed you would have known about it?" Mahoney replied, "Yes," to which Clark responded, mockingly, "You mean if the body had been found?" A swell of laughter rolled around the courtroom, and Wells had to call for order. In this way, Clark reminded the jury that perhaps the Windsor police were not as efficient as they let on. He also had more serious points to make. He argued that Edward Sears's evidence showed that the detectives had prejudged Sears's guilt and that perhaps "this confession is a complete forgery." The attending doctor confirmed that Sears had been in a state of "emotional upheaval" when he saw him at 2 a.m. If all this were true, then how reliable was this alleged confession?

Finally, the Crown called Dorothy Sears to the stand. Schoolmates recalled Dorothy as a beautiful blonde extrovert who could have had her pick of the boys. But since she had volunteered to talk to the police, the Sears family had all but cut her off, and while it was not known at the time, she was estranged from her husband, Ronald's twin brother, Donald. Perhaps even more than Ronald's own siblings, Dorothy had become his confidante. Now, she testified in her skittish tremolo voice about an unusual incident that had occurred the previous fall. Ronald had slipped her a note, the details of which she now had only a vague recollection, describing how he had murdered Sgt. Price. The following day, Ronald told her that it was all a joke, and the note was burned. Clark suggested to her that she had taken the incident as a joke, and she agreed.

Tuesday, September 17, was the defense's opportunity to present evidence, and Clark knew he would have to do something to counteract the impact of the confession. He adopted the tactic of portraying the boy's fragile state of mind as rendering him unable to give a reliable account of that traumatic night. On the stand, Ronald Sears certainly came across as a troubled youth. When Clark began with a simple question as to who had burned the note he had shown to Dorothy, Sears said that he did, and a moment later contradicted himself and said that his brother did it. As he recounted his evening in the police cells, Ronald agreed that the officers had left him at peace. But when he was recalled to the interrogation room he denied that they read him any caution, and anyway, "I didn't really understand what they were talking about. I was so mixed up. It more or less went in one ear and out the other."[24] After 9 p.m., he insisted that everything was a blank. For that matter, he had no recollection of events the following Sunday or at his court appearance that Monday. Clark raised with him that part of the confession where he claimed to have been attacked when he was nine. "If anything did take place it is so long ago I don't remember," he replied. Not only did he deny the killings, he was even denying the Crown a motive.

All of this testimony would be put to the test by the prosecution, and it would be a test Sears would be hard-pressed to survive. His story was that he recalled nothing, even those things he had admitted on the stand the previous Thursday. On that day, he had identified his signatures on the confessions. Now, he was not sure that he had signed them at all. Sporadically during his testimony, his memory would improve. Awrey suggested, for example, that it was quite a hot night when Sears was questioned, and Sears agreed that it was. "I was about the only one that drank a lot of water," Sears said. If he could recall that kind of detail, why was everything else a blank? Awrey expressed his incredulity at this vacuum in recollection: "When did your memory go bad so that you did not remember anything at all?" The young man fidgeted in his chair. "I can't remember when my memory went bad," he said.

Rex White of the *Detroit News* described Sears's floundering attempt to tell a coherent story: "His memory did acrobatics. He remembered saying some of the statements and not others. . . . He smiled, he wept. He pressed his forehead with long, slender fingers."[25] According to the *Star* reporter covering the case, Sears "testified in so low a voice he had to be cautioned repeatedly. His teeth flashed into a smile now and then."[26] If Clark had been trying to paint a picture of a bewildered youngster abused by overbearing detectives, much of his work had been undone by his client's demeanor, for Ronald Sears came across as an individual with a lot to hide. If he could recall the weather and who was drinking water, it was likely that he was perfectly aware of what had gone on in the interrogation room. The lasting impression was that he just preferred not to say. Remarkably enough, the defense's chief evidence was presented in about half an hour. While Clark knew it was essential that Sears take the stand in order to deny the Crown's case, he had done his best to keep Sears's testimony as brief as possible.

While Clark had not raised the possibility of an insanity defense, the question of the boy's inexplicable memory loss was now at issue. Therefore, Awrey called to the stand the psychologists who had interviewed Sears shortly after his arrest. Dr. Charles Tennant advised the Court that while Sears may have been confused, there was no reason to believe that he had experienced total memory loss. Dr. David Lynch confirmed that when he had talked with Sears, the suspect had been able to accurately describe events on the night he was interrogated.

On Wednesday morning, September 18, the lawyers prepared to sum up their case, and the *Star* advised its readers that a verdict could be expected later in the day. What seems remarkable to us now but was unremarkable at the time is the speed with which the trial began and ended. Murder trials in Canada in the nineteenth century were frequently dealt with from beginning to end in one day.[27] Witness examinations were short and to the point. Objections were few and were dealt with summarily by the judge. Moreover, in the absence of the *Canadian Charter of Rights and Freedoms*, Courts would not be confronted with any lengthy constitutional challenges to the admission of evidence. In 1946, the criminal trial was much like those of the preceding century, a concise review of the facts in an attempt to discover the truth. It was indeed "90 percent facts and 10 percent law."

There was another marked difference between a trial in 1946 and one more than half a century later. In 1946, it was almost impossible to analyze bloodstains, fiber particles, or bodily fluids and come up with any useful information. Jurors accepted that in most cases there would be little direct evidence and that the most important issue would be the credibility of the witnesses. However, by the beginning of the twenty-first century, a jury would expect extensive forensic analysis. A steady diet of police dramas on television would give the general public a rudimentary understanding of how police investigate crimes. Had the Sears's trial occurred today, the jurors would expect the prosecution to put on the stand an expert who would give a detailed account of the bloodstain on Sears's raincoat and to conclude whether it matched the DNA of any of the victims. Not only would jurors today expect to receive such evidence, it might well determine the outcome of the case.[28] But in 1946, that level of forensic examination was far in the future, and jurors were left with their own fallible if not capricious evaluation of the various stories told by the witnesses.

Good counsel—and James Clark was one of the best of his time—use their summations to put the finishing touches on an image they have already painted for the jury. The final summation was Clark's last chance to draw all the loose strands of evidence together and present them to Sears's best advantage. In the nineteenth century, the jury address had often been a theatrical display. As the jurors were used to musical hall performances with broad melodramatics, they expected the same from the barristers who presented cases in court. However, by the mid-twentieth century, the jury address had become more of a "man to man talk; its purpose is to convince the jury that your client is innocent or that, at least, there is too much doubt about his guilt to convict him."[29]

Clark began his summation by asking the jurors to forget the scream-ing headlines they had seen in the *Star*. In his view, these stories had been leaked "with the planned purpose of prejudicing the minds of prospective jurors." By raising this issue, Clark appealed to the jurors' sense of fair play and encouraged them to go against the grain of this biased publicity. But the heart of his defense lay in showing that Brand and McLauchlan were frauds and liars. Harping on the inconsistencies in their testimonies, he hinted that they had made up the confession. "Being ambitious I suppose they would do their best," he said—their best, that is, to crack the case. But just what mischief had been going on in the Inspector of Detectives office that night? "Why you couldn't get pushed in there with a bull-dozer. Mahoney stayed away from it as if it was the Black Hole of Calcutta, a pest hole. A hot night, two officers with [Sears]. Hour after hour." With-out doubt, Clark said, the jurors had been reading all summer about the crazed menace that had stalked Windsor. Did his client resemble that menace? When first arrested, he had asked the officers if he would be re-leased in time for a wiener roast. "Is that the reaction of a human monster? A de-ranged creature?" Clark thundered.

In contrast, Awrey's response was an appeal to the jurors' minds: "If Sears was right, then the officers have perjured themselves. . . . I ask you to determine if these officers could be called persecutors." It was a clever strategy, for now the jurors would have to choose whose story they be-lieved, the officers with impeccable reputations and largely clear recollec-tions or the young man who had hedged and dodged and denied. Lastly, Awrey observed, "These kinds of cases are repulsive." Everyone knew what he meant. The Sears trial had exposed an underworld of homosexual ac-tivity that good people in Windsor pretended did not exist. It had opened for display the fact that there were homosexuals in their midst who lived secret lives and that such men could be found anywhere, even among the heroes returning from Europe.

The last word was left to the trial judge. Wells solemnly told the ju-rors that it was the "golden thread" of British justice that the Crown had to prove guilt beyond a reasonable doubt. Investigators at the scene had shown that Price, a big man, had been dragged a significant distance. Yet, nowhere in his statement to the police had Sears mentioned drag-ging his victim. Did this raise a reasonable doubt? Moreover, without the confession, there was nothing connecting this accused to the crime. As for the detectives, the judge was impressed by their powers of recollection. Admittedly, there were some discrepancies in their testimonies, but "I do not think it is unreasonable that two men looking at the same act observe different things." On the critical issue of the detectives' credibility, the judge came down on the side of the prosecution, for it was apparent to him that the officers had not led or induced Sears and that "there is nothing in these questions that suggested the answers that came." Still, if the jurors believed Sears's confession, could they substitute a verdict of manslaughter for murder? Were the "depraved and horrible suggestions—perverted suggestions" enough to infuriate the accused? Almost regretfully, Wells said that they were not and that if the jury accepted Sears's signed statement, they also had to accept that he had deliberately lured Price to his doom. By 4:15 that afternoon, Wednesday, September 18, the jury retired.

No one seemed to anticipate an early verdict, and there was an unusually sparse crowd in the courtroom when, only a little over an hour later, the jury returned. Florence Sears, the only family member present when the jurors filed in, sat as close as she could to the prisoner's dock. As the judge took his place, the only sound in the courtroom was the ticking of the clock. Jury foreman Grover Johnson rose and in a low voice announced, "Guilty." A gasp rose from the crowd. Sears had not caught the verdict and turned to his guard to find out. "They found you guilty of murder," the guard replied. There was no sense in prolonging matters, for there was only one sentence for this crime. Justice Wells ordered the young man to rise:

> I do not propose to add to your present distress. I think you have had a fair trial
> and you have been found guilty. The sentence of this court upon you, Ronald
> George Sears, is that you are to be taken from here from whence you came and
> there to be kept in close confinement until Tuesday, the third day of December,
> 1946; upon that day you be taken to the place of execution and there hanged by
> the neck until you are dead, and may God have mercy upon your soul.

10

"NOT BRITISH JUSTICE"

Immediately after the sentence, Ronald Sears was moved to the death cell to await his execution. A special guard was mounted to keep watch both day and night to prevent suicide attempts. In the weeks that remained to him, a few extras would be provided, including special meals and unlimited family visits. The mournful edge of the days was further eased by a group of Salvation Army girls who took it upon themselves to visit Sears in his cell and on Sunday evenings stand outside the jail and serenade the condemned young man with hymns. Throughout the wait, Sears remained cheerful and remarkably optimistic that somehow he would avoid the gallows.

On September 19, the *Star* for the first time reported details on the connection between the Sears case and the homosexual subculture that existed in Windsor. It had become apparent to the police "that the stabbings, all down around the Government Park area on the waterfront, belonged to the half-world of sex perversion." Now that the Slasher hysteria had abated, the *Star* could reveal that there was nothing random about these attacks but that the killer was targeting homosexuals at "a particular section of the riverfront which had become established as a rendezvous for persons sexually abnormal."[1] Thankfully, the recent parks cleanup and the volunteer patrols had eliminated Government Park as a site for such unsavory meetings.

Yet there was unease that even with this happy result homosexuality had not been completely stamped out in Windsor. A month after the Sears conviction, *Star* columnist W. L. Clark wrote, "Just because one pervert has been sentenced for murder and because a couple of other perverts were murdered, it does not mean that Windsor or any other community is free from perversion." Clark's brutally callous comment suggested that the only way to rid the community of the homosexual menace was to eliminate all of them and thereby "clean up this whole sordid traffic." This problem was not unique to Windsor, Clark advised his readers. "Every community," he wrote, "is becoming more and more aware of the presence of perverts in its midst."[2] Getting rid of three of them was not enough; they must all be removed from society. The fact that a major newspaper would advocate the elimination of a subgroup simply because of its lifestyle was undoubtedly extreme, but it gives some notion of the threat of violence and social ostracism that homosexuals faced in Windsor society.

News of this shocking case was carried by the Canadian Press to newspapers across Canada. The story was also eventually picked up by *Time* magazine (Canadian edition). "Windsor's police were peacock proud," the magazine reported, to have arrested the notorious Slasher. Unlike just about every other magazine, *Time* actually commented on the homosexual aspects of the case, that "At first, [Sears] denied the stabbings. But he finally made a confession, with homosexual trimmings out of Krafft-Ebing."[3] *Official Detective Stories,* one of the pulp crime magazines widely read across the United States, also picked up the case, and its November 1946 edition featured a report on the "Mad Slasher of Windsor." This largely fictionalized account of the police investigation introduced American readers to Ronald Sears, who killed to protect the "persecuted." The magazine carried a fanciful account of the interrogation as conducted by Inspector Jim Yokum, who in reality was not present during the questioning:

"What would you do, Ronald, if anyone hurt a child you knew pretty well?"

Sears said, "I'd kill him! I'd slash him to ribbons!"[4]

One factual detail of the case that resonated with the Canadian public was that the condemned youth had been assaulted when he was only nine. As a result, there was considerable public sympathy for him, and several letters were sent to the federal minister of justice asking that the death sentence be remitted. A letter from a woman in London, Ontario, advised the minister, "The Police knows where most Sexual Perverts are and yet nothing is done about it until they have done something terrible." As for Sears's victims, she wrote, "In my opinion they need stabbing," and furthermore, "Sexual perverts should be turned over to the children's father they have damaged for punishment. Too much mercy is being shown in wrong places."[5] The letter echoed *Star* columnist W. L. Clark's idea that the problem was the very existence of homosexuals, not those who preyed upon them. Above that, the letter reflected an objection to the homosexual lifestyle, with its supposed tendency to corrupt children. In his own self-revealing comment, Sears had admitted that he had not thought much of the homosexual aspect of the encounter from his youth but that it was only over time that he had discovered by talking with others how revolting these acts were. That is, he had likely been socialized into believing that all male-male relationships were heinous, and not just those in which a child has been violated by an adult.

The apprehension and conviction of the Slasher should have been a notable triumph for the Windsor Police. With few clues at their disposal, they had solved the mystery and obtained signed confessions to all the Slasher attacks. Only the slaying of the night watchman Davies remained unresolved. It was apparent that this murder was unconnected to Sears or the Slasher and would remain a mystery. However, any sense of victory that the police enjoyed would be short lived. In mid-November 1946, a new scandal erupted over allegations that influential men were being excused from criminal misconduct and having their entries on the police blotter erased. Additionally, it appeared that certain well-connected brothel owners were being tipped off on imminent raids. Even when these owners were brought before the courts, they were given minimum or even less than minimum sentences. The far-from-pristine conditions in the Windsor justice system were raised at a meeting of the police commission in November 1946. Mayor Reaume sat on the commission, and at his insistence, the press was excluded while the problem was discussed. However, the accusations of police partiality could not be swept under the rug, and at a subsequent city council meeting, aldermen Ernest Davenport and Thomas Brannagan urged the provincial attorney general to conduct an inquiry, for, as Brannagan proclaimed, "People are demanding this be cleaned up."[6]

Added to charges that the Windsor Police Department was corrupt were allegations that they were incompetent. At a recent Hamilton murder trial that for pure public spectacle had overshadowed that of Ronald Sears, Evelyn Dick was accused of murdering her husband and depositing his limbless torso on Hamilton Mountain. The Torso Murder Case featured the pretty, photogenic twenty-six-year-old accused, who denied all charges and at one point inferred that her husband had been murdered by Windsor gangsters. Provincial Police Inspector W. A. Scott even lent some credibility to her story with his observation that Windsor mobsters were a notorious breed and that "Windsor men have been operating in many parts of the country."[7]

If the Windsor police suffered one embarrassment after another, the Sears family faced the frustrating dilemma of how to finance an appeal. They remained steadfast in their view that Ronald was innocent. "It just couldn't have been him," Florence Sears insisted to reporters. James Clark urged them to file a document *in forma pauperis* to insure that the appeal court in Toronto was aware that they wanted to keep up the fight. Ronald and his family hastily put together a kitchen-table document that perhaps says more about what they really felt than any refined legal document would. "In the first place, I'm not guilty of such a crime," Ronald began and continued, "When they first came and took me to the Court-house I wondered what it was all about I was dumb-founded to hear what they wanted me for." He then repeated many of the claims that Clark had raised that the detectives' stories were contradictory and that he was not able to recollect what had happened after 9 p.m. He had learned that Voligny had failed to identify him as his attacker and therefore claimed, "The whole thing was absurd." Lastly, Sears begged the Court of Appeal to accept this document, writing, "My father was only able to pay Major Clark $100 for the trial, so I can't ask him to pay for the evidence and handle the appeal for nothing." On September 9, 1946, Edward and Florence Sears had signed a mortgage for 261 Cameron over to Clark for $1,200, a figure that represented about half their equity in the property.[8] This was a large sum for 1946, but it seems most likely that Clark was holding the mortgage for the time being and had only been paid $100 to date.

The formal right to appeal to a higher court in criminal matters was a relatively recent innovation. In the early twentieth century, the absence of appeals cast a substantial burden on juries whose verdict on guilt or innocence was likely to be final. In 1907, Britain created an appeal system, and in 1923, a similar arrangement was finally enacted in Canada.[9] Another safeguard existed in addition to the option to appeal. In capital cases, the judge was required to give an account of the trial, and two weeks after the hearing's end, Justice Dalton Wells submitted a lengthy report to Justice Minister Louis St. Laurent. To Wells, the pivotal issue of the case was whether any threat or promise had improperly induced the confession, and on this point, the evidence was clear that no such evidence existed. Wells did point out that there were some discrepancies between Sears's statement and the murder scene, such as Sears describing a wounded Price staggering deeper into the weeds while the blood trail indicated that he had stumbled toward Sandwich Street. These conflicts had been pointed out to the jury, who had nevertheless convicted Sears.

One startling aspect of the report was Wells's revelation that he had privately consulted with the psychiatrists who had examined Sears and who believed "that Sears himself suffers from sexual aberrations, probably of a homosexual and sadistic character." As unusual as it seemed for a judge to make his report based on information he had gleaned from outside the courtroom, these unsworn, casual conversations had profoundly affected Wells, since they had led him to doubt that "[Sears] is morally responsible for what he had done. In my opinion, Sears is a diseased person both in mind and possibly in body." It was such a diminished level of responsibility that Wells did not think that execution was justified. The additional factor of Sears's youth brought Wells strongly to the conclusion that clemency should be allowed.[10] With such a strong recommendation from the trial judge, it seemed almost inevitable that the death sentence would be commuted.

However, none of this information was communicated to the Sears family or their lawyer, and by mid-November, only two weeks remained before the scheduled execution. James Clark was a fine trial lawyer; however, on an appeal, it was crucial to obtain the services of a Toronto counsel who regularly argued cases before the Court of Appeal. As the Sears family had declared their inability to pay, G. Arthur Martin was appointed by the Court to argue the appeal. It might have seemed a mere face-saving effort to entrust a man's life to a thirty-two-year-old lawyer who had only been practicing for eight years. But whether the Sears family knew it or not, Ronald's fate was now in the hands of perhaps the finest criminal defense lawyer in the country. While most young men with Arthur Martin's high level of skill went into corporate or civil law, he had devoted himself to the defense of accused criminals. When asked why, he replied, "Because the penal system of this country is so awful, I believe I have a moral obligation to keep as many people out of it as possible."

Ontario's justice system in the 1940s could well be described as Dickensian. Most people could not afford a lawyer, and so they were routinely convicted and subjected to a harsh penal regime that had originated in the nineteenth century. The Archambault Report of 1938 had revealed the barbarity of the penal system; however, any change was put aside for the duration of the war, and reforms were still years away. During this period, "You'd go up to the courts in the morning to act for someone," Martin recalled, "and there'd be literally a cage full of people. You'd end up trying to help anyone you could."[11]

Martin's first notable case came in 1939, when he defended Donald "Mickey" McDonald, who had been convicted of murder. Five eyewitnesses identified McDonald as the killer, and most lawyers considered the appeal to be futile. Not Martin, who went painstakingly over the evidence and raised a substantial doubt as to the validity of the identification. Not only did the Court of Appeal order a new trial, they made an unprecedented observation on the "brilliant manner" in which the appeal had been handled.

Since then, Martin had used the same process over and over again. He would meticulously comb through the file until the facts were second nature to him. Then he would point out the flaws in the prosecution's case that weighed in his client's favor. All the while, he did so in a quiet, unassuming manner and tried to avoid any publicity. In the recent blaze of newspaper coverage over Evelyn Dick and the Torso Murder case, Martin had defended one of the accused, William Bohozuk. While the other defense counsel (whose clients were convicted) appeared regularly on the front page, Martin remained nearly anonymous but got an acquittal for Bohozuk.

To an extraordinary degree, Martin's life was devoted to the accused persons he defended. He did not engage in any practice other than criminal defense. He did not own a car, nor did he go out to any clubs. As far as anyone knew, he worked seven days a week and rarely took a vacation. He lived with his sister, who also served as his office manager. No other contemporary lawyer had the ability to be such a master of the facts and the law and to apply them with such a single-minded devotion to his client's benefit.

As the clocks outside Osgoode Hall in Toronto began to strike eleven o'clock on the morning of Tuesday, November 18, 1946, the appeal for the life of Ronald Sears began. The Court of Appeal sat in one of the ornate chambers reserved for legal argument. With only limited room for spectators, it looked less like a courtroom and more like an elite gentlemen's club—which in 1946, it very much was. All of the justices were older men who had enjoyed considerable success and wealth in law practice. They had secured judicial appointment by their eminence and impeccable political connections. As there would be only verbal argument, with no witnesses or evidence presented, there was no point in having the accused present. He would remain in the Sandwich jail while his fate was debated in Toronto. As Martin and his adversary, Crown Attorney C. R. Magone, stood in silence, the chief justice of Ontario, Robert Robertson, and four fellow justices entered the courtroom.

Martin took the judges back to the scene of the crime. He put before them a photostatic copy of a diagram showing the area where Price's body had been found. On the diagram, the police had marked a twenty-three-foot line along which the killer had dragged the victim's body. At no time in Sears's statement had he said that he had dragged Price's body. A post-mortem examination had shown two stab wounds on the left side of the back. In his statement, Sears had said that he had stabbed Price in the back on the left and right sides. The judges listened intently as Martin pointed out as many detailed discrepancies as he could between the confession and the police reports, his purpose being to raise doubts as to the reliability of the confession.

But the heart of Martin's appeal, one not typical for him, would be an emotional argument that the conduct of the Windsor police was abhorrent and that the "callous and heartless" way in which the confession had been extracted should have rendered it inadmissible. Throughout, Martin's argument would be animated by a fierce condemnation of every step the police had taken, beginning with the arrest and confinement of Sears in the squad car. Not only was he not told why he was being arrested, the officers had refused to answer his questions, and he was treated with "stony silence," which could "quite reasonable terrify him, an 18 year old boy." Later, after they went off to have their dinners, the detectives never thought of providing any food for their prisoner. Most cruelly, they had refused to let Edward Sears see his son.

Ultimately, Martin's every word challenged the fact that this eighteen-year-old boy faced execution solely on the basis of some words he was supposed to have said to the officers. There was no direct evidence at all that connected him with the murder. "The jury should have been told," said Martin, "that even if a confession is given voluntarily it might not have been true because [Sears] had previously shown to have a morbid imagination." It was not unheard of, Martin argued, for persons to confess to crimes simply to attract attention. It was well known that many individuals who could not possibly have done the deed had confessed to the kidnapping of the Lindbergh baby in 1932. Exhibitionism alone might lead a youth of limited intellect such as Sears admit to things he had never actually done.[12] But this possibility had never been explained to the jury.

An appeal is not a recitation of a set speech but rather an exchange of ideas between the advocates and the judges. The lawyer who can best respond to the judges' questions is often the one who will carry the day and win the appeal. Chief Justice Robertson pointed out to Martin that the Crown had stated that the motive for the killing was that Price was a homosexual, and yet "there is not a title of evidence that the sergeant was a homosexual." Martin confirmed this fact and argued that therefore, there was no apparent reason why Sears should have attacked Price.

By failing to lead any evidence as to Price's homosexuality, the Crown lawyers had left a gaping hole in their case, namely, no evidence of a motive. The subsequent question from the seventy-five-year-old chief justice seemed most peculiar. He asked why there was no evidence of blood on Sears's clothing and why Florence Sears had not been called to the stand to testify on this point. That Mrs. Sears would have said anything to defend her son seemed obvious to everyone but the chief justice. Her testimony would have been to the effect that there was never any blood on her son's clothing and seemed so self-serving that the defense had not bothered to call her.

The chief justice continued with another unusual observation: "It is also strange that almost every time Sears sat on a park bench, a homosexual pervert came along and sat beside him." This comment betrayed a naiveté that bordered on willful ignorance. Homosexual gathering places existed in all major cities, and Government Park was one such place in Windsor. Many of the single men who went there late at night did so for a reason: to meet other men. For Ronald Sears, it was the place he allegedly had gone to identify homosexuals and kill them. But it seemed the chief justice was unfamiliar with the concept of a homosexual meeting place—such matters were not discussed in proper social circles—and consequently they did not exist. Therefore, the chief justice interpreted Sears's assertion that he was constantly accosted in the park as just another piece of adolescent fantasy that added to the unreliability of the boy's story.

It was an attitude that was headed in Martin's favor, and he fostered it. "My lords," he said, "it is highly dangerous to support this conviction for murder. There was no corroboration and sitting in this courtroom every day you know that in 999 cases out of a thousand there is." Justice William Henderson interjected with a rhetorical question: "Can you imagine five officers taking this 18 year old boy, handcuffing him and taking him to the station?" Martin was quick to agree that it was difficult to imagine. Henderson continued, "The father should have been allowed to be present [in the interrogation room]. It certainly casts grave suspicion on this statement." Once again, Martin was eager to concur, and he added "Yes, and the stony silence of the officers and being left in the cells for the two hours before being returned at nine o'clock must have had an effect on Sears." The justices were taking a critical view of practically every step the police had taken. It was a strange inversion from the actual trial, during which the officers had been examined and cross-examined, and for the most part their conduct had been approved. However, the mood in the Court of Appeal chamber, so far as the police were concerned, was distinctly hostile. By the time he sat down, Martin was assured that at least the chief justice and one other justice were on his side.

The attorney for the prosecution, Clifford Magone, known as the "ex office boy who became a legal authority," had begun his career as a civil-service clerk, and at the age of thirty-three (Martin's age when he argued the Sears appeal) he began his legal studies. In due course, he became an authority on criminal and constitutional matters and continued to work for the Attorney General's Department.[13] For the past several weeks, he had been in England arguing a case before the Privy Council and had had little time to familiarize himself with the facts of the Sears case. On behalf of the prosecution, he reminded the judges that after being brought to police headquarters, Sears had denied attacking Voligny or Gelencser. It surely demonstrated that he was not terrified or intimidated if "he didn't make any admission up to 7:15 p.m.," Magone argued. Furthermore, Magone said, his denial "shows that the five officers who arrested him had no effect on him."

Unlike the regular interruptions that had occurred during Martin's address, Magone's initial remarks were received in ominous silence. He continued by noting that instead of treating the suspect brutally, the officers had brought in sandwiches and coffee for Sears later in the evening. As Magone continued, the judges increasingly inserted themselves into the argument. Justice Hogg perused a copy of the confession and noticed the word "poised." This was an unusual choice of words for a boy with limited education. The rest of the statement seemed oddly coherent. "I wonder if words were not put into the boy's mouth by the two officers," he mused.

It was the manner in which the statements had been taken that most offended the justices. Justice R. E. Laidlaw was an engineer as well as a lawyer, and he was a renowned authority in commercial matters. However, he had had little contact with criminals or the police. Nevertheless, in his view, "By surviving the whole thing from the time five policemen arrested him and refused to give him any information—why until his collapse eight hours later it doesn't have the appearance of justice." Justice Henderson was even more outraged, saying, "The fact that this boy was held in this room and questioned, then brought back at nine o'clock and questioned until he collapsed and not given anything to eat is fantastic." Magone tried to point out that Sears had indeed been given refreshment and that, given the gravity of the situation, the questioning was not unduly prolonged. Henderson would have none of it: "I deny the right of a policeman to take a person into a private room without anyone there. He had a right to have his father there, and he was in the police station at that time. This is not British justice. I can't believe these statements were voluntary."

By now, Arthur Martin could rest assured that the Court was solidly behind him. In a revealing comment, Chief Justice Robertson added, "It seems ridiculous to think that a 17 year old boy could stalk the streets of Windsor killing two men, yet appearing to lead a normal life and not being suspected before." It was a remarkable observation, one that revealed more about the minds of the judges than that of the convict. To Robertson, and likely to his fellow judges, what appeared to be normal had to be normal. A multiple murderer had to be the drooling, blood-lusting maniac that the *Star* had originally predicted. But what the justices failed to understand was that what appeared to be ordinary might well be extraordinary. By the later part of the twentieth century, society would have sufficient experience with deranged killers to appreciate that they could present themselves as conventional members of society, that deep-seated abnormality could hide in plain sight. It might even be possible that the harmless neighborhood boy might be taking instructions from his cat to hunt down homosexuals. But in 1946, the justices of the Ontario Court of Appeal would have none of it, and if Ronald Sears *appeared* to be innocent, then he must be innocent.

On the morning of Wednesday, November 19, the Court returned with its verdict. In three short paragraphs, with little explanation or embellishment, the justices ruled that the confession had not been freely made and should not have been admitted into evidence. As the decision was unanimous, the Crown was barred from appealing to the Supreme Court of Canada. The five justices, none of whom had heard any testimony, overruled the trial judge's evaluation as to the voluntary nature of the confession. Even considering Arthur Martin's persuasive magic, the fact remained that there was no evidence of force or threat of force against young Sears and that at no time had he ever hinted that the police had mistreated him. Perhaps the unspoken reasoning at the heart of the Court of Appeal decision was that the judges did not want to send a troubled eighteen-year-old to the gallows solely on the basis of an uncorroborated confession.

There may have been other motivating factors left unsaid by the Court. Newspapers of the time regularly carried reports describing how American police had used inappropriate means to obtain evidence. In 1945, New York police had taken a suspect to a hotel room, stripped him, and begun an interrogation. After three hours, he was given a blanket to wear. After seven hours of interrogation, he confessed.[14] Was this the trend for Canadian police as well? In an Ohio case that bore some similarities to Sears's, a fifteen-year-old was interrogated for five straight hours. He was held in isolation for three days after the confession and denied access to a lawyer his family had hired.[15] One legal commentator later noted, "As our society becomes more clearly North American—as British influence becomes less distinct and familiar, and as influences from the United States grow more direct and stronger—the need for protection of the citizen against violence, ill treatment and bullying and other misconduct by the police grows greater."[16]

While on the face of it, the Windsor police had not seemed to have crossed the line into bullying tactics, by denying Sears the comfort of his father and by keeping him under questioning so long, had they actually departed from the standards of British justice? The Court of Appeal thought so, and its members were not prepared to accept that this youth could be made the deluded instrument of his own conviction. The Sears family received the news with quiet jubilation. "We always knew that Ronald was never guilty, and this proves it," his mother announced. She hurried down to the Sandwich Jail, and as she arrived, a guard called out down the cellblock, "Here she comes now, kid." Ronald already knew about the acquittal, and he told his mother "See Ma, I told you not to worry, everything's going to be all right." His first question was about his cat. He worried that Ginger would not recognize him when he got home. Later, back at 261 Cameron, the Sears family held court before the press and friends. "I only hope the ugly business ends soon," Florence pleaded, "and Ronald is back home with us again. We miss him so."[17]

However, Ronald would not soon be rejoining his family and his cat. Despite the opinion of the appellate bench, there was no question among local law enforcement that the Toronto judges had just ordered the exoneration of a multiple killer. While technically the decision only applied to the Price case, it made it next to impossible to apply the confessions on the remaining charges. The only direct evidence remaining to the prosecution was Joseph Gelencser's identification of Sears in a police lineup. On Monday, November 25, 1946, E. C. Awrey announced the prosecution's decision that Ronald Sears would remain in custody and that the Crown would proceed with the remaining charges. "There's nothing else to do," he added with little enthusiasm.[18]

In the wake of the Court of Appeal's decision, the city was charged with debate. Some felt that a self-confessed serial killer had just been acquitted on what appeared to be a technicality. Others sensed that the police might have been overly enthusiastic and that Ronald Sears, the mild son of a respectable family, could not possibly be the infamous Slasher. Columnist W. L. Clark wrote, "The case of Ronald George Sears, 18, is a topic of general conversation. People argue it in living rooms, on the buses and wherever they gather."[19] The acquittal came only a few days before Windsor's first postwar election. The Sears case, the presence of deviants in the parks, and allegations of police corruption were all issues that might have but did not feature in the election. Instead, the housing crisis and fallout from the Ford strike dominated the campaign. Arthur Reaume reminded voters that while over 12,000 people had been involved in the great strike, "there was not one drop of blood spilled." His challenger, Controller Arthur Mason, did raise the presence of vice in the city and hinted that he had been gathering information from unnamed sources on illegal gambling and prostitution. However, none of his accusations were substantiated, and Reaume was easily reelected.

As Christmas 1946 approached, Ronald Sears remained in his jail cell innocent of any charges. The only person convicted and imprisoned of a serious offense arising out of the Slasher incident so far was Alexander Voligny. His staunchly Roman Catholic family had been mortified by the publicity when he was convicted of gross indecency, and it was clear that he could never return to Windsor.[20] In any case, he still had six months of imprisonment ahead of him.

11

A MOST UNUSUAL YOUNG MAN

Defending Ronald Sears against the charge of the attempted murder of Joseph Gelencser would prove considerably more challenging for James Clark than his defense of Sears for the Price murder. The Price trial had been relatively straightforward, for the only real question had been the admissibility of the confession. But in the Gelencser case, several possible defenses presented themselves, and Clark had to select which one had the greatest chance of success. If he chose incorrectly, the consequences for his client could be disastrous. As he said later, "If counsel make a decision that is wrong, and I thought I made it wrong," there would be no going back.[1] What Clark had to wrestle with was the confession his client had made in the early evening of July 6. In that statement, Sears described Gelencser as aggressively solicitous: "He was talking about jacking off and wanted to know if I would let him suck me off." Sears's response was, "I told him I didn't think anyone would do a thing like that," at which point Gelencser urged him to come down to the dock by the river where they would be undisturbed.[2]

Why not let the Crown admit this exchange into evidence? Such a gambit would catch the prosecution off guard and might have a devastating effect on their case. It would reveal the Crown's main witness, who in his statements characterized himself as a conventional married man, as one of the deviants that infested the city's parks. It would hold him up as the worst kind of pervert who accosted young men and cajoled them into disgusting acts such as oral sex. In Sears's statement, the alleged victim was practically begging the youngster to submit to these acts. Then the Crown Attorney would be compelled to put Gelencser on the stand, where he would state that it was Sears who had propositioned him. Whom would the jury believe? If they believed Sears's confession, might they conclude that he was entirely justified in stabbing Gelencser? The jurors read the newspaper, and they undoubtedly knew that the police and prosecution put great store in the confession, a confession that characterized the Crown's prime witness as a sexual deviant.

Admitting the confession muddied the waters and made the trial a complicated proposition. It also provided the Crown with a shortcut, an admission by the accused that he had committed the act of attempted murder. Keeping the confession out limited the Crown's evidence to the knife and Gelencser's identification of Sears. Would that be enough for a conviction? James Clark spent the early part of 1947 grappling with these alternatives.

His task was not made any easier by the realization that the police knew a lot more about this case than they were divulging to the defense. Two days after Sears's original conviction, Clark had discovered a police bulletin that had been circulated after the Mannie stabbing, which described the assailant as "a person 25 to 30 years of age, 5 feet 10 inches tall, slim build, small moustache, a light-skinned Negro." Ronald Sears was fair-skinned, seventeen years old at the time, with long brown hair and blue eyes. This description would have been most useful to Clark in his cross-examination of the detectives to show that the youth they had grilled that night did not fit the description of the suspect they were after. Also, after the conviction, Clark learned that the police had recorded the statements made by witnesses at the identification lineups. Clark sought out the detectives who had handled the Voligny lineup and asked to see the statement. The police demurred. The trial was over and done with, Clark was told, and there was no point in sharing the Voligny statement with anyone. It was not difficult for Clark to track down Voligny, who was still in jail. Clark said that Voligny "assured me definitively that Sears was not the man who attacked him."[3]

As a result of this startling admission, Clark could have little confidence that the police were giving him all the relevant information in their possession. Little did he know how much the police actually knew about Gelencser's secret life and how reluctant they were to share this information with him. This level of secrecy stood in stark contrast to the theoretical role of the Crown in presenting all the facts so that justice might be done. As early as 1838, a British court had noted that the duty of the prosecutor "is to be assistant to the Court in the furtherance of justice, and not to act as counsel for any particular person or party." Almost a century later, the Ontario Court of Appeal echoed these sentiments, writing that "a criminal prosecution is not a contest between individuals, nor is it a contest between the Crown endeavouring to convict and the accused endeavouring to be acquitted" but rather "it is an investigation that should be conducted without feeling or animus on the part of the prosecution, with the single view of determining the truth."[4] Noble sentiments aside, the police held information that would have made Sears's defense golden. For example, only the police were aware of Haley Friend's sexual relationship with Gelencser. But no laws in 1947 compelled the Crown officers to share this file with Clark, and he would remain unaware that the chief prosecution witness harbored a weakness for male prostitutes.

Curiously, there are two separate files on Joseph Gelencser in the Windsor police records. One is the standard Crown file with all the relevant witness statements that the prosecutor would use in assembling his case for trial. This file would be shared with the defense counsel. The other is an investigative file that contains all of the information on Gelencser's secret life and the telephone numbers and addresses of his male friends and the prostitute he had hired. The police would never divulge this file to Clark.[5] It is even possible that Crown Attorney Awrey was unaware of its existence.

While James Clark wrestled with the tactics he would use in the next round, Windsor was finally putting the trauma of the war and the bitterness of the Ford strike behind it. By February 1947, rationing was finally being phased out. This recovery led to outrages such as sixty-five-cent haircuts, but at least private industry was again churning out products and houses. Dr. Faludi's plan to renovate the riverfront and get rid of the isolated, dangerous parks and convert them into a large open space for the public was endorsed by the city council. So many things belonged to the past, including the Slasher killings. The hysteria and novelty that had made the first trial such a spectacle had, in the absence of any further killings, given way to indifference. Only a small gallery of the curious would gather at the Sandwich Courthouse for the second trial.

Justice Daniel Patrick Kelly would preside. In a province that was still very much a Protestant bastion, Kelly was one of the few Roman Catholics ever to serve on the Supreme Court of Ontario. He was also a very principled man with a firm idea of his own correctness. Just how fixed he could be in his opinions would become apparent during the course of the second trial. On Wednesday, February 5, 1947, Ronald Sears pleaded not guilty to the attempted murder of Joseph Gelencser. If the crowd was much smaller, certain things were predictable. Florence and Edward Sears sat in the front row, as close as they could to the prisoner's dock. Awrey began by outlining for the jury how the victim and the accused had met on Sandwich Street and walked to a secluded spot on the riverbank, where "a certain proposal of an improper nature" was made, and the accused plunged a knife into the victim's back.

It is difficult to appreciate what pressure Joseph Gelencser was under when he took the stand that afternoon. He must have been aware that the authorities had checked him out thoroughly and that they knew all about Friend and his real life. The police knew the most intimate things about him and that the loss of his male prostitute he had forced him to troll Government Park and assume the risks of that subculture. It was a narrative that Gelencser desperately wanted to keep from coming out at trial. If only a particle of his secret emerged, his life would be ruined; his double life would be revealed and he would be reviled in his neighborhood and at work as a deviant. So far, the police had kept quiet about what they knew, and, unlike Alexander Voligny, Gelencser was not in jail for gross indecency. It was vital that he keep up the pretense that it was Sears who was at fault and that Gelencser was the innocent bystander who was assaulted by a frustrated pervert. One way to maintain this lie would be to take the offensive and fend off any questions about his manhood.

Awrey took Gelencser through the story he had repeated so many times: He had gone for a healthy walk after work and encountered a young man who offered to accompany him to Ambassador Park. This stranger offered to show him a shortcut, and the two of them walked down a stairway to the river. Once there, the youth threw himself on the ground. "I got scared," Gelencser related, and then the stranger asked "if I had any kind of cigar on me." The *Star* report of the trial discreetly omitted the rest of the discussion. As he turned away, Gelencser felt a blow to his back, and moments later drew a butcher's knife from his wound. In the courtroom, he pointed to Ronald Sears as the young man who had attacked him.

As Clark went to work on him, Gelencser's guard was fully up. Clark wondered why, after a full shift at the Chrysler plant that had begun at seven o'clock that morning, Gelencser was taking a walk practically across the city at 10:30 that night. He replied that his doctor had recommended that he take walks to improve his circulation. Even so, it was most unusual, Clark persisted:

"Why did you go to this park for?"

"Why do different people go to the parks?" countered the witness.

"Different people go for different reasons," said counsel.

"Well, I did not go for the purpose you are thinking of," flared back the witness. "You are trying to insinuate things."[6]

While Clark had said nothing about his character, Gelencser was overly sensitive about any question related to his motives. Clark suggested that Gelencser had read about the case in the newspapers. Had these reports stimulated his memory? After all, it was late at night when he had encountered the stranger. How could he be so sure that it was Sears who had attacked him? Gelencser hotly denied that he could be mistaken and refuted the charge that he had seen the newspapers. In order to avoid overstimulation, his doctor had ordered him to avoid reading about the case. All the exchanges between Clark and the witness were electric, laden with acrimony and sarcasm, but it was apparent that Joseph Gelencser was not about to change his mind about anything.

On the following day, the police who had conducted the lineup were called. Detective Sam Royan described how they had selected eleven young men, mostly from Assumption College, who had similar height, hair and age as the accused. They recounted how Gelencser, still prone on a hospital gurney, had reached out and pointed to Sears. "That's the man, right there," he had said. Clark asked if any independent person had been present. Just police and Crown prosecutors, he was told, all in the "usual manner."

In addition to Gelencser's identification of Sears, the Crown had the weapon used in the assault. Dorothy Sears, her pretty face framed by a white bonnet, was called to identify it. Dorothy repeated the story of finding the unusual knife with the missing rivet and worn handle and tossing it into a kitchen drawer. When the judge asked that it be shown to the jury, Dorothy obligingly left the witness stand and brought it over to them. There was an awkward moment as she was politely asked to return to the stand and let the lawyers handle the evidence.[7] As she testified, Ronald "watched her, listened, his eyes blinking drowsily." He had seemed to deliberately place himself so that he directly faced her. Despite Dorothy's apparent uneasiness on the stand, she testified that she was sure that the knife Gelencser had drawn from his back was one and the same as the one she had found. Lastly, Awrey sought to introduce the Sears confession. Clark protested that the Court of Appeal had already pronounced this "not British justice" and that it should be disregarded. Justice Kelly reminded him that the appeal had only dealt with the Price murder charge and technically did not apply to any other cases. At that point, Justice Kelly excused the jury for another voir dire. Kelly asked the jurors not to discuss the evidence or read any newspaper accounts of the case.

Brand and McLauchlan again went through their account of the evening of July 6, 1946, of giving Sears the warning and his sudden change of story after nine o'clock that night. Sears testified that he did not recall anything after nine o'clock, that it was all a blank and that the statement was false. As Gelencser's identification of Sears was crucial to the case, Detective Sam Royan was put on the stand, and he described how the police had arranged the identification parade. Clark asked whether Royan had bothered to have any independent party present to verify the use of Assumption College students roughly similar to Sears in age and appearance. That was not proper procedure, Royan responded. As he spoke, lawyers who were waiting for divorce cases to be tried wandered into the courtroom and sat in the vacant jurors' chairs.

The only new element in the voir dire was Clark's indication that he would call Sheriff A. A. Marentette to describe Sears's condition when he was put in the county jail. "[Marentette] doesn't know it yet, but I plan on calling him as a witness," Clark quietly advised the reporters. They laughed appreciatively.[8] In the end, Marentette's evidence would have an impact even Clark would not have anticipated.

The following morning when called to the stand, Sheriff Marentette testified that Sears had appeared to be exhausted and disoriented when he was brought in from police headquarters. After seeing him for several weeks, Marentette thought that he had the mentality of a fourteen-year-old. Jail Governor John M. Robinson was also called, and in his view, Ronald Sears was a most peculiar death row inmate. He was "unusually cheerful and smiling," even as the date of his execution drew near. Dr. Markkanen testified that Sears had appeared to be "washed out" that evening, with a rapid pulse and on the point of exhaustion to the extent that he "might answer anything suggested to him."

The following morning, February 10, the defense and prosecution waited for the all-important ruling on the admissibility of the confession. Once that was determined, the trial would most likely be completed in a matter of a day or less. However, Justice Kelly had other plans. The trial judge had been struck by the evidence from the sheriff and the jail governor on Sears's mental state. While Clark had called these witnesses to show how addled Sears was at the time of his interrogation, the judge had drawn an entirely different lesson from it. How was it possible for a person to remain cheerful under sentence of death? Above all, Kelly had been impressed by Sears's demeanor in the courtroom. He did not seem to appreciate the seriousness of his situation, and Kelly thought he might have an overwrought mind or possibly a delusional personality. It was the Court's duty to guard against the trial of an insane person, for such a person could neither plead to a charge nor instruct a lawyer in his defense. As it appeared to Kelly that Sears might be mentally incompetent, he ordered a separate hearing to determine his fitness. This decision would necessarily require an adjournment and the determination of the present issue at a fresh trial at the May assizes.

The lawyers were taken aback. Justice Kelly's decision seemed based on offhand comments by the sheriff and the jail governor, neither of who were medical professionals with any qualifications to assess a person's mental state. During the course of this trial, as during the previous one, Clark had taken the position that his client was sane. He advised Kelly that shortly after his arrest, Sears had been tested by two "of the outstanding alienists in the province," both of who had concluded that he was of sound mind. "Well, I did not know that" Kelly replied.[9] He defended his actions by explaining that they were based on the evidence he had heard and his observations of Sears's reactions in the witness box. Clark protested as vigorously as he could that his client, who had already spent seven months in jail waiting for his trial, would be left in a state of suspense for another three months. But the judge had made up his mind. The case was put over till May.

Kelly's ruling (described by the *Star* as a "bomb-shell like development") was not without precedent. Section 967 of the *Criminal Code* provided for a hearing to decide whether or not an accused was insane and therefore unfit to stand trial. A maxim of the law—then and now—dictates that "the accused must not only be physically present but mentally present as well."[10] In the Gibbons decision in the previous year, Chief Justice McRuer had heard evidence from a psychologist that the accused was of unsound mind. As a result, he had invoked Section 967 and ordered a trial to determine if the accused had the mental capacity to instruct his lawyer.[11] Of course, in the Sears case, there was no expert evidence at all, only Kelly's impressions that Sears was a strange fellow. That suggestion was apparently enough to merit handing the prisoner over to the psychiatrists.

In some ways, it seems curious that the question of Ronald Sears's mental state had not arisen earlier. Considering the voices he heard that others did not, the conversations with his cat, and his obsession with knives and horror movies, one might have thought that Sears's sanity would have been a prime question from the beginning. It had been enough of a concern that the deputy attorney general had ordered psychiatric evaluations immediately after the arrest. The war years had been a boom time for psychiatrists, since their services were in demand for screening troops and treating the traumatic effects of combat. After the war, "a faith developed that psychiatry could promote prevention by contributing toward the amelioration of social problems that allegedly fostered mental disease."[12] During the conflict, one of the main functions of psychiatrists had been the identification and weeding out of homosexual recruits. Homosexuality was widely regarded in the psychiatric profession as a malady and one that "can be easily acquired and become ingrained." Homosexuals as an alienated group were deemed psychotic, for "psychopaths were visualized as a small group of men that suffered from a lack of power to control their sexual impulses."[13] The question before the psychiatrists retained in this case was whether or not Ronald Sears lacked this power of self-control.

In a terse report dated July 1946, just after Sears's arrest, the medical superintendent of the Ontario Hospital at St. Thomas, Dr. D. O. Lynch, had concluded that Sears was not mentally defective and was fit to stand trial. He had also noted that Sears "is quite effeminate in manner, shows a marked maternal attachment and expresses different neurotic complaints. He denied perverse sexual activities but has a knowledge of such acts." This last detail was likely gleaned from the confessions in which Ronald readily admitted that he was familiar with the language and gambits of gay courtship. Anyone so knowledgeable about terms such as "frenchies" and "cornholing" had more than a casual acquaintance with the queer scene.

Dr. C. S. Tennant, the director of the Ontario Hospital at Penetanguishene was also asked to evaluate Sears just after his arrest, and he gave a more detailed report. From his reading of Sears's account of these encounters, "I am very strongly of the opinion that he is a sexual pervert (homosexual). He denies it absolutely, however, declaring that he was never guilty of such practices."[14] As had Lynch, Tennant found no evidence of mental illness. Interestingly enough, the doctors' comments on Sears are very similar to the report on Chicago's Lipstick Killer, William Heirens: "This patient, in our opinion, is not suffering from any psychosis, nor is he mentally retarded. . . . He has a deep sexual perversion and is emotionally insensitive and unstable."[15]

While the reports from two of the most senior psychiatrists in the province would support Sears's fitness to stand trial, they would taint the first trial as well as all future proceedings, for there would be a strong hint that the individual in the prisoner's dock was a deviant, a homosexual. This suggestion added yet another dimension to the case, since even if Sears was sane, he might still be suffering from the disease of homosexuality, a condition that may have explained (or exacerbated) his conduct.

On the day after Kelly's surprise ruling, Awrey reported to the deputy attorney general that the peculiar conduct of the accused had led the trial judge to conclude that Sears might be unfit to stand trial. Awrey stood by the judge, saying that his ruling had been "amply justified." Awrey suggested that at some time before the May sittings Sears be taken away for mental observation. As a postscript, Awrey added a plea that, despite what the judges of the Court of Appeal might think, the accused presented a very real threat. "I feel," he wrote, "that this boy if he goes at large will be a menace to society and it will not be long before something else occurs which may be a great deal more horrible than the exterminating of the class of man that was attacked before."[16]

It was a horrible prospect to contemplate that the Slasher might be turned loose to attack normal people.

12

THIRD TRIAL

A NEWSPAPER CONVICTION

As the days passed in the county jail, Ronald Sears made an unusual friend. His cellmate, William Jewitt, was also a twin and a first-time offender. The other thing they had in common was murder. Jewitt was accused of killing his mother in Leamington in the fall of 1946. While Sears would socialize with the other prisoners, Jewitt kept completely to himself and talked only with his cellmate. The two young men would chat and play endless games of gin rummy.[1] By the spring of 1947, this relationship ended when Jewitt was found to be mentally incompetent to stand trial and was removed to a mental institution.

The loss of his companion was far from Sears's worst problem. The resources of the Sears family had long since run out, and in a desperate attempt to winkle funds out of the government, Edward Sears filed an affidavit stating that after he had paid Clark $100 for the Price murder trial in 1946, he had been unable to pay anything further. Clark wrote to attorney general Leslie Blackwell, "[Sears's] father just works at Fords three or four days a week and has a hard time keeping his little house together as is." The attorney general's department took this information under advisement and indicated that they would consider paying Clark's bills. There is no indication, however, that they did so. In the pre-legal-aid era, the chances of legal representation were uncertain at best.[2]

Officials had followed Justice Kelly's recommendation that Sears undergo a second round of psychiatric evaluations between February and May, the findings of which would be presented in court. On May 5, 1947, Sears faced a judge and jury for the third time. The protracted legal ordeal had had particularly severe effects on the accused. The months in jail seemed to be grinding him down. To the reporters in the courtroom, he looked ill, thin, and pale, and yet, "His reactions aren't different," they wrote. "He doesn't display emotions to any extent at all."[3]

A fresh panel of jurors were sworn in and instructed in Shakespearean tones that the young man in the dock "hath pleaded not guilty and for his trial hath put himself upon his country, which country you are." That is, the jurors were the conscience of the country, the embodiment of the principles of all Canadians. To the men on the jury panel, it must have been an impressive, if somewhat mysterious introduction to the trial process, for the criminal trial has its own mystique, enhanced by its formal rituals, all of which are intended to impress upon the minds of the participants the gravity of the occasion.

These same jurors had been exposed to massive pretrial publicity and most likely had already formed an opinion about the case. The *Star* had proclaimed time and again that with the arrest of Ronald Sears, the Slasher panic was over, and Sears's confession to the killing of Sergeant Price had been reproduced in the front section of the newspaper almost verbatim. One study of the interaction between the press and jurors has suggested that the right to an impartial trial is jeopardized "when the amount and intensity of general press coverage of a case becomes so significant and so partisan that the whole community atmosphere is permeated with passion sufficient to preclude a fair adjudication."[4]

In spite of these circumstances, Clark had made no attempt to change the trial venue. In Canada it had not even been possible to ask for a change of venue under the *Criminal Code* until 1927. Thereafter, it was still difficult to have a case tried in any county other than that where the crime had been committed. In a case decided the previous year, Chief Justice J. C. McRuer had ruled that a change in venue should only be granted in exceptional cases where an impartial trial was impossible.[5] Had Clark brought a motion for a change of venue, it likely would have failed.

The same cast of lawyers and police officers assembled for Sears's third trial, and everyone anticipated a repetition of the previous testimony with few variations. To the surprise of the prosecutor and the spectators, Clark was about to change the focus of the defense. Like a clever boxer throwing a counterpunch, he would lay off certain parts of the Crown's case, compliment certain witnesses he had previously vilified, and concentrate instead on new issues, which might prove decisive. If so many other elements that made up this third trial remained the same, there was also one significant new actor in the drama—namely, the judge.

In 1913, a brilliant young Toronto lawyer had come to Windsor, lured there by an offer from the Bartlet & Bartlet law firm. George A. Urquhart became a prominent trial lawyer and well-known figure in Windsor. During the First World War, he had served with Essex County's 241st Battalion. Later, he became a city alderman and a member of the library board. Professionally, he became a respected criminal lawyer and was named Essex County Crown Attorney in 1921. In 1925, he left Windsor and returned to a lucrative civil law practice in Toronto. However, he was still retained by the attorney general's office to handle thorny prosecutions, and in 1934, he had conducted the case against Harold Vermilyea for the sensational axe murder of his mother. Even after his appointment to the Supreme Court of Ontario in 1938, Justice Urquhart found it difficult to remain above the fray, and his frequent forays into the examination of witnesses from the bench betrayed his previous role as an advocate for the prosecution.[6]

The first order of business was Kelly's ruling on the insanity question. By necessity, the Court's attention now turned to the state of Ronald Sears's mind. Urquhart grumbled that Kelly should have dealt with the matter without the need for an entirely new trial. When he asked the defense if the prisoner's mental state would be raised as an issue, Clark replied, "There has never been any doubt of it, my Lord. . . . He is perfectly sane." The Crown had already provided the most recent psychiatric reports indicating that Sears was fit to stand trial, so the issue seemed beyond dispute.

Every professional who touched the file concerning Ronald Sears, be they detectives, prosecutors, or doctors, was keen to ensure that they would not be accused of mishandling this very public case. Already, the Court of Appeal had slammed the detectives, and now the medical professionals were becoming concerned that perhaps it was their turn to come in for criticism. Two weeks prior to the trial before Kelly, the deputy attorney general had warned Awrey against making any requests that Sears be remanded for psychiatric evaluation: "As two senior psychiatrists of the Department of Health, Dr. Tennant and Dr. Lynch, will not certify Sears as being mentally ill, it is feared that a serious problem will arise should such remand be made."[7] The integrity of the province's leading psychiatrists was at stake.

However, one member of the medical profession was prepared to question his seniors. Shortly after Kelly's ruling, Dr. J. N. Senn of Hamilton examined Sears and found the young man "indefinite" about many things and prone to change his mind. In his report, Dr. Senn wrote, "This man's personality is such that there is real doubt as to whether it should not be considered as a Pre-Psychotic Personality."[8] Dr. Senn's conclusions might have been influenced by the diagnostic procedures of the time, by which homosexuality could be located among a range of mental illnesses. However, at the beginning of Sears's third trial, Senn's misgivings were swept away by the expertise of Dr. C. S. Tennant of Penetanguishene, who took the stand to confirm his initial report that Sears was not suffering from any mental illness. There was no doubt in Tennant's mind that Sears was sane and able to conduct his affairs. Clark declined to take any part in the proceedings regarding Sears's sanity. After a short recess, the jury returned with a verdict that Sears was competent to stand trial.

At that time, Joseph Gelencser took the stand for the third time. The slight but feisty Gelencser repeated his story of meeting the stranger and going with him to the riverfront. Once again, Clark asked him why he had gone for such a long walk after working a full shift. And why had he not taken Mrs. Gelencser along? Clark then proceeded to examine what little he did know about Gelencser from the statement that Sears had given to the police on July 6, 1946. Meticulously, Clark went through each point raised in that statement and asked the witness if he agreed:

Q. Did you agree to let him suck off?
A. I did not agree to anything.

Q. Did he tell you that he knew a darker and a better spot?
A. He did not tell me anything.

Q. Did the party you were with take you under some trees on the embankment?

A. He was leading the way, on the lane, and when he came to a certain spot, he dropped himself right on the grass.

Q. Did you both instinctively sit down?

A. I did not.

Q. Did you get ready to take your pants off?

A. I did not.

Q. Did you take your pants down?

A. I did not.[9]

It was an effective tactic on Clark's part, for he now had the Crown's main witness, the only person who could identify Ronald Sears as the Slasher, stating categorically that the statement Sears had given to the police on the night of July 6 was false. Both the confessor and the subject of the confession denied its validity.

Next, Clark went to work on the inconsistencies between the description Gelencser had given the police and the appearance of the prisoner in the dock. Gelencser thought that his attacker was twenty to twenty-two years old and had black hair. Then in the police lineup a few days later, he had pointed to the eighteen-year-old chestnut-haired Sears as his assailant. Now in the witness stand, Gelencser thought his assailant had brown hair. Clark wondered aloud if the newspaper accounts of Sears's arrest had helped prod Gelencser's memory, a claim Gelencser heatedly denied, insisting once again that his doctor had ordered him not to read any accounts of the attack, as it would overstimulate his heart.

As Gelencser gave this explanation, James Clark strode about the courtroom with a copy of the *Windsor Daily Star*, which announced in shrill red headlines the arrest of Ronald Sears as the Slasher. Awrey interjected that Clark was deliberately showing the banner headlines to the jurors in order to mislead them. But Clark had already driven his point home. Gelencser's story was that he had read the newspaper but somehow avoided the blaring headlines and the story that announced the near-fatal attack on him. This possibility seemed far-fetched if not totally unbelievable. Moreover, Gelencser delivered his version of events in a defensive, belligerent manner that seemed to broadcast a need to conceal.

Having gotten what he needed from Gelencser, Clark made good headway with the next two Crown witnesses. Dr. Rutherford had attended Gelencser at that time, and he had no recollection of ever telling him not to read the newspapers. But it was the following witness who would cast real doubt on Gelencser's account. Lloyd Leo Lauzon, the cab driver who had driven Gelencser to the hospital, was the first person to talk with him after the attack. Lauzon, heretofore a minor figure in the Slasher drama, gave evidence that would significantly change the complexion of the case. As they sped toward Grace Hospital, Gelencser told him, "He was walking by a bush, and all of a sudden he got a shove, and he never saw his assailant, and the next thing he knew, he had a knife in his back."[10] Clark made no attempt to expand on Lauzon's response. He had what he needed. It was an admission from an independent witness that Gelencser had never seen his attacker, which, if true, meant that his supposed identification of Sears was all but impossible.

When Dorothy Sears was called to the stand, she once again identified the knife used in the attack as the same one with the missing rivet and worn handle that she had seen in the kitchen drawer at home. She denied having seen the picture of the knife in the newspaper until after the police officers had arrested Ronald Sears. When she went downstairs to make formula for her baby in the early morning of July 6, she distinctly recalled that this knife was missing. Obviously uncomfortable on the stand and frequently close to tears, she came across as a reluctant but truthful witness. But her testimony could not save the prosecution.

Perhaps realizing that the prosecution's evidence was thin, Awrey again tried to get Sears's confession admitted into evidence. Given the Court of Appeal's decisive rejection, it seemed a long shot at best. Once again the jury was excluded as the court went into a voir dire. The same ground that Brand and McLauchlan had traversed so many times before was gone over yet again. Urquhart frequently stepped in and took over the cross-examination himself. In fact, he already seemed to have formed an idea of the accused's personality. He asked Detective Hill, "In Ireland what do you call a young fellow who is perhaps not quite as smart as the rest of men? . . . There is the expression like 'daft'?" As a former Crown officer it must have seemed like second nature for the justice to evaluate prisoners and test the evidence himself. Yet it seemed strangely out of place for a judge to assume that investigative role and to ask the following questions of McLauchlan:

BY HIS LORDSHIP: Q. Was there any indication to him that it would be to his advantage to give you a statement?

A. No, sir.

Q. Nothing of that sort, or nothing that encouraged him in the belief that you might be helpful to him?

A. Absolutely nothing like that whatever.

Q. You are a much slighter man than the others who have given evidence here?

A. That is right.

Q. Why is it you were chosen? Why didn't Mahoney do the questioning?[11]

Urquhart was peeling away layers of facts to try and get to the bottom of why junior detectives had been assigned to this critical interrogation. Perhaps then he could understand why and how Sears had changed his story so abruptly. But the mystery stubbornly remained, and the best Awrey could offer by way of explanation was that Mahoney was occupied "looking after other matters."

Just below the surface of this and the two previous trials lay the unstated fact that the catalyst for each of the Slasher attacks was a homosexual encounter. Now, for the first time, Awrey attempted to raise this unspoken issue and look into this heretofore forbidden area. He began by asking McLauchlan about his experiences with gross indecency charges. To Awrey's surprise, McLauchlan testified that such cases were a low priority to Windsor Police and that he knew little about homosexuals or their activities. "Well anyway," Awrey persisted, "in the other slashing cases there was also a suggestion of acts of gross indecency?" McLauchlan agreed that it was so. Awrey then prodded, "You knew whether [gross indecency] was an objective towards which you were working in your questioning." "Before we questioned the accused," McLauchlan admitted, "I knew that the individuals who were involved were suspected of being that type of individual."

Having gotten that much, Awrey hoped to wrap up the line of questioning by confirming that the police anticipated arresting a homosexual who was lashing out after being refused by a prospective lover. "That was an objective you had in getting a statement from the accused, wasn't it?" Awrey asked. But as happens from time to time, the witness and the prosecutor had not gone over this area as thoroughly as they might have before questioning. McLauchlan's reply undercut the scenario Awrey was hoping to create: "Well, I was not working on that angle," McLauchlan said. "I did not anticipate anything, actually."[12] The Crown had failed again to demonstrate a motive for the attack; even the investigating officer conceded that it was a motive to which they had never given any credence.

In his testimony, McLauchlan also unwittingly added one detail that had so far been overlooked. During Sears's interrogation, he had noticed a small, fresh cut on Sears's hand directly under the little finger and an inch above the wrist line. Neither police officer had noticed any cut during Sears's first interrogation before 9 p.m. even though during that period he had signed two statements, with his hands in plain view. Upon reflection, McLauchlan considered that this was the kind of cut that could have been made by the worn handle of a butcher's knife where movement in the handle could pinch the skin.

There was one other piece of fresh evidence on the voir dire. Awrey asked Sears whether he had ever been in danger, and Sears replied, "[The police] would not like to beat me up," implying that they would if they had to.[13] It was the kind of statement bound to make James Clark cringe. An assertion this important should have been made right at the outset; it should have been the bedrock of a vigorous defense that the confession was founded on threats. To raise it almost casually in cross-examination was simply not convincing, and it cast further doubt on the young man's credibility.

Dr. Markkanen took the stand and recounted Sears's condition after his fainting spell. Once again, Urquhart inserted himself into the process with a peculiar set of questions. Instead of asking the doctor about the incident in the cells, Urquhart questioned him on his knowledge of homosexuals. The doctor agreed that it was true that "perverts" were emotionally unstable and therefore susceptible to pressure from those in authority:

Q. I am not saying that the accused is a man of that sort, but supposing he is a man of that sort, because he made the statement there apparently as the officers say . . . assuming that he is that type, is that type more pliable, and less qualified to stand up to questioning than an ordinary man who does not do that sort of thing?

A. I do not think there is anything general that you can say about that, sir as far as I know.[14]

The question was far more revealing than the answer. The judge was developing (or had already developed) an image of Ronald Sears as one of "that sort," one of those deviants who loitered about public lavatories. Urquhart had prosecuted many of these types for gross indecency over the years, and he believed that in addition to their sexual depravities they differed from other men in that they were weak and subject to domination. It was a stereotypical image that would color the remainder of the proceedings.

Late in the afternoon of May 7, Urquhart gave his ruling on the admissibility of the confession. Sears's suggestion that he had been threatened was judged patently untrue and summarily rejected. In a revealing comment, the judge found Gelencser's story entirely credible. "I am certain," he said, "that Gelencser was horrified at the suggestion that was made by his assailant." Perhaps if he had known a bit more about Joseph Gelencser, he would not have been so certain. In any case, if Gelencser was deemed a normal man, then someone else in the narrative had to be a deviant, which left only Sears. On that issue, Urquhart trusted his own keen perception of human motivations. "I have observed the accused very closely," he said, "particularly during the evidence of Gelencser, and have noticed that in those parts where he referred to sexual proposition, the accused had on his face what I might well call a very foolish smile." This detail meant a great deal to the trial judge, for, "having sized him up, I would say that, in my opinion, for certain reasons which I do not want to make public at the moment, he is not a man of fortitude. In my opinion, he would be like putty in the hands of the officers, and most susceptible to suggestion."[15]

While he had reached the same conclusion as Dalton Wells—that the police had not used threats or promises to extract the confession—Urquhart ruled that the confession should still be excluded on the basis that the declarant was a vulnerable individual. The prolonged questioning, the officers' use of notes that implied that they had information on the crimes, and above all, Sears's unusual emotional state made the statement unreliable. "I am forced rather reluctantly," the judge concluded, "by the nature of the evidence, to reject the statements." It seemed a novel result, for ever since the interrogation of the unfortunate Private Ibrahim, confessions had been assessed by how the prisoner had been treated by the authorities, not on the prisoner's particular personality. Urquhart's ruling took the evaluation of admissibility in a very new direction, one that required a subjective consideration of how the accused had felt. Urquhart had concluded that the accused was lacking in fortitude, that his statements to the police were not to be relied upon, and that the confession was therefore valueless.

The confession was out, and the jury would therefore never hear Sears's description of Gelencser as a desperate older man craving sex from another male who was barely older than a boy. Moments after making this ruling, Urquhart called a recess and summoned both lawyers to the bench. His comments to them were recorded in a note attached to the proceedings: "In his opinion the accused was a sexual pervert and probably a homosexual. In his five years as a Crown Attorney he had come across many such, and the accused presented many evidences which led him to the above conclusion."[16]

It was a remarkable assertion for a judge to make in the middle of a trial. First, it revealed that he believed he possessed some special sense borne of experience that enabled him to detect homosexuals. Some evidence—it was never disclosed which, exactly—had set off alarms and led Urquhart to conclude that Ronald Sears was sexually exotic and different from other men. Now, whenever Urquhart cast a glance at the prisoner's dock, there would be no doubt in his mind that the accused was guilty of being a deviant and likely a vicious criminal as well. There is no record of any comment by either lawyer to the judge's extraordinary pronouncement. There was little James Clark could do but continue with the defense.

The Sears trial entered its final phase on May 8, 1947, exactly two years after the end of the war in Europe. Once again, the proceedings had been remarkably efficient. Aside from the sanity hearing and the voir dire, the Crown's case had been presented in a day. The defense would take far less time than that. For the first time, Florence Sears took the stand. In addition to whatever evidence she would bring to the case, her presence was an added bonus for the defense. The jurors would see that the young man in the dock was not a weird loner but a much-loved son. That Florence's testimony would be heavily weighted in her son's favor was never in doubt. She stood in the witness stand dressed in a dark gray suit and gave her answers calmly, as her son "sat in the prisoner's dock a few feet away with his eyes avoiding hers."[17] According to Mrs. Sears, after Mahoney had shown the knife to Dorothy and then left the Sears home, Dorothy had turned to Florence and said, "Well, Mrs. Sears, I am not sure that was the knife or not that was found." Awrey did not cross-examine her.

Clark then called Ronald Sears. His entire direct examination proceeded as follows:

> Q. Mr. Sears, you have heard Gelencser say that he picked you out in a line-up as the person who stabbed him. Is that correct?
>
> A. Yes, sir.
>
> Q. Did you stab him?
>
> A. No sir, I did not.
>
> Q. Did you ever see him in your life before until you—
>
> A. I never did.

There was no need to say any more. It was essential in these circumstances for Clark to put his client in the stand to deny the charge. But to go into details with a witness as mercurial as Ronald Sears was to invite disaster.

In cross-examination, Awrey took Sears over his story of seeing a horror film at the Palace Theatre and then walking home along London Street. He had chosen this route rather than the riverfront, "since I learned about the slashings." As to when he had walked home, the answers seemed to vary from 11 o'clock to 11:30 to midnight. Sears was constantly averting his eyes, and Awrey had to ask him to look at him when he answered questions. As usual, Urquhart took over the cross-examination and asked a series of questions as to how Sears had arrived home. In response to one question, Sears blurted out that he had met a friend "Martin" along the way and stopped to talk with him for a few minutes. This was yet another startling revelation. If this was true, it meant that Sears had an alibi, for he could not have been chatting with Martin at the same time he was escorting Gelencser to their rendezvous at the riverbank. Urquhart was confused and asked why the defense had not raised this alibi earlier. There was no explanation forthcoming, most likely because James Clark heard this story at the same time as everyone else in the courtroom. There would be nothing further on this point, and no one would ever know who this mysterious Martin was, if he existed at all.

The defense had taken barely more than an hour to rest its case. Since Sears had testified, Clark would give the first summation. He had already laid a firm foundation for acquittal in his cross-examination of Gelencser and especially with the information gleaned from the cab driver, Lauzon. But the jury may not have appreciated the significance of that information, and the closing address would be his opportunity to weave these answers into a coherent whole. The presentation of an effective closing argument has been compared to the painting of a picture: "By properly assembling the evidence, by arranging it in the most effective order, by appropriate emphasis, the skilful lawyer can paint a meaningful picture in words."[18] G. Arthur Martin, one of the most skilled practitioners of this art, felt that while the jury address should be heartfelt, it should also be an appeal to reason. James Clark had invested a great deal of emotion in this case, and in addition to logic, his summation would be filled with fire and intensity.

He began by telling the jurors that he had no doubt that a grave crime had been committed and that crime had been committed right before their eyes in the courtroom by the Crown's principal witness Joseph Gelencser. Here was a man who "swore he knew nothing of the slasher case. He also swore that his doctor forbade him to read the papers. The doctor later denied it." Clark maintained that Gelencser was an unashamed perjurer who used the newspaper reports to assist him in identifying Sears. As for his story of walking along the riverfront at night for the good of his health, "He is a married man and he walks the slashing area." It was as close as Clark could come to insinuating that it was Gelencser who was on the prowl for sex that night.

Gelencser's initial description of the attacker contrasted with the appearance of the accused. While he had lied in the courtroom, Gelencser had told the truth to the cabbie when he said that he had not seen his attacker. The cab driver was an independent witness with no reason to lie, and his account of the event completely contradicted Gelencser's. The cabbie distinctly remembered Gelencser saying that he had not seen his assailant, "Then when he gets in court he cooks up an entirely different story." Pausing for effect, Clark burst out "Lying ... perjurer! I say gentlemen."[19]

Clark also asked the jurors to accept Sgt. Mahoney's comments on the police lineup. While Mahoney had endured a verbal drubbing during the Price murder trial, Clark now told the jurors that the sergeant was a "most reliable officer whose word is uncontested" and who had testified that Mannie and Voligny, both men who had seen the Slasher face-to-face, had stated that Ronald Sears was not the man. But Gelencser, with a little help from the newspaper, had made that identification. Lastly, Clark picked up the butcher knife and flashed it before the face of the jurors. "There is no evidence," he solemnly told them, "that this boy ever saw this knife or ever had it in his hands." The evidence against him was circumstantial, and in that case, the evidence had to be absolutely consistent with guilt to warrant a conviction.

However passionate and heartfelt Clark's plea may have been, how effective was it? Accusing a Crown witness of perjury was serious business, and Clark had little to actually substantiate his accusation. One defense lawyer who would later figure in the Sears case, Arthur Maloney, advised young lawyers that "[jurors] find it much less difficult to accept a submission that the witness was guilty of an honest mistake or of carelessness. I am always reluctant to brand a witness as a perjurer." Clark had shown no such reluctance. Again, he had made a tactical decision, and his client's fate rested on the wisdom of that choice.[20]

Awrey went through the Crown's evidence in less than half an hour. The defense had made much of the cabbie's testimony, but Awrey observed that Gelencser was not under oath at that time. He then proceeded to make an unusual suggestion to the jurors: "But supposing, just for a moment, that he was down there for some purpose other than he says. In such case he might well have told the cabbie the truth about being stabbed, but concealed the other reasons on the matter." Awrey had deliberately raised the unspoken issue of the homosexual encounter again, the same issue he had tried to get Detective McLauchlan to comment on. It was certainly a matter of importance to the judge, and even though the jurors had not heard Justice Urquhart's condemnation of the accused as a deviant, it was one matter that Awrey felt should be brought into the open. Ironically, the prosecutor was prepared to concede that it might have been Gelencser who had gone down to the riverfront in order to solicit male sex. It is even possible that Awrey, unlike Clark, had access to the second police investigative file, and thus it was possible that he knew all about Gelencser's secret life.

If the Crown Attorney was the wiser, he was apparently prepared to make an ethical compromise and keep this knowledge to himself, perhaps as a way of keeping a man he considered a serial killer off of the streets. In any case, the most Awrey would do was suggest to the jurors that it was possible Gelencser had lied about his reasons for going to the river. Even so, he argued, the victim's testimony about being stabbed and his identification of Sears as the assailant was true. Awrey's easily overlooked comment to the jury was the sole attempt to peel away the layers of unreality that obscured these proceedings and expose the real world that lay beneath. Otherwise, the case against Ronald Sears had been thoroughly "heterosexualized" to the extent that Gelencser was deemed normal, and it was Sears, the accused Slasher, who was the deviant.[21]

Awrey quickly went through the remainder of the prosecution's case. If the cab driver had been a good witness for the defense, Dorothy Sears had filled this role for the Crown. Here was a young woman, Awrey reminded the jury, who was obviously unwilling to testify against her own brother-in-law but did so in order that the truth should come out. She was firmly convinced that the butcher knife she had seen in her kitchen drawer was the same one Gelencser had pulled from his back. There was also the cut on Sears's hand that might have been caused by this knife.

"I never ask a jury to convict any man," Awrey concluded rather equivocally. "My business is to help you come to a proper conclusion." Perhaps his lack of enthusiasm had something to do with the fact that his main witness, Gelencser, was hiding something and had lied during part of his testimony. As for his identification of Sears during the lineup, it may also have been tainted. The butcher knife might have been in the Sears's kitchen drawer, but no one had ever seen Ronald with it. As for the small cut on Sears's hand, if it had existed at all, many things could have caused it. In sharing his final comments with the jury, Awrey must have appreciated the fact that his case was paper-thin. He could not have had much confidence that a verdict of guilty would be forthcoming.

While it is the jury's function to determine the facts in a case, a major influence on this process is the final instruction they receive from the trial judge. After a quarter of a century of advocacy in criminal trials, Urquhart was well aware of his obligations to lay out the issues for the jury. He suggested that they recall the Sherlock Holmes stories where that great, fictional detective had been able to determine a man's height and whether or not he had a game leg by studying cigar ashes on a carpet. The jurors should apply these Holmesian techniques to this case and make deductions based on what facts they knew to arrive at a conclusion. In the absence of forensic evidence of any kind, such as fingerprints or blood types, there was little else they could do but look at the few exhibits before them and evaluate the witnesses they had heard. On that point, Urquhart was critical of the Crown's main witness, for "on a good many occasions he was inclined to argue his point rather than giving the straight Yes or No." Urquhart continued, saying that "practically the whole case depends on your opinion of Gelencser, your opinion of his evidence, what manner of man he was, how he impressed you." The jurors would have to draw their conclusions, not from scientifically proven facts, but from inferences, from the winks and nods of the characters involved.

Throughout his summation, Urquhart attempted to toe the line between informing the jurors of the questions they would have to answer and suggesting the answers to them himself. As for the small cut on Ronald's hand, he asked, "Does that strengthen the evidence in any way?" On the cab driver's evidence, the judge seemed to lean in favor of the Crown when he told the jurors that after all, Gelencser was excited and the cabbie may have misunderstood his words. Then the judge reminded the jurors of the two other victims who had not picked out Sears in the lineup. It was Urquhart's last reference that drew an objection from the Crown that the summation was too partial to the defense.

Now the case was left with the one group that had been silent throughout these proceedings. Little is known of this jury other than that they were all men, mostly farmers, from Windsor or Essex County. They were about to embark on a task none of them had ever done before or likely would ever do again: in the confining atmosphere of the Sandwich Courthouse, they were to evaluate evidence against a fellow citizen that could send him to prison for the rest of his life. None of them had been trained in how to evaluate conflicting evidence, but it is something ordinary people do all the time—that is, draw inferences from facts and use common sense to arrive at a conclusion. The jurors in this case were undoubtedly drawing conclusions about Ronald Sears himself. Aside from the testimony of witnesses and the exhibits, the jury had observed an evasive, diffident young man who seemed to have a good deal to hide. Even before the trial, they had been bombarded with publicity about Sears's identity as the Slasher and his confession to the murder of Sgt. Price. In the words of his own confession, he was the monster who had lured men to secluded areas and savagely butchered them. However much the judge and the lawyers told them to put that publicity from their minds, it was natural that it would play a part in their deliberations. In spite of any good intentions the jurors may have had, and no matter how much they took to heart the admonition that they were the "conscience of the country," it was not only possible but likely that their minds were heavily weighted against the accused before the trial even began.[22]

Given the many issues to be sorted out, it was not surprising that the jury deliberations were prolonged. At 1:30 on the afternoon of May 8, the jurors were sequestered to consider their decision. By eight o'clock that night, they had a verdict. Again Ronald Sears stood to face a jury, and again, the decision was guilty as charged. Upon hearing the verdict, one of the Sears family fainted and had to be carried from the courtroom. When the hubbub in the courtroom died down, Urquhart thanked the jurors and told them, "I think the verdict is quite justified in the evidence."

It was a hard result for James Clark. Given the weakness of the Crown's case, he must have been hoping for or even anticipating an acquittal. Urquhart asked him if he wanted time to prepare submissions on the sentence. Clark brushed the offer aside and said that he was ready to proceed. Clark told the Court that Sears came from a decent family and that he had brothers who had served overseas. He had never been in trouble with the law before, and Clark suggested that a reformatory term of two years would be sufficient. Awrey replied that given the severity of the attack and that it had almost killed the intended victim, a term of not less than ten years was appropriate. Urquhart responded, "This is the very lowest I could think of."

During these submissions, Clark was hard-pressed to conceal his rage. At one point, he blurted out that the conviction was a "miscarriage of justice." Urquhart calmly replied that he thought the jury was correct and that Sears had deliberately, without provocation, set out to kill a man. The judge's comments only further aroused Clark, who insisted that the conviction was a travesty. "How the jury could arrive at this verdict," he said, "I do not know." One thing he did know was that before his trial in the courtroom ever began, Ronald Sears had been tried and convicted in the pages of the *Star*. "This case is a newspaper conviction," he fumed.[23]

Then, in a peculiar submission, Clark asked the judge to consider that it was really Gelencser who had caused these unfortunate events. It was young men such as Sears who were preyed upon by "moral perverts apparently trying to pervert the decent young boys in this community." Urquhart interrupted Clark and reminded him that the jury had found that it was Sears who had made the improper suggestion to Gelencser. The only evidence to the contrary was Sears's statement to the police that it was Gelencser who had initiated the homosexual encounter. Yet Clark had fought to exclude this statement. Now Urquhart reminded him, "You had the privilege of using it." Urquhart's comment was like rubbing salt in the wound. Perhaps Clark had made a tactical error by challenging the confession. If he had made a mistake, he asked the Court not to punish his client for his error.

Ronald Sears was ordered to stand and receive his sentence. Urquhart told him that the maximum sentence for his offense was life in prison. Ultimately, the charge of attempted murder had arisen because of Sears's sexual proposition of Gelencser, "the cause of all this trouble." Urquhart said, "I wish there was some place I could send you . . . where you could be treated, and where, if possible, you could be cured." That is, it was Sears's homosexuality that was the root of the problem, and if his homosexuality could be cured, he might be returned to society. The inevitable end result of reasoning like Urquhart's is that "having manufactured a homosexual, the homosexual can be fit into the theory of the case and found culpable. But homosexual culpability is of a special kind. It flows from the deviant character of the homosexual body itself and sets that body apart from civilized society."[24]

At that point, the solemn process of sentencing was interrupted by an unusual outburst. Sears called out from the prisoner's dock: "Your Honour, if I was given a chance, I would be all right, I am normal all right."

"I am not sure of that" Urquart responded. This briefest of outbursts was cut short by the firm hand of a policeman on Sears's shoulder. Sears's loss of control had revealed some of his innermost feelings. While he did not outwardly object to the conviction or the looming prospect of a lengthy prison sentence, what did profoundly bother him was Urquhart's publicly labeling him a homosexual. As he had confided to Dorothy in the privacy of his room, it was gay men who were the menace, and someone had to do something about them. To associate him with the evil that he was trying to eradicate was the worst possible insult.

However, Urquhart's mind was made up. "I think your trouble lies in sex," he told Sears. "I think it my duty to the community if the sentence was not a fairly long one."

Ronald Sears was sentenced to twelve years in Kingston Penitentiary, two years more than the Crown Attorney had requested.

13

THE MARKETPLACE OF FEAR

Another appeal was inevitable.

While the record was being prepared, the question arose as to whether or not Sears should be temporarily released on bail. Urquhart reported to the chief justice on the trial and advised him, "If I am right in my estimate of the accused and in my experience as a Crown Attorney, I have seen a good deal of men of that sort, I am of the opinion that the public would be in danger if bail was granted."[1] Urquhart even offered advice to the Crown law officer who would argue the appeal. Undoubtedly there was a good deal of ego at stake when one of Urquhart's decisions was being challenged, but to go to the extent of "assisting" the prosecuting officer seemed well beyond any propriety. His "Dear Bill" letter to the head of criminal enforcement William Common, who had replaced C. R. Magone at the attorney general's department, was like a collegial note from one prosecutor to another. Urquhart told Common that the jury charge had been taken from a case tried by Chief Justice Rose in 1937, and since then, judges in hundreds of cases had used similar wording.

On the issue of whether or not he had misdirected the jury on the question of reasonable doubt, Urquhart informed Common that Clark was an experienced defense counsel and that he would have been quick to object had anything inappropriate occurred. Solicitously, he invited Common to drop in before the argument for some last-minute preparation. "Another thing," he added, "don't overlook Sears's remark to be found on practically the last page when I was in the act of sentencing him. It sounded to me, although it doesn't read that strongly, as though it was a confession of his guilt."[2] It appeared that the trial judge had a vested interest in insuring that a man of "that sort" was not freed and that his own actions were vindicated.

Urquhart was not the only one who wanted to make sure that this conviction did not slip away. E. C. Awrey offered to assist with and be present at the appeal. Common appreciated the additional help and confidentially advised Awrey that he had been speaking with Sears's lawyer, who had "expressed little confidence in the success of the application."[3] The Sears family would need formidable resources to oppose the combined forces of the judge, the local Crown Attorney and the attorney general's department. And this time, defense attorney G. Arthur Martin would not be present to work his magic, perhaps as a result of a scheduling problem or Martin's reluctance to act for the same accused twice. Once again, without recourse to legal aid, the Sears family was in the hands of the government and whomever they chose to appoint to defend Ronald. They chose Arthur Maloney, a junior lawyer of only four years standing. While Maloney would ultimately be considered a leading criminal lawyer, in 1947, he had little experience in the criminal appeal courts. In fact, he had struggled just to qualify for the bar, and before the justices of the Court of Appeal he did not carry anywhere near the gravitas of someone like Arthur Martin.[4]

The summer and fall passed as the parties waited for the trial transcript to be prepared. That summer, the second since the end of the war, should have been one of relief and renewal. Instead, the uncertainties of the postwar world caused widespread anxiety. Western countries faced a threatening Soviet presence in Eastern Europe, and civil wars raged in Greece and China. In the shadow of these conflicts lay the threat of atomic weapons. The world after Hiroshima and Nagasaki seemed at the mercy of forces it could barely understand, let alone control.

The summer of 1947 also saw a series of reports of unidentified flying objects in the United States and Canada. In July 1947—the same month as the first UFO sightings—FBI Director J. Edgar Hoover published an article in *American Magazine* titled "How Safe Is Your Daughter?" The headline was a quote from the article: "the nation's women and children will never be secure . . . so long as degenerates run wild." The cover photo showed three little girls fleeing from a menacing male hand. The Canadian press seemed to accept without question that a wave of sexual attacks against females was sweeping the nation. In July 1947, *Maclean's* magazine printed "The Truth About Sex Criminals," an article that detailed "the growing problem of sex criminality."[5]

Perhaps more so than in any other major city in Canada, the Windsor press was focused on the sex-crime panic and the alleged threat posed by deviants. In September 1947, it was reported that a seventeen-year-old girl had been assaulted on Pillette Road. During the war, such an incident might have been routinely noted in the police record, but now it became a major issue. The lead editorial in the *Star* reported other assaults against little girls and asked why "the protection of children against monsters" was not a prime objective of the law.[6]

And yet, this renewed hysteria bore no relationship to any statistical rise in attacks against women or children. The reality that Canada was not undergoing any wave of sex crimes (or UFO landings) would not hinder the press in exploiting the topic to the fullest. Ronald Sears's next appeal would be heard in a context in which magazines and newspapers were constantly stressing the danger posed by deviants like him.

Defense attorney Maloney fashioned his appeal along traditional lines. In his written submissions, he raised the points that Clark had stressed, that Gelencser's identification of Sears was questionable and that Gelencser was an untrustworthy witness. The basis of the defense was the identification of Sears as the perpetrator, for which only flimsy evidence existed. In fact, Urquhart had failed to advise the jurors just how flimsy the evidence was and how significantly it conflicted with the testimony of an independent witness. It was not enough, Maloney argued, for the trial judge to have directed the attention of the jury to any conflicts; he should have impressed upon them the danger of relying on such questionable proof. Maloney closed his written arguments with an explanation as to why these errors had been committed: "It is submitted that the error of the trial judge in this respect is attributable to a conclusion—to an unwarranted conclusion—not supported by any proper evidence and arrived at by him during the course of the trial and before any evidence for the defence had been heard that the accused was a sex pervert."[7]

Maloney's approach, while direct, seemed a dangerous gambit. It was one thing to blame the police for a heavy-handed interrogation but another thing entirely to accuse a justice of the Ontario Supreme Court of bias and partiality against an accused. It was a direct attack on the integrity of the judiciary and the fairness of the trial process and might have been considered a perilous, if not foolish, strategy.

On October 16, 1947, Arthur Maloney argued the appeal before a three-judge panel at Osgoode Hall. All three of the judges, Henderson, Roach and Hogg, had sat on the first Sears appeal, and they undoubtedly remembered the young man who had confessed to two murders and three other knife assaults. Maloney began by arguing that it was unprecedented to instruct a jury that they should use the same techniques employed by Sherlock Holmes to decide an actual case. Citing the fictional detective only encouraged the jurors to draw inferences and to guess instead of properly evaluating the evidence before them. The judges permitted Maloney to go through his arguments with few interruptions—a bad sign, for their silence indicated a certain disinterest, a desire to get the appeal over with.[8] When Maloney suggested that the identification evidence was flawed, Justice Henderson merely noted, "But surely that's for the jury." The Court of Appeal adjourned and advised that it would give its decision later in writing.

In the final result, released on December 10, 1947, the judges chose to sidestep the volatile issues of Urquhart's partiality and Sears's alleged homosexuality and instead restricted their inquiry to the safe, conventional topics of reasonable doubt and circumstantial evidence. The allegation that Urquhart had failed to adequately point out to the jury that the evidence against Sears was mostly circumstantial was easily dismissed. Ever since Hodge's case of 1838, it had been a principle of British law that whenever the prosecutor was relying solely on circumstantial evidence that the jurors should be warned that it was dangerous to convict on such limited proof. But in addition to such circumstantial evidence as the scratch on Sears's hand, the Crown had relied on the direct evidence of Gelencser's identification. Therefore, there was no need to warn the jury about Hodge's case.

A more troubling question was whether or not Urquhart had adequately explained the concept of reasonable doubt to the jurors. It was never an easy concept to put into words. Urquhart had defined it as "a substantial doubt ... such a doubt as would influence you in your daily affairs." Justice Roach felt that this description mischaracterized the concept. In daily affairs, people tend to govern themselves on probabilities. However, in determining the guilt of a fellow citizen, they must act on the moral certainty that that person is guilty. It is not enough merely to weigh the probabilities and consider the person guilty. In spite of this error, Roach still concluded that the jury charge was fair and the jurors understood that their duty was no ordinary one. On several occasions, Urquhart had reminded the jurors that if they had any doubt at all as to Sears's guilt that he should be acquitted. Taken on the whole, he concluded that the jurors properly understood the gravity of their task.

It was a clean, clinical decision that neatly avoided the real issues. It did not address the inescapable and biased publicity that had more than likely led to a prejudgment of the facts; it avoided any discussion of whether or not Sears had been condemned for his alleged homosexuality instead of his alleged actions. Only Justice Roach dared say anything at all about this issue, but only to agree with Justice Urquhart's interpretation of Sears's outburst during sentencing. Roach also believed that instead of insisting on his heterosexuality, Sears had admitted to his own deviancy and therefore deserved a longer sentence. As one scholar observes, the Court of Appeal "reads the accused's own words as a confession of not only his guilt but also of his pervert status. . . . Sears's guilt is apparent from the truth of his homosexuality which has been revealed by the police and the judicial process."[9] The people of Windsor seemed satisfied with this result, for the man they were convinced was the Slasher was locked up, and the hysteria could therefore end. Except for a retrospective half a century later, the *Star* would no longer mention the Slasher case.

However, senior government officials had not forgotten. The judicial problems raised by the Slasher case could not be locked away or ignored. In 1947, Progressive Conservative critic of the justice system John Diefenbaker questioned in the House of Commons why so many confessions were being rejected by Courts of Appeal. Perhaps, he suggested, the principles guiding police interrogations should be made uniform and predictable. He cited as an example the Evelyn Dick case in Hamilton and particularly "the Sears case in Windsor, where persons had been convicted of murder, however the convictions were later quashed as the police had failed to follow accepted standards." Only a few days before Diefenbaker offered these comments, the Ontario Court of Appeal had set aside the conviction of a man who had confessed to the murder of a nine-year-old girl. As a result of this case, a *Windsor Daily Star* editorial suggested that "before public faith in the wisdom of trial judges is destroyed, admissibility of evidence should be definitely chalked up on the blackboard for the guidance of all concerned." As Diefenbaker said, cases including "the Sears case in Windsor have pointed up the confused and highly unsatisfactory state of the law in this matter."[10]

Neither were the judges pleased with this situation. The Evelyn Dick murder trial, one of the most publicized affairs in the country, had focused attention on the law's inadequacies. While the beautiful Mrs. Dick was a prime suspect in her husband's death, there was little evidence against her. In order to hold her, the police had charged her with vagrancy and under this pretext questioned her repeatedly. During her confinement, she gave detectives seven statements, some of which had been preceded by a caution and some of which had not. It therefore came as no shock when her conviction was quashed by the Court of Appeal. Chief Justice McRuer concluded that even though there was a divergence of judicial opinion, "Such a matter is more for the Legislature than for the Judge."[11] Various committees, both federal and provincial, examined the issue and recommended changes to the *Criminal Code* to mandate a procedure for the questioning of suspects. However, no consensus emerged, and the topic remained one of judicial interpretation. In 1949, Justice Ivan Rand, the same judge who had resolved the Ford strike in Windsor in 1945, expressed the view that would prevail in Canadian law: The investigation of crime should not be put into a straightjacket of artificial rules. Rather, confessions should be evaluated on the facts of each situation and admitted or excluded on the basis of their degree of volition.[12]

If the law concerning confessions defied change, there was still substantial public pressure to deal with the "pervert" problem. The postwar sex-crime panic had focused attention on the dangers of the pervert—the homosexual, the rapist, and the child molester—the distinctions between the different types being less important than the fact that they were all a menace. Popular belief now dictated that the law should create a special category, not of offense, but of deviant offender, with the purpose of separating these deviants from normal society. However, instead of simply imprisoning them, there was a possibility that these individuals could be treated and cured. In the atomic age, it seemed that science could do anything, so why not cure the sex criminal? Even at the end of the Sears trial, as Urquhart had levied his stern punishment, he had wished "that there were some place that I could send you ... where you could be treated, and where, if possible, you could be cured." In a similar sympathetic vein, *Star* columnist W. L. Clark wrote about Sears, "If a man with insane criminal tendencies is sent to prison what provision is there to make sure he will not be just as insane, just as dangerous when released?"[13] Medical texts of the time noted that so long as a homosexual was aware of his defects that he might be cured.[14] In fact, a letter from one such "reformed" gay man appeared in the *Star* in September 1947. He wrote that there was hope for homosexuals—"I know, because I was once one of them"—and described how he had been arrested in Detroit for gross indecency. "Thanks to a good talking by a detective-lieutenant of the Detroit Police Force," he wrote, "I was straightened out in time" and resolved to devote himself to rescuing others. He signed his letter "Cured."

Citizens' groups in Edmonton and Calgary sent urgent petitions to Justice Minister J. L. Ilsley begging the government to consider some method of treating and curing sex criminals. At the height of the 1946 panic in Calgary caused by the murder of Donnie Goss, the *Calgary Herald* pronounced that, "Sex Perverts are, in reality, mentally unbalanced. Men with this mental quirk are not responsible for their condition."[15] In October 1947, J. Alex Edmison, the president of the Canadian Penal Association, spoke in Toronto on the urgent need to control sex offenders. Significantly, he lumped homosexuals together with child molesters and thought it shortsighted that homosexuals convicted of indecent acts were given only thirty-day sentences. After citing several horrific cases across Canada, he observed, "The situation in Windsor was admittedly serious ... it has been given a lot of publicity since the Sears case."[16]

By the summer of 1948, the liberal government of Mackenzie King was prepared to act. The previous year, it had created the first category of criminal personality, the "habitual offender." Now, it was ready to define an even more specific type of objectionable individual, the "criminal sexual psychopath." Such a designation already existed in the laws of several American states, and there was enormous pressure for a similar provision to be put into the *Criminal Code*. John Diefenbaker observed, "This provision represents the first action on the part of the parliament of Canada to meet a type of offence that creates fear in the minds of mothers and fathers."[17] In defiance of available statistics, a Calgary member abhorred "the great increase in crimes of this kind, and by the brutality and bestiality of them."[18]

A series of moral panics across Canada from Vancouver to Montreal had created a consensus that persons convicted of a series of rapes or sexual assaults of a child should face life imprisonment. No consideration was given to the reality that the highly publicized incidents upon which the panic was based were actually the work of, at most, five men. The law reform was based on fear rather than reality and grounded in the premise, as it appeared in the *Star* headline, "Perverts a Menace."[19]

Considering the political climate, it was unsurprising that Ronald Sears remained in the Sandwich Jail until February 1948 pending the disposition of the remaining charges. That month, the outstanding charges were stayed, so that, as Awrey phrased it, "the records may be completed and Sears sent on his way to Kingston."[20] In the years to come, those individuals allowed to return to or remain in mainstream society, such as Alexander Voligny and Joseph Gelencser, would face the choice of either conforming or becoming even more discreet in their conduct.

14

THE COST OF PANIC

As the Sears appeal was being argued in Toronto, the film *Crossfire* was playing in Canadian theaters. This gritty story of a few American GIs who get drunk and murder a Jewish civilian was seen as a parable about anti-Semitism. However, in its original version, Richard Brooks's novel *The Brick Foxhole* (1945), the victim was homosexual.[1] Nevertheless, in 1947, no film could portray homophobic violence, or for that matter, homosexuality in any context. Indeed, homosexuality was so repulsive, a Windsor lawyer of the period observed, that "it was never mentioned . . . like bestiality."[2] After all, most people in respectable society would never meet an openly gay person, which made it easy to pretend homosexuality did not exist. The Slasher debacle, with its accounts of homosexual meeting places and male-male sexual relationships, brought a subject to the surface that most Windsorites would rather have kept repressed.

The legacy of the Slasher hysteria of 1945 and '46 was that gay men in Windsor became invisible, forced underground by the intensity of the official repugnance toward their lifestyle. Alexander Voligny and men like him knew now that their conduct was not only socially unacceptable but also carried harsh penal consequences. Voligny's case was a prime example of what could happen to any man who attempted to have consensual sex with another man. After he finished his prison term, Voligny found it impossible to return to Windsor. Ironically, he joined a Roman Catholic religious order. However, he left after a few years and moved to St. Catharines, where he finally conformed to the mainstream and married. He had no children and died in 1975.[3] His brother permitted no discussion of Alexander's past among family members. The revelation that a male member of a devoutly Catholic family had solicited sex from other men was supremely disgraceful and had to be suppressed by any means.

During the second wave of panic in 1946, gays in Windsor, who were already well aware of the consequences of being caught, suddenly had to consider as well the very real possibility of being murdered as they sought companionship. That the Slasher turned out to be a young man from a good family who had been sexually abused when he was nine years old significantly added to the press's portrayal of all homosexuals as dangerous to children. It was the element of child molestation, of the stealing of a child's innocent self, that was seized upon by the press to highlight the pervert menace. It was widely accepted at the time that once contaminated, a victim would pass on homosexual practices to others.[4] To many people in Windsor and beyond, Sears's youthful contamination justified his murderous crusade. When perverts rather than vagrants became the prime target of the police, civic-minded, quasi-vigilante groups closed the few gay gathering places that had existed in Windsor.

There is an ebb and flow to moral panics, and once Sears was in custody, Windsor quickly got over the Slasher scare. By 1947, few people even bothered to attend the trials. There seemed to be little ongoing concern about homosexuals or the threat they posed. And yet, the panics had served their purpose. As Stanley Cohen observed, even after widespread hysteria has subsided, "The deviant or group of deviants is segregated or isolated and this operates to alienate them from conventional society. They perceive themselves as more deviant, group themselves with others in a similar situation."[5] Being a gay man in Windsor after the panic meant not only the danger of arrest and prosecution but an even deeper social shame than had existed previously. "In the twentieth century pecking order," John Loughery noted, "nothing was lower than a self-confessed faggot."[6] A gay man living in Windsor felt that "right up to the '50s [homosexuality] was looked upon as a very taboo thing." It is therefore not surprising that charges of overt homosexual conduct or "gross indecency" declined in Windsor after the Slasher panic. These charges had averaged five or more during the war years. However, for 1947 and 1948, there were a miniscule two charges each year.[7]

To be gay and visible was to invite public vilification, a possible jail term, or a violent assault. For many gay men, their bachelorhood automatically made them suspect, and some sought marriage as a useful, if hypocritical, arrangement. After the war, the pressure to marry and conform intensified, for the consequences of being found out as queer had intensified as well. It was a sign of normalcy that a man settle down with a wife. Anyone who did not was classified as a "vocational drifter" or possibly worse.[8]

Another option open to homosexuals in Windsor was to seek anonymity in a larger setting. After his discharge from the Air Force, a local gay left the city and moved to Toronto, where he found that "a lot of [gay men] came from smaller communities. They felt that in Toronto they could let their hair down, which they did." Within a larger community of gay men, "you seemed to get more of the real gay types real flamboyant. . . . They seem to have a lot of nellie bars."[9] For those who stayed in Windsor, the existence of a larger gay community a few minutes away in Detroit made it possible for Windsor homosexuals to live conventional lives on their side of the border. It also resulted in a paradoxical cross-border migration of gay Canadians going to Detroit for sex, while Americans in search of illicit heterosexual relations came to Windsor.

Moral panics would continue to flare up throughout the late 1940s. A small number of brutal crimes could always be widely reported and give the impression that there was a widespread problem.[10] In 1949, a series of rapes in Cleveland gave that city "a hair trigger psychology." Sensational journalist Howard Whitman reported that in the late 1940s, Detroit "was plagued by the homosexual problem . . . he infests the most beautiful parks. Police know that such men are dangerous—that when trapped they may kill." On his travels with Detroit Police Commissioner Harry S. Toy, Whitman was told that every sixth call on the police network was a "sex call." At Belle Isle Park and Palmer Park Woods, the police had to prune the shrubbery around the women's rooms "to keep sex offenders from hiding in the bushes," Toy declared. To Whitman, men who committed sexual acts against girls were pedophiles while those who committed similar acts on boys were homosexuals.[11]

Fear of Detroit homosexuals was seemingly borne out in 1949, when a young man with homosexual proclivities and a penchant for horror movies murdered a six-year-old.[12] Ten years after the Windsor Slasher, Boise, Idaho, would be gripped by a similar witch-hunt when it was alleged that members of an underground of prominent men were preying on teenage boys. "Crush the Monster," screamed a local headline, and the public encouraged the authorities to eradicate all homosexuals. In the end, it turned out that there was no ring of homosexuals trying to contaminate local youth. A panic fed by the press and led by local officials had created an artificial concern that had no basis in fact.

It has been suggested that what happened in Boise was a panic manipulated by an elite to its own ends.[13] This theory suggests that an element of organization and control might exist during a panic. However, no such coherent purpose seemed apparent in Windsor. Without doubt, the hysteria was fed by a compliant municipal government and a press that avidly over-reported events. The *Star* even went so far as to report rumors of additional Slasher killings that had never occurred. They gave extensive coverage to the inflammatory writings on washroom walls, even though it was clear they were the work of cranks. To a certain extent, the press purposely exaggerates events to stimulate public interest and boost circulation.[14] And yet, the Slasher threat was real, men did die, and the public was genuinely aroused. None of these events was necessarily directed by some superior force to its own ends; rather, it happened with some degree of spontaneity and reflected widespread and preexisting feelings that homosexuals presented a material danger.

Troubled times seem to fuel such panics.[15] Fear over the destructive power of the atom bomb, the hostile intentions of the Soviet Union, and the internal threat of espionage made the late 1940s and early 1950s an uneasy era.[16] Easy solutions included concentrating public hostility on an agreed-upon target, a scapegoat. By participating in panics, members of mainstream society acted out their response to powerlessness. Scapegoating homosexuals was a way to take control, to redraw societal boundaries by saying, "This conduct is intolerable."

Motivated by the panic, the actions of Windsor police officers in the Slasher case had hardly been commendable at any point in the process. The initial arrest of scores of innocent men had revealed a heavy-handed and misguided investigation. The police failure month after month to collect any evidence or arrest any credible suspects had been an ongoing embarrassment. Then their questionable interrogation of Ronald Sears had resulted in the dismissal of a murder charge. Being publicly humiliated by the Court of Appeal for their alleged brutish conduct only added to the department's frustrations. However, the ultimate downfall of Windsor's senior law enforcement officers, barely two years after the Sears case was finally closed, was their toleration of the vice trade.

If anything, Windsor's reputation as an open city had gotten worse during the late 1940s. Even Detroit authorities had begun to complain that Windsor was the source for illegal racetrack wire services. Everything came to a head on January 1, 1950, when the Ontario Provincial Police raided the Howard Avenue operations of the "King of Bootleggers" Joe Assef. There, the OPP discovered a sophisticated business setup that supplied thousands of dollars' worth of illegal alcohol to locations across the city. Among the items seized were accounts that showed Windsor police constables as the recipients of gifts. Magistrate Arthur Hanrahan, the same official who had presided over Sears's preliminary inquiry, gave Assef the maximum sentence and in passing castigated Windsor police for laxness and corruption.[17] An illegal trade of this magnitude could only have been carried on with their tacit approval. When an internal investigation of the Windsor department by the police commission accomplished nothing, the province stepped in.[18] Attorney General Dana Porter fired most of the police commissioners, including Chief Renaud, Deputy Chief Neale, and even Crown Attorney E. C. Awrey. Awrey, who had done everything he could to get a multiple killer convicted and off the streets, found his career as a prosecutor summarily cut short in 1950.

The new police chief, Carl Farrow, was an OPP Inspector, and his deputy was the former detective-sergeant John Mahoney. Their mandate was to shut down vice, and their chosen instrument was Inspector John Burns. As head of the Morality Division (later Special Investigations) Burns would vigorously go after the bordellos and blind pigs. While vice would never be completely rooted out, turning a blind eye to it became a thing of the past. To the dismay of some of its citizens and many American visitors, Windsor ceased to be an open city.

Perhaps the Windsor police force of the 1940s was being held to an impossible standard, for the Slasher case presented a dilemma that no police department of the time could have handled. A serial killer at work in a major Canadian city was a bizarre, unprecedented phenomenon in 1945. That the killer was targeting homosexuals made this case especially challenging to Windsor detectives unfamiliar with the subculture. It was not until the late twentieth century that modern investigative techniques such as those used by the FBI's Behavioral Science Unit brought profiling techniques to bear on identifying serial killers. Modern criminal investigation methodically reviews all known facts, shares data with other police forces, and develops a criminal profile and an investigation based on that profile that narrows the list of likely suspects.[19] Such techniques enable police to avoid such methods as mass roundups. But in 1945, a young man like Ronald Sears was an unknown quantity to the Windsor police, and in his early attacks, he left few clues. Even the most sophisticated profiling would not likely have detected him until the attacks in 1946.

Fortunately, serial killers are a rare breed, and Canadian police would not often have to confront this problem. But when it did occur, finding the killer continued to be a frustrating ordeal. In September 1956, two Toronto boys were murdered within the span of nine days. Three weeks later, another boy was murdered. It was a tough assignment for Toronto police, and one innocent suspect was charged before seventeen-year-old Peter Woodcock was apprehended. To outward appearances, Woodcock appeared to be a normal, law-abiding young man, but he was leading a secret second life as a killer. He was found not guilty by reason of insanity and sent to a mental institution. In 1990, he was paroled and within hours had murdered again.

In the early 1990s, prostitutes began to go missing from Vancouver streets. An RCMP task force finally made a link between the local disappearances and the bodies of sex trade workers found near Mission, British Columbia. Despite the number of victims, the police seemed unable to make any headway in their investigation. As no one on the RCMP task force had any experience hunting serial killers, the officers had to travel to Washington State to consult with American investigators. As in the Sears case, it took one fortuitous event to result in an arrest. When police went to the farm of Robert Pickton in February 2002 with a search warrant looking for firearms, they found evidence of the remains of several of the missing women.[20]

In many respects, Pickton's case resembles that of Ronald Sears. Both of them were unassuming individuals with no record of violence, and this mask of normalcy enabled them to stalk and kill over an extended period. Moreover, both men's victims came from a despised and vulnerable group whose lives were not valued by mainstream culture. However, in stark contrast to the Sears case, Robert Pickton did not have to stand trial until January 2007, almost five years after his arrest. By the late twentieth century, the speed of justice in Canada had slowed to a glacial pace, as criminal trials took years to prepare, and *Charter of Rights* motions and appeals promised to extend the proceedings over several months, if not years.[21]

In 1948, Ronald Sears's first year in prison, a remarkable assault on the sexual norms of the postwar world was published. Alfred Kinsey's study of sexual behavior among thousands of white Americans disputed the notion that the vast majority of people only engaged in heterosexual intercourse. Kinsey's finding that homosexual activity and oral eroticism were more widespread than previously thought challenged conventional ideas of what was normal. The report even suggested that between 4 and 10 percent of men were exclusively homosexual and that 37 percent of the male population had had a homosexual experience at some time in their lives. The report generated considerable moral outrage. A number of people "simply refused to believe these statistics."[22]

None of these controversies penetrated Ronald Sears's cell walls. There is no record of what psychiatric treatment, if any, he received after 1948. While Dr. Tennant remained solidly convinced of Sears's sanity, few shared his opinion. Even as Sears was being taken to Kingston Penitentiary, the governor of the Essex County Jail, John Robinson, was worried that his condition was deteriorating. "After [Sears's] last appeal failed," Robinson said, "he became silent and brooding. He was getting worse daily and said very little to anyone."[23] When Sears had been in Kingston Penitentiary barely a month, the commissioner of penitentiaries expressed his grave misgivings to the attorney general's department. In his view, this young man should have been sent for psychiatric treatment instead of to a penal institution.[24] The prison did not have any psychiatric facilities, and the commissioner was clearly uncomfortable keeping him in the cellblock. On July 2, 1948, Sears was transferred to the Ontario Hospital at Penetanguishene, where he was diagnosed as schizophrenic. He had served only five months in prison and would never return there. In December 1948, he was diagnosed with pulmonary tuberculosis and was transferred to the chest division of the Woodstock hospital.

There remained persistent questions as to Sears's guilt. The Sears family never accepted the police version of events, and some of them continued to consider Ronald's confession to be simply another manifestation of his bizarre sense of humor. Without doubt, the validity of his final trial before Urquhart could be challenged on a variety of grounds, including the lack of any substantial evidence, the likely perjury of the main Crown witness, the withholding of key evidence from the defense, and lastly, the vigorous pretrial publicity that practically preordained the outcome. Perhaps worst of all was the trial judge's early conclusion that Sears was a deviant. From there, it was only a short step to finding Sears guilty of a crime.

Despite the inadequacies of the trial, the question remains of actual guilt versus legal guilt. The reality was that Sears seems to have freely confessed, without any police pressure, to the murder of two men and the attempted murder of three others. On the day after this confession, he had not recanted his words but repeated them and willingly gone with the police to walk over the attack sites and recount in detail how he had carried out the knifings. These were no spur-of-the-moment statements or deluded ramblings. Whatever the Court of Appeal had concluded, his confessions were fair, lucid admissions. Regardless of the legality of the confessions, in trying to resolve the question of legal versus actual guilt, there is one striking detail, largely overlooked during the court process that seems to answer the question.

In his conversations with the police, Sears had recounted the killings and included details that could later have been recounted by anyone who read the *Windsor Daily Star*. It is for this reason that prudent investigators keep certain information back from the media, so that only those who are directly involved know these crucial details. When he described the events leading up to his assault, Alexander Voligny had told police that he and the assailant had been arguing over what kind of sex they would engage in. This information was considered far too depraved to be printed in the newspaper, and as a result, the public had never heard about it. Yet during his confession, Ronald Sears recalled how, "[Voligny] became a little angry because I wouldn't let him suck me off."[25] This minor detail, never commented on by lawyers or detectives, but commented upon by both Sears and Voligny, seems to inextricably link Ronald Sears to the killings, for only a person who had actually been there would know that the dispute had occurred. If Sears's legal guilt was questionable, this detail seems to confirm his actual guilt.

Even if he was guilty, the question remains, why did he do it? In his own mind, Ronald Sears seemed to feel entirely justified in what he had done, even characterizing it as a mark of good citizenship to rid the parks of sexual deviants. Sears solidified his motive by admitting that, as a child, he had been the victim of a pedophile. While such abuse is undeniably traumatic, not every boy who has been abused by an older man ends up as a homicidal young adult. In Ronald's case, his actions might well have been caused or at least encouraged by serious underlying psychological factors. The accounts of Ronald's talks with his cat, his fascination with knives, and his increasing withdrawal from contact with other boys all point toward a troubled personality. It has been suggested that some homophobes actually suffer from a true phobia, a delusional paranoia that explains their profound hatred of gay men.[26]

Underneath Ronald's stated motive that he was simply seeking revenge may have lurked a more compelling reason. Sears had spent considerable time hanging about Government Park and learning the conventions of how to meet a gay man. There may have been a separate thrill to this chase, to the unknown possibilities of what might happen that was even more powerful than the act itself. He may have become addicted to this theatrical thrill, unable to prevent himself from dressing up, announcing that he was off to the movies but instead heading to the meeting place, where he knew some chance encounter would culminate in a bloody but justifiable act of vengeance. Even the final act, with the knife poised over the prostrate, unsuspecting body, may have fulfilled a deep-seated sadistic impulse that Sears was compelled to satisfy.

In the years following Ronald's imprisonment, as his life slowly trickled away, the Sears family did what they could to comfort him. Edward and Florence regularly drove up to see him in Woodstock, where he was being treated for tuberculosis. In 1952, his parents wrote a plaintive note to the attorney general begging for Ronald's pardon and his transfer to a Windsor sanitarium where it would be possible for family and friends to visit him. "Would it be asking too much to grant Ron this and have him come home here while he is still alive if just of a while."[27] However, there would be no pardon, and as there was no branch of the Ontario Hospital in Windsor, Sears would remain in Woodstock. His young nephew recalled visiting him in the early 1950s, saying, "He was very slender . . . he looked ill." In the spring of 1956, the tuberculosis became more virulent and he began to experience pulmonary hemorrhaging. Ronald Sears died on May 11, 1956.

The Windsor Slasher panics took place in a series of panics that led to the enactment of the criminal sexual psychopath law of 1948. Seen in the context of its times, this law may have had a progressive aspect, namely that it was intended not only to lock up "deviants" but also to offer medical treatment to heal sexual offenders.[28] Over time, it became something much darker. In 1954, when abhorrence of homosexuality had gained even greater momentum, an amendment to the *Criminal Code* made it possible for a person to be declared a criminal sexual psychopath after two convictions for gross indecency.[29] With this amendment, all homosexual activity, even that of a consensual, nonviolent nature could lead to life imprisonment. It is a fair observation that this law, "participated in constructing homosexuality as a criminal sexual danger."[30]

At a time when Canadians were striving to return to a normal postwar world, in which women worked in the homes tending traditional families, homosexuals were increasingly seen as a threat. During the "lavender scare" of the 1950s, there was even more government action to curb this peril. In the name of national security, gender roles would be reestablished, and lisping bureaucrats would be put in their place. Based on the fear that all gays were a security threat, the RCMP assiduously combed through the files of civil servants to ferret out gays or suspected gays, and in 1952, homosexuals were classified among those undesirable persons who could not emigrate to Canada.[31]

While a panic has the influence to, for a brief time, reestablish social boundaries and state what is and what is not acceptable, the morals of a previous age are always vulnerable to historic change. The old scenario of the 1940s and 1950s would evolve as new standards of acceptable social conduct emerged.[32] After the end of World War II, most Windsor residents tried to return to their prewar lifestyles and roles but found that their world views had changed in subtle, almost imperceptible ways. So many young men had been displaced by the war, some never to return, while others had been exposed to a new lifestyle they could not leave behind. Women had been given glimpses of new possibilities, including that they could be integrated into the permanent work force. At the same time, laborers had rediscovered the power of organization to influence the most formidable industries.

In keeping with this subtle shift, not long after the criminal sexual psychopath laws had been enacted, doubts were raised as to their legitimacy. The incidence of sexual assaults was far smaller than the press let on, and there was no evidence that these new laws were effective.[33] Eventually, it even became possible to question the extent to which the law should be used to regulate private sexual behavior. In Britain, the release of the Wolfenden Report in 1957 revolutionized thought on government control of homosexual conduct.[34] In Canada, the Wolfenden Report would be cited as the source for the novel idea that "there must remain a realm of private morality and immorality which is, in brief and crude terms, none of the law's business."[35] For the first time, a major government report argued that the law had no place in enforcing morality. It is remarkable to contrast the "Perverts a Menace" editorial of 1946—which warned, "as long as these perverts are allowed to run free, they are a menace to everyone"—with the Parliamentary debates of 1968, during which Justice Minister John Turner maintained, "All that is immoral has not been and is not now criminal."[36] Eventually, in 2003, the Ontario Court of Appeal ruled that the ban on same-sex marriages was unconstitutional.[37] Public acceptance of the legal status of homosexuality was such that in 2005, the federal act governing marriage was amended to permit same sex couples to marry.

In the summer of 2005, the Windsor police station was demolished. The old station, which had been incorporated into a newer building, was briefly exposed before it too was knocked down. The small, airless interrogation room and the cells to the rear of the station had been carted away as rubble by the end of that summer. At the same time, adjacent to the former station, in Windsor's City Hall, the nation's first same-sex marriages were being officially performed.

NOTES

CHAPTER 1

1. Don Brown, "City's Celebration Impromptu, Merry," *Windsor Daily Star,* May 9, 1945.
2. Don Brown, "Thousands Welcome Veterans Home," *Windsor Daily Star,* July 13, 1945.
3. The Windsor Police files on this investigation are hereinafter cited by title and file number as they appear in the Slasher investigation binder. "George Mannie stabbed July 24, 1945," Windsor Police Records, file 4; "Police Investigating Mysterious Stabbing on Water Front," *Windsor Daily Star* July 24, 1945.
4. Report of July 25, 1945, Windsor Police Records, file 8.
5. J. L. Robinson, *Windsor Ontario: A Study in Urban Geography* (Syracuse University MA Thesis, 1942), 31. On Windsor's growth, see Trevor Price and Larry Kulisek, *Windsor 1892–1992: A Centennial Celebration: An Illustrated History* (Windsor: Chamber of Commerce, 1992).
6. On the development of Ford of Canada, see David Roberts, *In the Shadow of Detroit: Gordon M. McGregor, Ford of Canada, and Motoropolis* (Detroit: Wayne State University Press, 2006).
7. See Leon Paroian, interview with the author for the Osgoode Society, August 1997.
8. Report of Mahoney and Carter, August 8 1945, Windsor Police Records, file 9.
9. "Unidentified Man Stabbed to Death," *Windsor Daily Star,* August 9, 1945. "First Theory of Robbery Abandoned," *Windsor Daily Star,* August 11, 1945.

10. See City of Windsor Police Department Annual Reports, 1941–1944, R.G. 8 CII/19, Municipal Archives, Windsor Public Library. For this four-year period, there are two years, 1941 and 1944, in which no charges for murder were laid. There were two charges of murder made in 1942 and two in 1943. During the same four-year period, there were only three rape charges filed.

11. "It was just wild," Hugh Fulford, former Windsor police officer, interview with the author, November 2, 2005; "Pitt Street was," Fred Brannagan, former Windsor police detective, interview with the author, November 18, 2005; "that old gal," Jim Ure, former Windsor police detective, interview with the author, January 20, 2006.

12. "Bookies Operating Full Blast Again," *Windsor Daily Star*, September 18, 1946.

13. Gerald Hallowell, *Prohibition in Ontario, 1919–1923* (Ottawa: Ontario Historical Society, 1972). See also Chris Edwards, "Mobsters, Mayhem and Murder," *Windsor Times*, May 2003.

14. "Windsor Pictured as 'Monte Carlo' at Border Inquiry," *Toronto Globe and Mail*, November 2, 1927. David Rossell, *Windsor Justice Facility* (Windsor: 1999): "For years [Thompson] was dogged by complaints. Some alleged he protected criminals. Others claimed he directed money to himself. And then there were the ever-persistent morality issues of the Roaring Twenties," 14.

15. "Deliriously Happy Folk Fill Streets," *Windsor Daily Star*, August 15, 1945.

CHAPTER 2

1. "Man Beaten to Death in Windsor Garage," *Windsor Daily Star*, August 16, 1945.

2. R. M. Harrison, Now, *Windsor Daily Star*, September 18, 1946. On the *Star*'s circulation, see their edition of October 5, 1946. With regard to the impact of the *Star*, I am grateful for Melanie Namespetra's comments in her master's thesis, *The Windsor Slasher: Homosexuality as a Changing Discourse in Media, Police and Legal Records in Windsor, Ontario, 1945–1946* (Windsor: University of Windsor MA thesis, 2004), chapter two.

3. "Authorities Believe Robbery Was Motive in Killing of Watchman," *Windsor Daily Star*, August 16, 1945.

4. City of Windsor Police Department Annual Report, 1944, R.G. 8, C II/19, Municipal Archives, Windsor Public Library.

5. On police ethnicity, see Nicholas Rogers, "Serving Toronto the Good: The Development of the City Police Force, 1834–1884," in *Forging a Consensus: Historical Essays on Toronto*, ed. Victor Russell (Toronto: University of Toronto Press, 1984). On the statistics for morality arrests, see Annual Reports of the Chief Constable, 1941–1945, R.G. 8, CII/19, Municipal Archives, Windsor Public Library. On the spike in activity against bawdy houses in 1944, see the congratulatory note from Major John Leroux of the army medical service to Chief Renaud, "Police Morality Squad's Drive On Disorderly Houses Praised," *Windsor Daily Star*, September 22, 1944.

6. See Bruce Macdonald, interview with the author for the Osgoode Society, September 1984.

7. Former Windsor detective Jim Ure, interview with the author, January 20, 2006.

8. Fred Brannagan, interview with the author, November 18, 2005.

9. Ibid.

10. Ibid.

11. "Feel Slayer May Have Been Injured," *Windsor Daily Star,* August 17, 1945.

12. On Hugh Price's background, see Tom Brophey, "Third Windsor Man Slain: Victim is Army Sergeant," *Windsor Daily Star*, August 18, 1945.

13. Report of Royan and Hill, August 18, 1945; Windsor Police Records, file 7; and Statement by Ernest White, August 18, 1945, Windsor Police Records, file 7.

14. See note 12, Brophey.

15. Fraser MacDougall, "Knife Killer Threatens Girl to Be Fourth Windsor Victim," *Toronto Globe and Mail,* August 20, 1945.

16. For accounts of the panic, see "Murder Epidemic Said City's Worst," *Windsor Daily Star,* August 18, 1945; "Several Homicides Reported," *Windsor Daily Star,* August 20, 1945; "Police Speed Search for Mad Killer," *Detroit Free Press,* August 21, 1945. On Murray Rossell: Inspector David Rossell, interview with the author, January 30, 2006.

17. Editorial, *Windsor Daily Star,* August 20, 1945.

18. "It caused everyone," former Crown Attorney John Whiteside, interview with the author, October 28, 2005. "Everyone was fearful," Fred Brannagan, interview with the author, November 18, 2005.

19. "False Murder Rumors Spread Terror Through City," *Windsor Daily Star,* August 20, 1945.

20. A. M., interview with the author, May 30, 2008.

21. Stanley Cohen and Jock Young, *The Manufacture of News: Social Problems, Deviance and the Mass Media,* rev. ed. (Beverley Hills: Sage Publications, 1973), 265.

22. Stanley Cohen, *Folk Devils and Moral Panics: The Creation of the Mods and Rockers* (London: MacGibbon & Kee, 1972), 16.

23. On the criteria for a moral panic, see Erich Goode and Nachman Ben-Yehuda, *Moral Panics: The Social Construction of Deviance* (Oxford: Blackwell, 1994), 31–37.

24. Tea Garden and Belmont Café Reports, August 18, 1945, Windsor Police Records, Investigating Officer's File, file 2.

25. On Reaume's compassion during the Depression, see his inaugural speech in 1933, "New Sandwich Mayor Asks Assessment," *Border Cities Star,* January 9, 1933: "The government has a duty to protect the interest of the man on relief as well as the more fortunate taxpayers". On wartime housing, see "Reaume Will Be Candidate for 4th Term," *Windsor Daily Star,* November 10, 1946: "It was through my efforts with the support of city council that we were able to bring to Windsor 2,500 Wartime Housing Limited Dwellings and 114 Housing Enterprise of Canada Limited Units."

Reaume had insisted, over the objections of others, on hiring a black lawyer, James Watson. In 1950, Reaume would promote Watson to become Windsor's city solicitor. He became the first black man to hold that position in Canada.

See James Watson, interview with the author for the Osgoode Society, December 1989.

26. "City Posts Reward in Slaying," *Windsor Daily Star*, August 18, 1945.

CHAPTER 3

1. Editorial, "This Fiend Must Be Caught," August 20, 1945.
2. "Two Killers Sought in 3 Border Murders; One Said Sex Maniac," *Toronto Globe and Mail*, August 22, 1945.
3. "3 Charged with Having Concealed Weapons," *Windsor Daily Star*, August 20, 1945. The way in which the *Star* described the suspects—"The three accused, all shabbily dressed . . . in work shirts, top buttons opened, and their hair awry"—illustrates how the climate of fear made appearance the most important indicator of a person's character.
4. Stuart Hall, Chas Critcher, Tony Jefferson, John Clarke, and Brian Roberts, *Policing the Crisis: Mugging, the State and Law and Order* (New York: Holmes and Meier, 1978), 52.
5. "Statement made by a citizen of Windsor," August 20, 1945, Windsor Police Records, file 2.
6. Undated note, Windsor Police Records, file 2.
7. Report from John Quinlan, August 19, 1945, Windsor Police Records, file 2.
8. J. Burns to D. MacNab, Report on L./C. Eugene Doe. Windsor Police Records, file 7.
9. R. M. Harrison, Now, *Windsor Daily Star*, August 20, 1945.
10. A. M., interview with the author, May 30, 2008.
11. "Killer Suspect Man of Weird Interests," August 24, 1945.
12. Ibid.
13. Blair Crawford, "Slasher Case a Study in 'Horrifying' Intolerance," *Windsor [Daily] Star*, May 10, 1997.
14. Tom Brophey, "Investigation Continues in 3 Cases," *Windsor Daily Star*, August 22, 1945.
15. Tom Brophey, "Detroit Girl Gets Threatening Call," *Windsor Daily Star*, August 22, 1945.
16. Letter postmarked from Detroit, August 21, 1945, Windsor Police Records, file 2.
17. "Detroit Detectives Join Slasher Hunt," *Detroit Free Press*, August 22, 1945.
18. See note 11, "Killer Suspect."
19. "Link Local Slayer with U.S. Fiend," *Windsor Daily Star*, August 21, 1945.
20. Report of officer Henry Bird, August 31, 1945, Windsor Police Records, file 2.
21. Report of Blair and Carter, September 2, 1945, Windsor Police Records, file 2.
22. "For Better Police Protection," letter to the editor, *Windsor Daily Star*, August 22, 1945.
23. "Fly Trap Finnegan," letter to the editor, *Windsor Daily Star*, August 25, 1945.
24. Editorial, "Let's Have a Real Cleanup," *Windsor Daily Star*, August 23, 1945.

CHAPTER 4

1. Report on Maureen Crone, August 22, 1945, Windsor Police Records, file 2.
2. Report on Tecumseh Road incident, August 18, 1945, Windsor Police Records, file 2.
3. "Many Sex Crimes," August 29, 1945; "Prosecutions Few," August 31, 1945.
4. Annual Reports of the Chief Constable, 1941–1945, R.G. 8 CII/19, Municipal Archives, Windsor Public Library.
5. Angela McRobbie and Sarah L. Thornton, "Rethinking 'Moral Panic' for Multi-Mediated Social Worlds," in *Critical Readings: Moral Panics and the Media,* ed. Chas Critcher (Maidenhead: Open University Press, 2006), 273.
6. *New York Herald Tribune,* September 26, 1937, quoted in Estelle B. Freedman, "'Uncontrolled Desires': The Response to the Sexual Psychopath, 1920–1960," *Journal of American History* 74 (June 1987): 94.
7. See note 6, Freedman, 94.
8. William N. Eskridge Jr., "Law and the Construction of the Closet: American Regulation of Same-Sex Intimacy, 1880–1946" *Iowa Law Review* 82 (1997): 1065. See also George Chauncey, "The Postwar Sex Crimes Panic," in *True Stories from the American Past,* ed. William Graebner (New York: McGraw-Hill, 1993), 160–70.
9. See note 8, Eskridge, 1019.
10. See note 6, Freedman, 87. On the social purity movement, see Mariana Valverde, *The Age of Light, Soap and Water: Moral Reform in English Canada, 1885–1925* (Toronto: McClelland & Stewart, 1993). On the seduction of young women, see Patrick Brode, *Courted and Abandoned: Seduction in Canadian Law* (Toronto: University of Toronto Press/Osgoode Society, 2002), chapter six.
11. Steven Maynard, "'Horrible Temptations': Sex, Men and Working-Class Male Youth in Urban Ontario, 1890–1935" *Canadian Historical Review* 78 (June 1997): 193. "In contrast to the condemnation of the law, as well as of police and reformers, stood a working class moral economy that nourished a wider range of understandings and responses to sex between boys and men," 226.
12. Ibid., 219–21.
13. Paroian, interview with the author for the Osgoode Society, August 1997.
14. "May Add 50 Officers to Staff," *Windsor Daily Star,* September 5, 1945.
15. Mary E. Baruth-Walsh and G. Mark Walsh, *Strike! 99 Days on the Line: The Workers' Own Story of the 1945 Windsor Ford Strike* (Windsor: Penumbra Press, 1995), 70. See also Herb Colling, *Ninety-Nine Days: The Ford Strike in Windsor, 1945* (Toronto: N.C. Press, 1995).
16. "Note Writers Convicted," *Windsor Daily Star,* September 5, 1945.

CHAPTER 5

1. Report of Royan and Hill, August 23, 1945, Windsor Police Records, file 2.
2. Retired Windsor detective Fred Brannagan, interview with the author, November 18, 2005.
3. Report of John Mahoney, December 18, 1945, Windsor Police Records, file 8.

4. *Capital Punishment Act*, 1833, 9 Geo. IV, c. 31, s. 7. Daniel Ellsworth was condemned to death for buggery in 1829. See Patrick Brode, *Sir John Beverley Robinson: Bone and Sinew of the Compact* (Toronto: University of Toronto Press/Osgoode Society, 1984), 173.

5. Canada, *House of Commons Debates* (May 25, 1892), p. 2969.

6. Gary Kinsman, *The Regulation of Desire: Homo and Hetero Sexualities*, 2nd ed. (Montreal: Black Rose Press, 1996), 131.

7. On the enforcement of gross indecency laws and the Toronto chief constable's comments, see Steven Maynard, "Through a Hole in the Lavatory Wall: Homosexual Subcultures, Police Surveillance, and the Dialectics of Discovery: Toronto, 1890–1930," *Journal of the History of Sexuality* 5 (1994): 230–31. On gays as "biological freaks" see Jay Hatheway, *The Gilded Age Construction of Modern American Homophobia* (New York: Palgrave MacMillan, 2004), 194. On lobotomies as a cure for gay men, see David B. Cruz, "Controlling Desires: Sexual Orientation Conversion and the Limits of the Knowledge of the Law" *Southern California Law Review* 72 (1999): 1297. "Even body parts such as the neck and lower back have been targets of medical attempts (in the form of cauterization) to extinguish homosexuality": 1305.

8. Steven Maynard, "Through a Hole in the Lavatory Wall: Homosexual Subcultures, Police Surveillance, and the Dialectics of Discovery: Toronto, 1890–1930," *Journal of the History of Sexuality* 5 (1994): 235. On Portland, Oregon, see Peter Boag, *Same-Sex Affairs: Constructing and Controlling Homosexuality in the Pacific Northwest* (Berkeley and Los Angeles: University of California Press, 2003), 115. On New York City and Central Park, see George Chauncey, *Gay New York: Gender, Urban Culture and the Making of the Gay World, 1890–1940* (New York: Basic Books, 1994), 182.

9. Allan Bérubé, "Social Theory and Gay Resistance," in, *American Gay*, ed. Stephen O. Murray (Chicago: University of Chicago Press, 1996), 48. On the gay experience in the Canadian military during World War II, see note 6, Kinsman, *The Regulation of Desire*, 154–57.

10. Paul Jackson, *One of the Boys: Homosexuality in the Military during World War II* (Montreal, Kingston: McGill-Queen's University Press, 2004) 152–53.

11. Diana Flavelle, "Homosexuality destroyed decorated soldier's career," *Toronto Star*, March 15, 1986.

12. S. R. Mattson, "The way it was in Windsor: An interview about gay life since the 1930s," *Outspoken* 6, no. 1 (Winter 1996).

13. See note 10, Jackson, 231.

14. See note 3, Report of John Mahoney.

15. Chief Constable Reports for 1936–1940 and 1941–1945, R.G. 8, CIII, Municipal Archives, Windsor Public Library.

16. *R. v. Sears* Trial Transcript I, 1946, Ontario Archives, R.G. 4-32, 167.

17. See note 12, Mattson.

18. Retired Detroit police officer Jack Brode, interview with the author, April 26, 2008.

19. See note 12, Mattson.

20. "Criminal Appeals," May 27, 1895.

21. James Melvin Reinhardt, *Sex Perversions and Sex Crimes* (Springfield, Il-

linois: Charles C. Thomas, 1957), 113.

22. Havelock Ellis, *Studies in the Psychology of Sexes: Sexual Inversion* (London: 3rd ed., 1915), 80.

23. Report of MacLaren and Patterson, July 5, 1946, Windsor Police Records, file 6.

24. Marc Stein, *City of Sisterly and Brotherly Love: Lesbian and Gay Philadelphia, 1945–1972* (Chicago: University of Chicago Press, 2000), 92.

25. William T. Rasmussen, *Corroborating Evidence: The Black Dahlia Murder* (Santa Fe: Sunstone Press, 2005); and Lucy Freeman, "*Before I Kill More . . .*" (New York: Crown Publishers, 1955).

26. Books on Jack the Ripper are legion, but see especially Terence Sharkey, *Jack the Ripper: 100 Years of Investigation* (London: Ward Lock, 1987); and Donald Rumbelow, *Jack the Ripper: The Complete Casebook* (Chicago: Contemporary Books, 1988). On Dr. Cream, see Angus Maclaren, *A Prescription for Murder: The Victorian Killings of Dr. Thomas Neill Cream* (Chicago: University of Chicago Press, 1993), 73.

27. Philip Jenkins, *Using Murder: The Social Construction of Serial Homicide* (New York: Aldine de Gruyter, 1994), 33.

28. Roger Lane, *Murder in America, A History* (Columbus: Ohio State University Press, 1997), 319. See also Ronald M. Holmes and James DeBurger, *Serial Murder* (Newbury Park: Sage Press, 1988), 20: "Through stealth and the typically nonaffiliative nature of their contact with victims, such killers may lead 'normal' lives."

29. "Winnipeg Strangler Case," *Toronto Globe and Mail,* November 7, 1927.

30. Joel Norris, *Serial Killers: The Growing Menace* (New York: Dolphin, 1988), 77. See also Elliott Leyton, *Hunting Humans: The Rise of the Multiple Murderer* (Toronto: McClelland and Stewart, 1986).

31. Robert D. Keppel and William Birnes, *The Psychology of Serial Killer Investigations: The Grisly Business Unit* (New York: Academic Press, 2003).

32. Editorial, "Are Reefers Back?" *Windsor Daily Star,* December 8, 1945.

33. J. J. Dingman, "Over 3,500 New Units Are Needed," *Windsor Daily Star,* February 6, 1946.

34. Windsor Police Records, Slasher file.

35. Tomas Guillen, "Serial Killer Communiqués—Helpful or Hurtful," *Journal of Criminal Justice and Popular Culture* 9 (2002): 41.

CHAPTER 6

1. On 359 Brant, see *Windsor Daily Star,* "359 Brant is Raided," June 5, 1946; and "Two Month Sentence Is Probed," June 14, 1946.

2. On the tornado, see "Death Toll 15: Damage Mounts After Disaster," *Windsor Daily Star,* June 19, 1946; and Jim Ure, interview with the author, January 20, 2006.

3. Report of P.C. Gordon Preston, June 22, 1946, Windsor Police Records, file 3.

4. Harrison, Now, *Windsor Daily Star,* June 24, 1946. Editorial, June 25, 1946.

5. Report of Brand and Anderson, June 23, 1946, Windsor Police Records, file 3.

6. Statement of Alexander Voligny, July 13, 1946, Windsor Police Records, file 3.

7. Peter Boag, *Same-Sex Affairs: Constructing and Controlling Homosexuality in the Pacific Northwest* (Berkeley and Los Angeles: University of California Press, 2003), 117–18.

8. Steven Angelides, *A History of Bisexuality* (Chicago: University of Chicago Press, 2001).

9. A. M., interview with the author, May 30, 2008.

10. Erich Goode and Nachman Ben-Yehuda, *Moral Panics: The Social Construction of Deviance* (Oxford: Blackwell, 1994), 31.

11. "Mayor Reaume Pleads With Married Women to Leave Jobs," *Windsor Daily Star*, January 23, 1946.

12. "Aunt Marissa," letter to the editor, *Windsor Daily Star*, July 2, 1946.

13. David Hajdu, *The Ten Cent Plague: The Great Comic-Book Scare and How It Changed America* (New York: Farrar Straus and Giroux, 2007). On Riverside comic books, see "Riverside Puts Ban on Six Comic Books," *Windsor Daily Star*, August 28, 1946.

14. See "Brothers Jailed for Curb Cruising," *Windsor Daily Star*, September 3, 1946.

15. Mary Louise Adams, *The Trouble with Normal: Postwar Youth and the Making of Heterosexuality* (Toronto: University of Toronto Press, 1997), 91–92.

16. July 8, 1946.

17. See chapter 5, note 6, Kinsman, *The Regulation of Desire*, 193–94.

18. "Cleanup of Parks is Needed," *Windsor Daily Star*, July 8, 1946.

19. On the intolerance shown toward homosexuality by Christianity, see John Boswell, *Christianity, Social Tolerance, and Homosexuality: Gay People in Western Europe from the Beginning of the Christian Era to the Fourteenth Century* (Chicago: University of Chicago Press, 1980).

20. Report of Bird and Hall, July 6, 1946, Windsor Police Records, file 1.

21. Report of Ouellette and Preston, July 6, 1946, Windsor Police Records, file 1.

22. "Knife Wound Requires 14 Stitches," *Windsor Daily Star*, July 6, 1946.

23. Report of Bird and Hall, July 6, 1946, Windsor Police Records, file 1.

24. David S. Bimbi, "Male Prostitution: Pathology Paradigms and Progress in Research," *Journal of Homosexuality* 53: 12–13. On male prostitutes and "hoodlum homosexuals" see Kerwin Kaye, "Male Prostitution in the Twentieth Century: Pseudohomosexuals, Hoodlum Homosexuals, and Exploited Teens," *Journal of Homosexuality* 46 (2003): 1–59.

25. Statement by Hailey Friend, July 6, 1946, Windsor Police Records, file 5.

26. S. R. Mattson, "The way it was in Windsor: An interview about gay life since the 1930s," *Outspoken* 6, no. 2 (Spring 1996).

27. On gay men "passing" as heterosexuals, see Erdwin H. Pfuhl and Stuart Henry, *The Deviance Process*, 3rd ed. (New York: Aldine de Gruyter, 1993), 196. See also Jean S. Gochros, "Homophobia, Homosexuality and Heterosexual Marriage," in *Homophobia: How We All Pay the Price*, ed. Warren J. Blumenfeld (Boston: Basic Books, 1992), 134–36.

28. Report of Tellier and Paget, July 6, 1946, Windsor Police Records, file 5.

CHAPTER 7

1. See chapter 4, note 6, p. 94: Letter "Marty" to "Howard" in the possession of Allan Bérubé, as quoted in Estelle B. Freedman, "'Uncontrolled Desires.'"

2. Dolores Kennedy, *William Heirens: His Day in Court* (Chicago: Bonus Books, 1991).

3. Report of John Mahoney, July 6, 1946, Windsor Police Records, file 1.

4. Jim Ure, interview with the author, January 20, 2006; and Fred Brannagan, interview with the author, November 18, 2005.

5. Statement of Sears on Voligny, completed 6:45 p.m., July 6, 1946, Windsor Police Records, file 3; Statement of Sears on Gelencser, completed 7:15 p.m., July 6, 1946, file 1.

6. Statement of Dorothy Sears, July 6, 1946, Windsor Police Records, file 6.

7. Saul M. Kassin and Lawrence S. Wrightsman, eds., *The Psychology of Evidence and Trial Procedure* (Beverly Hills: Sage Publications, 1985), 73. See also Alfred W. McCoy, *A Question of Torture* (New York: Metropolitan Press, 2006).

8. James W. Williams, "Interrogating Justice: A Critical Analysis of Police Interrogation and Its Role in the Criminal Justice Process," *Canadian Journal of Criminology* 42 (April 2000): 216.

9. Statement of Sears on Gelencser, completed at 10:15 p.m., July 6, 1946, Windsor Police Records, file 1.

10. Statement of Sears on Voligny, completed at 11:15 p.m., July 6, 1946, file 3.

11. William and Nora Kelly, *Policing in Canada* (Toronto: MacMillan, 1976), 216.

12. Statement of Sears on Price, completed at 12:45 a.m., July 7, 1946, Windsor Police Records, file 7.

13. Statement of Sears on Sciegliski, completed at 1:30 a.m., July 7, 1946, file 9.

14. Joel Norris, *Serial Killers: The Growing Menace* (New York: Dolphin, 1988), 216–17. On the method behind a serial killer's conduct, see Peter Vronsky, *Serial Killers: The Method and Madness of Monsters* (New York: Berkley Books, 2004), particularly chapter 8, "The Killing Times: The Method to Madness."

15. Mark Selzer, *Serial Killers: Death and Life in America's Wound Culture* (London: Routledge, 1998), 44.

16. *R. v. Sears* Trial Transcript I, September 11, 1946, Justice Dalton Wells, p. 311, Windsor Police Records.

CHAPTER 8

1. Sears's schoolmate Evelyn Hillman, interview with the author, April 24, 2006.

2. Statement of Ronald Robinson, July 10, 1946; and statement of Clifford Surgent, July 11, 1946, Windsor Police Records, file 6.

3. Statement of Fred Raby, July 11, 1946, Windsor Police Records, file 6.

4. Wayne Lockwood, "Asserts Son Robin Hood," *Windsor Daily Star,* July 8, 1946.

5. Rex G. White, "Slasher, A Quiet Boy Who Loved His Cat, Tortured By

Voices Only He Could Hear," *Detroit News*, July 8, 1946.

6. See Joshua Dressler, "When 'Heterosexual' Men Kill 'Homosexual' Men": Reflections on Provocation Law, Sexual Advances and the 'Reasonable Man' Standard," *Journal of Criminal Law and Criminology* 85 (1995): 726.

7. Statement of Sears on Mannie, completed at 9:15 a.m., July 7, 1946, Windsor Police Records, file 4.

8. Report of McLauchlan and Brand, July 7, 1946, file 3.

9. Wes Gaul, "Ronald Sears, 18, Faces Court after Confession," *Windsor Daily Star*, July 8, 1946.

10. "Police Sigh in Relief—Slasher Terror Ended," *Windsor Daily Star*, July 10, 1946.

11. *R. v. Sears* Trial Transcript I, September 11, 1946, Justice Dalton Wells, p. 175, Windsor Police Records.

12. "Cringing Slasher Suspect Charged with 2 Murders," *Toronto Globe and Mail*, July 9, 1946; arraignment described in Gaul, *Windsor Daily Star*, July 8, 1946.

13. Evelyn Hillman, interview with the author, April 24, 2006. On the background of Edward Sears, see his grandson, Barry Sears, interview with the author, September 12, 2006. On Edward Sears's comments to the Detroit newspapers see "Evidence Bears Out Youth's Confession," *Detroit News*, July 8, 1946. On his comments to the Windsor press, see "Asserts Son Robin Hood," *Windsor Daily Star*, July 8, 1946.

14. July 9, 1946.

15. See chapter 2, note 18, Stanley Cohen, *Folk Devils and Moral Panics*, 31–34.

16. A. M., interview with the author, May 30, 2008.

17. Now, July 9, 1946.

18. See C. Jenny, T. A. Roesler, and K. L. Poyer, "Are Children at Risk for Abuse by Homosexuals?" *Pediatrics* 94 (1994): 41–44; and Stephen J. Clark, "Gay Priests and Other Bogeymen," *Journal of Homosexuality* 51 (2006): 1–6.

19. See chapter 2, note 18, Stanley Cohen, *Folk Devils and Moral Panics*, 28: "Societies appear to be subject every now and then, to periods of moral panic. A condition, episode, person or group of persons emerges to become defined as a threat to societal values and interests; its nature is presented in a stylized and stereotypical fashion by the mass media; the moral barricades are manned by editors, bishops, politicians and other right thinking people."

20. "Praised for Their Efforts," *Windsor Daily Star*, July 29, 1946.

21. John Marshall, "Pansies, Perverts and Macho Men: Changing Conceptions of Male Homosexuality," in *The Making of the Modern Homosexual*, ed. Kenneth Plummer (Totowa, NJ: Barnes & Noble, 1981), 150.

22. "Cleanup Of Parks Is Needed," July 8, 1946.

23. Erich Goode and Nachman Ben-Yehuda, *Moral Panics: The Social Construction of Deviance* (Oxford: Blackwell 1994), 36.

24. John Loughery, *The Other Side of Silence: Men's Lives and Gay Identities: A Twentieth Century History* (New York: Henry Holt, 1998), 168. For examples of American magazines' response to the sex-crime panic of the 1940s, see "The Biggest Taboo," *Colliers*, February 1947, and "What Can We Do About Sex Crimes?" *Saturday Evening Post*, December 11, 1948, 31: "Until the laws are changed and some method is devised for the rigid control of constitutional

psychopathic inferiors, dreadful sex killings will continue to be frequent."

25. "Man Accosts Another Youth," *Winnipeg Tribune*, January 10, 1946.

26. "Prisoner Also Admits Killing Vancouver Boy," *Calgary Herald,* August 19, 1946.

27. Harvey Hickey, "Study Launched to Curb Sex Criminals," *Toronto Globe and Mail,* October 16, 1947; Sidney Katz, "The Truth about Sex Criminals," *Maclean's,* July 1, 1947.

28. On Wilson Park, Fred Sorrell, interview with the author, March 22, 2006; "The city's manager of parks," see "Parks Here Are Safe, Committee Told," *Windsor Daily Star,* July 31, 1946.

29. Philip Jenkins, *Moral Panic: Changing Concepts of the Child Molester in Modern America* (New Haven: Yale University Press, 1998), 53–55, 65.

30. See the Reports of the Chief of Police for Windsor, Windsor Municipal Archives; Ottawa Police Department Annual Reports, City of Ottawa Archives; Police Department Annual Reports, City of Vancouver Archives; Toronto Chief Constable Reports, Toronto Police Museum—all for the years 1944–48. On the statistical decline in crime in Canada, see *The Canadian Yearbook, 1950* (Ottawa: King's Printer, 1950). The Dominion Bureau of Statistics reported in 1947 that the rate of serious or indictable offences had increased by one percent since 1938. During the same period, Canada's population had grown by 14 percent.

31. C. L. Snyder to E. C. Awrey, July 11, 1946, Ontario Archives, R. R. Sears, R.G. 22-1890.

32. Lavery Statement of September 7, 1946, and Sears Statement of September 14, 1945, Windsor Police Records, file 6.

33. Identification Parade Document, Windsor Police Records, file 1.

34. "Youth's Father Retains Counsel," *Windsor Daily Star,* July 10, 1946.

35. "Reformatory for Voligny," *Windsor Daily Star,* October 12, 1946.

36. Statement of George Mannie, July 9, 1946, Windsor Police Records, file 4.

37. On the Shemko case, see G. Arthur Martin, "Reflections on a Half-Century of Criminal Practice," in *Counsel for the Defence,* ed. Edward Greenspan (Toronto: Irwin Law, 2003), 160. Comments on James Clark, "was a no nonsense person," see John Whiteside, interview with the author, October 28, 2005; and Dalton Charters, interview with the author, November 29, 2005.

38. S. R. Mattson, "The way it was in Windsor: An interview about gay life since the 1930s," *Outspoken* 6, no. 2 (Spring 1996).

CHAPTER 9

1. Wes Gaul, "Ronald Sears Committed," *Windsor Daily Star,* July 24, 1946.

2. July 30, 1946.

3. John Whiteside, interview with the author, October 28, 2005. For more on Dalton Courtwright Wells, see Ontario Bar Biographical Research Project, Law Society of Upper Canada Archives.

4. *R. v. Sears* Trial Transcript I, September 11, 1946, Justice Dalton Wells, p. 18, Windsor Police Records.

5. Ibid., 69.

6. Ibid., 80.

7. Ibid., 106–7.

8. "Boy's Confession Held Voluntary By Prosecutor," *Windsor Daily Star,* September 13, 1946.

9. See note 4, *R. v. Sears* Transcript I, 149.

10. Ibid., 182.

11. Ibid., 183.

12. See note 8, "Boy's Confession."

13. See note 4, *R. v. Sears* Transcript I, 203.

14. *Ibrahim v. The King* (1914), A.C. 599 at 609. On the history of the use of confessions, see John Henry Wigmore, *A Treatise on the System of Evidence in Trials at Common Law* (Toronto: Little Brown, 1905), 818–22; and T. D. Macdonald and A. H. Hart, "The Admissibility of Confessions in Criminal Cases," *Canadian Bar Review* 25 (1947): 823–53.

15. *Gach v. The King* (1943), 79 C.C.C. 221 at 225.

16. See note 4, *R. v. Sears* Trial Transcript I, 259.

17. C. G. Schoenfeld, "A Psychoanalytic Approach to Plea Bargains and Confessions," *Journal of Psychology and the Law* 3 (1975): 466.

18. See note 4, *R. v. Sears* Trial Transcript I, 266.

19. "Sears Confession Is Read," *Windsor Daily Star,* September 14, 1946.

20. Ibid.

21. Ibid.

22. Editorial, "Morbid Curiosity," *Windsor Daily Star,* September 17, 1946.

23. See note 4, *R. v. Sears* Transcript I, 361.

24. Ibid., 442.

25. "Ronald's Flip-Flop Memory Baffles All at Slasher Trial," September 13, 1946.

26. "Expect Sears Verdict Today," Sept 18, 1946.

27. M. L. Friedland, "A Century of Criminal Justice," *The Law Society Gazette* 16, nos. 3 & 4 (1982): 336: Of the three 1882 murder cases discussed here, one was tried in a day and the others in two and three days. In that year, there were only eight murder convictions in all of Canada.

28. Max M. Houck, "CSI: The Reality," *Scientific American* 295 (July 2006), 84: "jurors schooled on *CSI (Crime Scene Investigation)* . . . now demand unreasonable levels of physical evidence in trials."

29. G. Arthur Martin, "Closing Argument to the Jury for Defence in Criminal Cases," *Criminal Law Quarterly* 10 (1967–68): 37.

CHAPTER 10

1. "Jurors End Terror Reign," *Windsor Daily Star,* September 19, 1946.

2. As We See It, *Windsor Daily Star,* October 16, 1946.

3. "British Justice," *Time* (Canadian edition), December 2, 1946. Richard von Krafft-Ebing was the author of *Psychopathia Sexualis* (1886), the first widely read book on sexual perversity. His writings were influential throughout Europe and America and spread his view that the purpose of sexual desire was procreation. Any other form of desire was a perversion. See H. Kennedy, "Re-

search and commentaries on Richard von Krafft-Ebing and Karl Heinrich Ulrichs," *Journal of Homosexuality* 42: 165–78.

4. William Gentry, "Find the Mad Slasher of Windsor," *Official Detective Stories* 15 (November 1946): 12.

5. Amy C. Taylor to Minister of Justice, Library and Archives of Canada, R.G. .13, vol. 1659, File cc611. On perceptions of homosexuals as weak and effeminate, see Richard A. Posner, *Sex and Reason* (Cambridge: Harvard University Press, 1992), 300.

6. "People Demand It, Council Is Told," *Windsor Daily Star,* November 20, 1946.

7. "Renaud Doubts Killers Here," *Windsor Daily Star,* October 16, 1946.

8. Mortgage No. 44-44146 on lot 19, Plan 260, Essex County Land Registry Office. On the appeal filed *in forma pauperis* in October 1946, see Ontario Archives, R.G. 4-32, 1946, No. 773.

9. *Criminal Code Amendment Act, SC* 1923, c. 41, s. 1012; and Alan D. Gold, "Criminal Appellate Advocacy," in *Advocacy in Court,* ed. Franklin Moskoff (Toronto: Canada Law Book, 1986), 89.

10. Report of Dalton Wells to Minister of Justice, October 1, 1946, Library and Archives of Canada, R.G. 13, vol. 1659.

11. Susan Kastner, "Arthur Martin Deserves to Be a Household Word," *Toronto Star,* May 15, 1988. Also on G. Arthur Martin, see Law Society Archives, Toronto, Ontario, Past Members Database; Ray Corelli, "G. Arthur Martin to be Appointed to Court of Appeal," *Toronto Star,* February 14, 1973; Max Rosenfeld article in *Maclean's* magazine, July 1, 1953. On Martin's appointment to defend Sears, see Charles Smith, Registrar of the Supreme Court of Ontario to AG's Department, November 1, 1946, Ontario Archives, R.G. 4-32.

12. The newspaper report of Martin's address to the Court of Appeal was carried by the *Windsor Daily Star*: Wayne Lockwood, "Sears Judgment Reserved Today," November 19, 1946. On the possibility that an innocent person could confess to a crime see, C. G. Schoenfeld, "A Psychoanalytic Approach to Plea Bargains and Confessions," *Journal of Psychiatry and the Law* 3 (Winter 1975): 465: "unconscious exhibitionistic tendencies may cause some persons to confess to crimes they could not possibly have committed."

13. Biographical material on Clifford R. Magone, Law Society of Upper Canada Archives, Toronto, Ontario, Past Members Database.

14. *Malinski v. New York* (1945) 324 U.S. 401.

15. *Haley v. Ohio* (1948) 332 U.S. 596. See also Steven Penney, "Theories of Confession Admissibility: A Historical View," *American Journal of Criminal Law* 25 (1998): 309.

16. Stuart Ryan, "Involuntary Confession," *Criminal Law Quarterly* 2 (1959–60): 398.

17. "Happy, Thankful at Jail is the Mother of Sears," *Windsor Daily Star,* November 21, 1946.

18. "To Proceed with Sears Cases," *Windsor Daily Star,* November 25, 1946.

19. As We See It, *Windsor Daily Star,* November 21, 1946.

20. A. B., interview with the author, April 17, 2008.

CHAPTER 11

1. *R. v. Sears* III, Ontario Archives, R.G. 22, file 1890, 373.
2. Sears Statement of July 6, 1946, Windsor Police Records, file 1.
3. Affidavit of James Howard Clark, November 7, 1946, Ontario Archives, R.G. 4-32, 1946, No. 773.
4. *Regina v. Thursfield* (1838), 8 C. & P. 269, 173 E.R. 490; and *Rex v. Chamandy* (1934), O.R. 208 at 212. However, the obligation of the prosecutor to disclose was in 1946 limited to a general outline of the case he would present at trial: see *Rex v. Bohozuk* (1946) 87 C.C.C., 125, McKay J.: "There is no rule directing that the names of witnesses which the Crown may call should be given to the accused. . . . Counsel for the appellant referred to the interest of the accused; the interest of the accused is not a matter with which the Court should be concerned," 126.
5. Joseph Gelencser, Windsor Police Records, files 1 and 5.
6. "New Sears Trial Is Opened," *Windsor Daily Star*, February 5, 1947.
7. "Sears Case Jury is Excluded," *Windsor Daily Star*, February 6, 1947.
8. "Still Argue Evidence As Jury Barred," *Windsor Daily Star*, February 7, 1947.
9. "Order Sears Stand Trial for Sanity," *Windsor Daily Star*, February 10, 1947.
10. Hy Bloom and Richard Schneider, *Mental Disorder and the Law: A Primer for Legal and Mental Health Professionals* (Toronto: Irwin Law, 2006), 60. On the "bomb-shell like development," see "Order Sears Stand Trial for Sanity," *Windsor Daily Star*, February 10, 1947.
11. *Rex v. Gibbons* (1946), 86 C.C.C. 20.
12. Mark S. Micale and Roy Porter, *Discovering the History of Psychiatry* (New York: Oxford University Press, 1994), 273. See also Bernard H. Hall, ed., *A Psychiatrist for a Troubled World: Selected Papers of William C. Menninger, M.D.* (New York: Viking Press, 1967).
13. See chapter 5, note 6, *Kinsman, The Regulation of Desire*, 184. Homosexuality as ingrained, see Colin Spencer, *Homosexuality in History* (New York: Harcourt Brace, 1995), 355–56.
14. Report of D. O. Lynch, July 12, 1946, and Report of C. S. Tennant, July 12, 1946, Ontario Archives, R.G. 22.
15. Robert M. Allen "On the 'Psychiatric Study of William Heirens,'" *Journal of Criminal Law, Criminology and Police Science* 39 (1948): 49.
16. E. C. Awrey to C. R. Magone, February 11, 1947, Ontario Archives, R.G. 22.

CHAPTER 12

1. Wes Gaul, "Sears and Jewitt Pass Time With Gin Rummy," *Windsor Daily Star*, February 11, 1947.
2. C. R. Magone to James Clark, March 18, 1947; Affidavit of Edward Sears, April 21, 1947; and J. H. Clark to A. G. Leslie Blackwell, February 28, 1947, Ontario Archives, R.G. 4-32.
3. Wes Gaul, "Genencser Names Sears As His Knife Attacker," May 6, 1947.
4. Alfred Friendly and Ronald L. Goldfarb, *Crime and Publicity: The Impact of*

News on the Administration of Justice (New York: Twentieth Century Fund, 1967), 86. See also Fred S. Siebert, Walter Wilcox, and George Hough III, *Free Press and Fair Play: Some Dimensions of the Problem* (Athens: University of Georgia Press, 1970). This study indicates that there is no definitive answer as to how press coverage may affect a jury.

5. *Rex v. Adams* (1946), 86 *Canadian Criminal Cases:* 425. This case concerned a Soviet official accused during the Gouzenko affair. It had been widely publicized in Ottawa, and the defense asked for a change in venue. Chief Justice McRuer refused and noted that instead the accused could challenge any tainted jurors.

6. Biographical material on George Urquhart, Law Society of Upper Canada Archives, Toronto, Ontario, Past Member Database; "Well Known in Windsor" *Windsor Daily Star,* January 26, 1938.

7. C. L. Snyder to E. Awrey, January 16, 1947, Ontario Archives, R.G. 4-32.

8. Report of Dr. J. N. Senn to Director Hospitals Division, Toronto, February 24, 1947, Ontario Archives, R.G. 4-32.

9. *R. v. Sears* III, Ontario Archives, R.G. 22, file 1890, 31. On the opening of the trial, see Wes Gaul, "Genencser Names Sears as His Knife Attacker," *Windsor Daily Star,* May 6, 1947.

10. *R. v Sears* III, Ontario Archives, R.G. 22, file 1890, 72.

11. Ibid., 157.

12. Ibid., 167–68.

13. Ibid., 249.

14. Ibid., 262–63.

15. Ibid., 277–78.

16. Ibid., 280.

17. "Sears Case Goes to Jury," *Windsor Daily Star,* May 8, 1947.

18. G. Arthur Martin, "Closing Argument to the Jury for the Defence in Criminal Cases," *Criminal Law Quarterly* 10 (1967–68): 35.

19. "Sears Case Goes to Jury," *Windsor Daily Star,* May 8, 1947.

20. Arthur Maloney, "Addressing the Jury in Criminal Cases" *Canadian Bar Review* 35 (1957): 389; Clark's jury address is noted in "Sears Case Goes to Jury," *Windsor Daily Star,* May 8, 1947.

21. On references to the "heterosexualization" of the case, see Canadian Gay and Lesbian Archives, Toronto, Ontario; and Robert Champagne, "Still a Menace: Murder, Sex and Perversion in Windsor, 1945–47" (paper for Law and Sexuality, December 22, 1998), 25–26.

22. On the impact of previous convictions on jurors see Anthony Doob, "Psychology and Evidence," in *Courts and Trials: A Multidisciplinary Approach,* ed. Martin Friedland (Toronto: University of Toronto Press, 1975), 40: "The jury member may shift his criterion of the standard of proof necessary to determine guilt and feel that it would not be so bad to find an innocent accused guilty if he had a criminal record."

23. *R. v. Sears* III, Ontario Archives, R.G. 22, file 1890, 371.

24. See note 21, Champagne, "Still a Menace," 38.

CHAPTER 13

1. Report of Urquhart to Chief Justice of Ontario, June 20, 1947, Ontario Archives, R.G. 4-32, 1946, No. 773.

2. G. A. Urquhart to W. B. Common, August 22, 1947, Ontario Archives, R.G. 4-32, 1946, No. 773.

3. W. B. Common to E. C. Awrey, September 17, 1947, Ontario Archives, R.G. 4-32, 1946, No. 773.

4. Sears Appeal, May 29, 1947, Ontario Archives, R.G. 4-32, 1946, No. 773. On Arthur Maloney, see Arthur Edward Martin Maloney, Law Society Archives, Toronto, Ontario, Past Members Database; and Charles Pullen, *The Life and Times of Arthur Maloney: The Last of the Tribunes* (Toronto: Dundurn Press, 1994).

5. J. Edgar Hoover, "How Safe Is Your Daughter?" *American Magazine* 144 (July 1947); David G. Wittels, "What Can We Do About Sex Crimes?" *Saturday Evening Post* 221 (December 11, 1948); Sidney Katz, "The Truth About Sex Criminals," *Maclean's* (July 1, 1947).

   On the anxiety of the postwar period, see "Hiroshima's Lesson Yet to be Digested," *Vancouver Sun,* August 5, 1947; "The Atom Bomb Race is Officially Open," *Ottawa Journal,* April 1, 1948, 5; J. Griffin, *Toronto Daily Star,* August 20, 1947: Dr. Griffin comments on a mental-hygiene service established in Toronto: "The world is equipped with weapons to destroy itself before it has gained mental maturity. Some psychiatrists agree that the world has but five years to grow up or else it will be annihilated." See also William Graebner, *The Age of Doubt: American Thought and Culture in the 1940s* (Boston: Twayne Publishers, 1991).

   On the sex-crime panic of the late 1940s, see Estelle B. Freedman, "'Uncontrolled Desires': The Response to the Sexual Psychopath, 1920–1960," *Journal of American History* 74 (June 1987): 96: "The postwar years . . . provided a climate conducive to the reemergence of the male sexual psychopath as a target of social concern."

6. Editorial, "Fiend's Victim," *Windsor Daily Star,* September 24, 1947.

7. "Memorandum of Points of Facts and of Law," Ontario Archives, R.G. 4-32, 1946, No. 773.

8. A report of the argument of the appeal is found in "Sears' Case Being Heard in Toronto," *Windsor Daily Star*, October 16, 1947. On the questioning of lawyers during an appeal, see Alan D. Gold, "Criminal Appellate Advocacy," in *Advocacy in Court: A Tribute to Arthur Maloney, Q.C.*, ed. Franklin R. Moskoff (Toronto: Canada Law Book, 1986), 95: "The questions by a court are not designed to trap counsel or make them look unknowledgeable. Rather, they are an opening into the mind of the listener; it is valuable information for counsel seeking to persuade."

9. *Rex v. Sears* (1947) 90 *Canadian Criminal Cases*, 159. See also chapter 12, note 21, Champagne, "Still a Menace", 42.

10. Canada, *House of Commons Debate,* July 3, 1947, 5027 and 5029. R. M. Harrison, Now, *Windsor Daily Star,* May 10, 1947.

11. *Rex v. Dick* (No. 2) (1947) 89 *Canadian Criminal Cases,* 312 at 315.

12. *Boudreau v. The King* (1949) 94 *Canadian Criminal Cases,* 1 at 9: Rand: "It

would be a serious error to place the ordinary modes of investigation of crime in a straight-jacket of artificial rules; and the true protection against improper interrogation or any kind of pressure or inducement is to leave the broad question to the Court. Rigid formulas can be both meaningless to the weakling and absurd to the hardened criminal; and to introduce a new rite as an inflexible preliminary condition would serve no genuine interest of the accused and but add an unreal formalism to that vital branch of the administration of justice."

On the controversy over the status of confessions in the late 1940s, see T. D. Macdonald and A. H. Hart, "The Admissibility of Confessions in Criminal Cases," *Canadian Bar Review* 25 (1947): 845; and J. L. Saltiero, "Form of Warning to the Accused," *Canadian Bar Review* 27 (1949): 67.

13. As We See It, *Windsor Daily Star,* May 10, 1947. Even before many American states, Ontario courts were using psychiatric evaluations to judge persons accused of gross indecency. See Steven Maynard, "On the Case of the Case: The Emergence of the Homosexual as a Case History in Early-Twentieth-Century Canada," in *Explorations in Social History,* ed. Franca Iacovetta and Wendy Mitchinson (Toronto: University of Toronto Press, 1998), 65.

14. Wilhelm Stekel, *The Homosexual Neurosis* (New York: Emerson Books, 1950), 306: "The homosexual must be genuinely willing to be cured."

15. Editorial, "Only Two Years for Indecent Assault," August 2, 1946.

16. "Hope for Curbing Sex Criminals," *Windsor Daily Star,* October 17, 1947. Edmison was a former Crown Attorney from Montreal who attracted the support of police chiefs and prominent medical officers to seek changes to the *Criminal Code* on sexual offenses. On the origins of the criminal sexual psychopath designation, see Elise Chenier, "The Criminal Sexual Psychopath in Canada: Sex, Psychiatry and the Law at Mid-Century," *Canadian Bulletin of Medical History* 20 (2003): 75–101.

17. Canada, *House of Commons Debates,* June 14, 1948, 5196.

18. Ibid., 5198 (Smith).

19. Editorial, *Windsor Daily Star,* July 8, 1946. See also Patrick Brode, "Perverts a Menace: The Development of the Criminal Sexual Psychopath Offence, 1948," in *Essays In the History of Canadian Law, Volume X: A Tribute to Peter N. Oliver,* eds. Jim Phillips, R. Roy McMurtry, and John T. Saywell (Toronto: University of Toronto Press/Osgoode Society, 2008) 107–28.

20. E. C. Awrey to W. B. Common, January 31, 1948, Ontario Archives, R.G. 4-32.

CHAPTER 14

1. Edward Dmytryk, RKO Pictures, 1947.

2. Windsor lawyer W. Willson, interview with the author, November 8, 2006.

3. A. B., interview with the author, April 17, 2008.

4. A prominent article—"Commitments under the Criminal Sexual Psychopath Law in the Criminal Court of Cook County, Illinois," *American Journal of Psychiatry* 105 (1948)—held that adults who had homosexual contact with children corrupted them, and "The minors in turn corrupted other minors

. . . ": see chapter 4, note 6, quoted in Freedman, 104.

5. See chapter 2, note 22, Cohen, *Folk Devils*, 18.

6. See chapter 8, note 23, Loughery, *The Other Side of Silence*, 180.

7. Annual Reports of the Chief Constable, 1947–1948, R.G. 8 CII/19, Municipal Archives, Windsor Public Library. S. R. Mattson, "The way it was in Windsor: An interview about gay life since the 1930s," *Outspoken* 6, no. 1 (Winter 1996).

8. On the failure of men to marry, see Barbara Ehrenreich, *The Hearts of Men: American Dreams and the Flight from Commitment* (Garden City: Anchor Press, 1983), 11–13.

9. S. R. Mattson, "The way it was in Windsor: An interview about gay life since the 1930s," *Outspoken* 6, no. 1 (Winter 1996).

10. Philip Jenkins, *Moral Panic: Changing Concepts of the Child Molester in Modern America* (New Haven: Yale University Press, 1998), 54.

11. Howard Whitman, *Terror in the Streets* (New York: Dial Press, 1951), 147.

12. "19-Year-Old Admits Killing Boy, 6," *Windsor Daily Star*, April 21, 1949.

13. John Gerassi, *The Boys of Boise: Furor, Vice and Folly in an American City* (New York: MacMillan, 1966): The author suggests that the Boise panic was directed by a conservative clique to frustrate a more reformist political group.

14. See Terry Ann Knopf, "Media Myths on Violence," *Columbia Journalism Review*, Spring 1970: 20.

15. Eriche Goode and Nachman Ben-Yehuda, *Moral Panics: The Social Construction of Deviance* (Cambridge, Mass.: Blackwell, 1994): 32: "It is almost axiomatic in the literature that moral panics arise in troubled times, during which a serious *threat* is sensed to the interests or values of the society as a whole or to segments of a society."

16. Mary Louise Adams, *The Trouble With Normal: Postwar Youth and the Making of Heterosexuality* (Toronto: University of Toronto Press, 1997), 22: "At the very least, Canadians and Americans shared both a fear of and a fascination with the bomb."

17. "Solicitor Takes Complaint on Hanrahan to MacMillan," *Windsor Daily Star*, March 8, 1950.

18. "Queen's Park Wants Thorough Vice Probe," *Windsor Daily Star*, March 24, 1950.

19. Peter Vronsky, *Serial Killers: The Method and Madness of Monsters* (New York: Berkley Books, 2004), 329–33.

20. Pickton's case was reported in dailies across Canada in January 2007. See for example, *Toronto National Post*, January 23, 2007.

21. See Cristin Schmitz, "Lawyers Told to Take Responsibility to Prevent Radical Criminal Reforms," *The Lawyers Weekly*, April 11, 2008, 27: "The Ontario government had appointed 2 experts to look into the dysfunctional system . . . Justice Moldaver, 'Murder trials that would have been tried in five to seven days now take five to seven weeks or months.'"

22. See chapter 5, note 6: Kinsman, *The Regulation of Desire*, 159. On Kinsey, see Alfred C. Kinsey, *Sexual Behavior in the Human Male* (Philadelphia: Wardell, 1948).

23. "Sears Sent to Kingston," *Windsor Daily Star*, February 17, 1948.

24. Commissioner of Penitentiaries to W. B. Common, March 4, 1948, Ontario Archives, R.G. 4-32-773.

25. Statement of Alexander Voligny, July 13, 1946, Windsor Police Records, file 3: Voligny states that he and Sears were arguing because Voligny wanted to "frenchie" Sears, but Sears preferred "cornholing." Statement of Sears on Voligny, completed at 11:15 p.m., July 6, 1946, Windsor Police Records, file 3. Another factor indicating Ronald Sears's guilt might be found in the note to the police of March 1946. While the writer was prudent enough to print the note, he slipped into cursive writing while addressing the envelope. Several letters from the address, notably the *p* and *l,* are identical to the handwriting of Ronald Sears.

26. Martin Kantor, comment in *Journal of Homosexuality* 43 (2002): 136: "Serious homophobes are often quite troubled psychologically and their homophobia reflects their psychopathy. Sometimes they suffer from a true phobia of gays and lesbians."

27. Edward Sears to Attorney General, July 23, 1952, Ontario Archives, R.G.-4-31-773-46; W. B. Common to Edward Sears, July 30, 1952, Ontario Archives, R.G.-4-31-773-46.

28. On the progressive objective of the 1948 law, see Elise Chenier, *Strangers in Our Midst: Sexual Deviancy in Postwar Ontario* (Toronto: University of Toronto Press, 2008).

29. *Criminal Code Amendment Act,* Statutes of Canada, 1953–54, c. 51, s. 659.

30. See chapter 5, note 6, Kinsman, *The Regulation of Desire,* 183. The original statute creating the designation of "criminal sexual psychopath" is *Criminal Code Amendment Act*, S.C. 1948, c. 39, s. 43.

31. Philip Girard, "From Subversion to Liberation: Homosexuals and the Immigration Act, 1952–1977," *Canadian Journal of Law and Society* 2 (1987): 1. On the prosecution of gays in the early 1950s, see David K. Johnson, *The Lavender Scare: The Cold War Persecution of Gays and Lesbians in the Federal Government* (Chicago: University of Chicago Press, 2003); and John D'Emilio, "The Homosexual Menace: The Politics of Sexuality in Cold War America," in *Passion and Power: Sexuality in History,* eds. Kathy Peiss, Christina Simmons, and Robert A. Padgug (Philadelphia: Temple University Press, 1989), 232: the anti-gay animus of the 1940s was "one front in the widespread effort to reconstruct patterns of sexuality and gender relations shaken by depression and war."

32. Jon Teaford, *The Metropolitan Revolution: The Rise of Post-Urban America* (New York: Columbia University Press, 2006): 7: "The certainties of post-war America gave way to the ambiguities of the 1990s, the 'new scenario.'"

33. Edwin H. Sutherland, "The Diffusion of Sexual Psychopath Laws," *American Journal of Sociology* 56 (1950): 146.

34. *The Wolfenden Report* (London: Her Majesty's Stationery Office, 1962).

35. Canada, *House of Commons Debates,* January 23, 1969, 4723: Justice Minister John Turner speaking on the introduction of *Criminal Code* amendments to decriminalize consensual homosexual conduct.

36. Ibid., 8576.

37. *Halpern v. Canada* (Attorney General) (2003) 65 Ontario Reports (3d) 161.

INDEX